MIRACLES IN ENLIGHTENMENT ENGLAND

MIRACLES IN ENLIGHTENMENT ENGLAND

Jane Shaw

YALE UNIVERSITY PRESS
NEW HAVEN AND LONDON

For information about this and other Yale University Press publications, please contact:
U.S. Office: sales.press@yale.edu   yale books.com
Europe Office: sales&yaleup.co.uk   www.yaleup.co.uk

Set in Caslon by J&L Composition, Filey, North Yorkshire
Printed in Great Britain by St Edmundsbury Press Ltd, Bury St Edmunds

Library of Congress Cataloging-in-Publication Data

Shaw, Jane, 1963–
   Miracles in Enlightenment England/Jane Shaw.
      p. cm.
   Includes bibliographical references and index.
   ISBN 0–300–11272–6 (alk. paper)
   1. Miracles—England—History—17th century.   2. Protestant churches—England—Doctrines—History—17th century.   3. England—Religious life and customs.   I. Title.
   BR757.S44 2006
   231.7'3094209032—dc22   2006011985

10 9 8 7 6 5 4 3 2 1

For my mother, Joyce Shaw, and in
memory of my father, Jack Davies Shaw (1915–1997)

Contents

Acknowledgements

In researching this book, I have been most grateful for the help of librarians in the Bodleian Library, the British Library, the Houghton Library at Harvard, the Huguenot Library in London, Dr Williams's Library in London and the Bancroft Library at the University of California, Berkeley. Particular thanks to Sue Mills, the Librarian at Regent's Park College, for her enthusiastic assistance in the college's Angus archives as I researched chapter 2.

I have received much helpful feedback in various university, conference and other settings when I presented sections of this book in seminar papers and lectures. I am grateful to warm and responsive audiences at Princeton University, Rutgers University, Barnard College, Manchester University, Birmingham University, Cambridge University, Oxford University, two seminars at the Institute for Historical Research at the University of London, the Center for Advanced Study of the Behavioural Sciences at Stanford, the Norfolk Theological Society, the colloquium on Missiology in Paris organised by Alan Kreider and Neal Blount (1996), the colloquium on Religion and Modernity at the Rockefeller Centre in Bellagio, organised by Phyllis Mack (1998), and several meetings of the American Academy of Religion and the American Society for Eighteenth-Century Studies. I thank those who kindly invited me to present my work to them and all those – too numerous to mention – whose comments sharpened my thinking about this book.

Many kind friends and colleagues encouraged me to keep on writing this book, even as my attention was called to other things and I found myself repeatedly putting this manuscript to one side. They are probably almost as relieved as I am that it is at last finished. For their encouragement, for their conversation and the sparking of ideas, and for helpful leads and references, I thank: Marilyn McCord Adams, Henry Chadwick, Lisa Forman Cody, Miranda Curtis, Natalie Zemon Davis, Catherine Gallagher, Barbara Harvey, Carla Hesse, Tom Laqueur, Rebecca Lyman, Phyllis Mack, Henry Mayr-Harting, Ernest Nicholson, Fred Quinn, Sarah Ogilvie,

Sheldon Rothblatt, Vincent Strudwick and Donna Tartt. I also remember with gratitude the encouragement given to me by the late Bill Bouwsma, and the numerous discussions he and I had about early modern religion. Deborah Madden, Kate Shuttleworth and Philip Lockley all provided excellent research assistance at particular moments when I most needed it. Special thanks go to those friends and colleagues who read chapters as I was completing the manuscript, whose critical attention to my work has undoubtedly improved it, and whose kindness in engaging with my work, especially when they were often so busy themselves, I greatly appreciate. Diarmaid MacCulloch and Vincent Strudwick read chapter 2, and gave me the benefit of their Reformation expertise in their comments and references. Fred Quinn read chapters 3 and 4 and helped me clarify some of my terms. Marilyn McCord Adams read chapters 1 and 7, and Robert Merrihew Adams read chapters 7 and 8: both helped relate a philosopher's approach to the eighteenth-century debate on miracles to this historian's approach. An anonymous reader for Yale University Press gave me immensely useful and stimulating comments, for which I am very grateful. Lisa Forman Cody, Tom Laqueur, Phyllis Mack and Sarah Ogilvie, long-time friends, conversation partners and my best critics, all read significant portions of the book and prompted me to think through the whole project with greater clarity. I am grateful for their close attention to my work, and their kindness.

I am grateful to Robert Baldock for his faith in the project and kind editorial steering, Candida Brazil and the staff at Yale University Press.

The book is dedicated to my mother and to the memory of my father, in gratitude for their endless kindness and support.

CHAPTER 1

Miracles, Protestantism and the Enlightenment:
An Introduction

In the 1650s, independent and Baptist churches began to heal according to a biblical injunction and Quakers claimed they could heal and raise the dead; at the Restoration of the monarchy in 1660, Charles II touched more of his subjects for the ulcerous and itchy illness known as the King's Evil (*scrofula*) than any of his predecessors had; in 1665–6, an Irishman named Valentine Greatrakes healed hundreds of people in Ireland and England by stroking the pain out of their bodies; a year or so later, a young woman in Derbyshire, named Martha Taylor, survived without food for over a year; in the 1690s, four women in London were healed when reading the Bible; in the first decade of the eighteenth century, a group of Protestant prophets from southern France arrived in London and claimed they could perform miracles – healing the sick, walking through fire unscathed, raising the dead. These claims of miracles, over a period of about sixty years, provoked investigation, discussion and debate at all levels of society: amongst fellows of the Royal Society, small-town physicians, nonconformist ministers, Anglican clergy and bishops, printers and booksellers, philosophers and theologians, as well as the neighbours, family members and friends of those who claimed they were cured, raised from the dead and had survived for a prodigiously long time without food.

These miracle stories and the responses to them form the overarching narrative of this book. They suggest that, despite the sixteenth-century Protestant doctrine of the cessation of miracles, which said that miracles had ceased after the early church had been established, some Protestants began to incorporate a belief in, and experience of, miracles into their religious practice and theology. Secondly, this set of miracle stories, which claimed the attention of theologians and proponents of the new philosophy several decades before the famous philosophical debate in the first half of the eighteenth century, questions the starting point of Enlightenment discussion about miracles, and suggests that not only intellectuals but also ordinary people and their religious practices played a part in determining its course.

When we think of miracles and the Enlightenment in England, we automatically think of the philosophical debate, emblematic of the wider Enlightenment discussion of the relationship between revelation and reason, which began in the 1690s and largely culminated in Hume's influential text on the subject, 'Of Miracles' of 1748. In this book, I suggest that a broader and longer discussion about miracles started several decades before that philosophical debate. It began in the seventeenth century with people's lived experiences, when those who were sick, suffering, in pain and experiencing anguish found themselves relieved of those ills and agonies, and believed that God had cured them. It began when some independent churches in the 1650s wished to follow to the letter a particular biblical text about healing, and radical sectarians claiming apostolicity announced that they could heal the sick and raise the dead. In short, it began when there was a revival of miracles in the second half of the seventeenth century. Because that revival occurred in a Protestant context, where officially miracles were said to have ceased, and where miracles had been polemically associated with the 'misguided' ways of papists, such miracle claims *necessarily* generated comment and controversy. Nevertheless, in the intellectual context of the second half of the seventeenth century, the investigations that such miracle claims and their attending controversy provoked went beyond the intra-doctrinal and opened up significant questions about truth, evidence and the nature of God.

Taking both doctrine and practice into account in this way reveals that there were three major attitudes, or 'streams', within Protestantism to miracles in seventeenth-century England. These fed into the eighteenth-century philosophical debate in direct and indirect ways. First, it was a commonplace notion that miracles had ceased with biblical times. This was an idea inherited from sixteenth- and early seventeenth-century Protestants who, when confronted by Roman Catholic claims that their ongoing miracles were signs that they were still the true church, turned their back on miracles and came to regard scripture as the only trustworthy foundation for faith, all that was needed for belief in Jesus Christ. Those Protestant thinkers argued that God *no longer* needed to work miracles to convince people of the truth of the gospel. They did not question that God might be able to work miracles if he wished; nor did they question the validity of the biblical miracles as revelations that supported Christian doctrines, especially the incarnation and the resurrection of Christ. In that sense, they were not questioning the role of God as miracle-worker, as a God who could intervene – and had intervened – in human affairs, whether in the universe or the human body, to demonstrate his nature, power and existence. They simply suggested that there had been a limited age of miracles. However, they opened the way for more radical thinkers in the Enlightenment, most notably the deists, to ask questions about the very nature of God and whether God had indeed ever been a miracle-worker. Some deists, as part of a larger challenge to the authority of the Bible, argued against the reality of the biblical miracles, claiming that the truth of Christianity lay not in Jesus' miracles but in his ethical message. This first stream of Protestant thought and the scepticism which ultimately emerged from it begin and end this book: the Protestant doctrine of the cessation of miracles is discussed in chapter 2, and the deist contribution to the eighteenth-century philosophical debate is discussed in chapter 7. It literally forms the 'bookends'.

A second and different approach to miracles emerged amongst some groups of Protestants in the mid-seventeenth century, when some of the independent churches and radical Protestant sects that flourished in the civil war and Interregnum began to claim that they had experienced divine healing, and could work miracles. They challenged the Protestant orthodoxy that miracles had ceased with the biblical times. Indeed, for some, such as the Quakers, their claim to be able to work miracles was evoked as a sign of their authority: as in the early church, miracles were regarded as a sign of the Holy Spirit working favourably amongst them, and therefore a sign of the truth of their message. Some of the most fervent miracle claims amongst these groups ended after the Restoration of the monarchy in 1660, but claims of miracles continued to be made long after this. They prompted investigations by members of the Royal Society, and debate and discussion amongst nonconformist and Anglican clergy and many others in pamphlets and coffee houses. Ironically, these many cases of miracle claims, for some commentators and observers, also ultimately pointed the way towards doubt. For too many miracles, and too ready a belief in all wonders as miracles, also made people sceptical. This was exactly what some Anglican divines feared; as Thomas Sprat put it, in his 1662 history of the Royal Society: 'the Enthusiastic goes neer to bring down the price of the True, and Primitive Miracles, by such a vast, and such a negligent augmenting of their number'.[1]

There was, then, an attempt to develop a middle way: this argued that miracles were plausible, but only with very great evidence. This might be regarded as a third attitude towards miracles within later seventeenth- and early eighteenth-century Protestantism. This became the orthodox position held by many Anglican apologists (though others still held to the view that miracles had ceased with biblical times). Both atheism (no miracles at all) and enthusiasm (too many miracles) were to be avoided. This 'middle way' emerged out of a series of responses to miracle cases in which the developing techniques of experimental philosophy were used to test miracles. On the one hand, very great evidence was required because of a widespread distrust of Roman Catholic miracles – regarded as 'superstitious' – and the apparatus surrounding them, and an equal distrust of those Protestant 'enthusiasts' who discredited miracles by believing in them too readily. On the other hand, to refute the possibility of any miracles at all was a step towards the 'atheism', which, by the late seventeenth century, Anglicans (and dissenters of a moderate stripe) feared. In proposing this 'middle way', reasonable Anglicans did not question the view that God could and did intervene in the natural world to work miracles; indeed they rethought the doctrine of cessation and came to believe cautiously (but necessarily, they believed, in the face of the other options) in the possibility of miracles in their own day.

Despite this careful attempt to steer a middle course between 'atheism' and 'enthusiasm', it was not possible to hold the larger question – whether God worked miracles at all – at bay. The way had been opened for philosophical, indeed cosmological, questions to be asked about God's very nature as a miracle-worker, and thus for even the biblical miracles to be challenged. The deists and other sceptics took that step at the end of the seventeenth century, challenging all streams of Protestant thought about miracles: the doctrine of the cessation of miracles after apostolic times (which kept the biblical miracles intact); the ready belief in contemporary miracles that was to be found amongst some of the sectarian and dissenting Protestant groups; and the belief that miracles were plausible, indeed possible, but only upon very great evidence, found amongst Anglican apologists and experimental philosophers alike. The deists and sceptics made this challenge not only by questioning the very notion of God as miracle-worker, but also by asking whether there was any evidence good enough for either biblical or contemporary miracles; thus the debate continued in a different mode, a philosophical mode, conducted primarily through pamphlet and text, to which the miracle events and claims of the preceding few decades had formed a vital backdrop.

Those miracle claims generated discussion, controversy and – frequently – competing explanations, brought to the wider public in pamphlets and other printed texts, some of considerable length. This wealth of material included: first-hand narratives of miracle events; sermons; ballads; accounts of 'scientific' investigations of miracle claims, often accompanied by explanations of the miraculous happenings; reports and letters in the *Transactions* of the Royal Society; general discussions of the plausibility of miracles, with reference to specific events; spoofs and satires. Authors of such texts included Anglican and nonconformist ministers, printers and publishers, as well as those involved in the new philosophy and the experimental method. There are, of course, many examples of one- or two-page pamphlets from this period, sold for a penny, which invoked the term 'miracle' rather loosely in their titles, whether speaking of a miraculously gigantic ear of corn on display in a coffeehouse, a bumper harvest or a whole range of monsters, prodigies, and marvels.[2] Such phenomena always incited interest and short pamphlets about them would always make money for their publishers.[3] These are not the pamphlets I am discussing in this book, for while they indicate that there was an appetite for wonders – and we can understand the wider interest in miracles as part of that larger appetite for wonders – they reveal little to us about the broader theological landscape. Rather, I focus on the miracle stories and events that generated discussion amongst people in various levels of society – a discussion which emerged in different sorts of printed materials – suggesting that this early Enlightenment period was one of shifting and changing ideas about miracles, and was therefore a moment when divergent schools of thought about the miraculous emerged and co-existed.

By taking the miracle stories, and the debates that they generated, as the initial sources for the narrative told here, I ask what those miracles meant to the people involved.[4] The interpreters of these miracle claims certainly came from a wide range of backgrounds and included the ordinary people who claimed they had been healed of long-standing illness; the men (and occasional women) who claimed they could perform miracles; the neighbours who rushed hither and thither telling news of a 'miraculous' cure or a prodigious survival without food; members of the Royal Society, Anglican bishops and doctors of the Royal College of Physicians who inspected the healed, and presented their results; and the small-town physicians and gentlemen amateur scholars who offered their natural explanations of such miracle claims, in competition with the ministers who claimed them as true miracles, signs of God's providence or indications of the approaching apocalypse.

All of this occurred in just the place and at just the moment when the public sphere was opening up.[5] Such a debate was therefore enabled and enhanced by the new media of the Enlightenment: coffeehouses where conversation was plentiful, where newspapers and periodicals could be read and demonstrations of scientific experiments witnessed; increased and ever-increasing print culture (books, pamphlets, and newspapers); lending libraries, lecture series and public gardens, as well as the learned academies and societies whose membership was carefully controlled, such as the Royal Society and its provincial spin-offs. All of these joined with the more traditional spaces of the pulpit and alehouse to create an environment in which ideas were more freely and more regularly discussed; the participation of the public in political and other debates was broadened.

Of course, some of these 'media' of the public sphere overlapped and some did not. Some had their own particular clientele. The coffeehouse (central to

Habermas's notion of the public sphere) was a new form of gathering place, with its origins in Interregnum Oxford (and soon spreading to London) at just the moment when a new 'scientific' community was forming in Oxford; this meant that the Oxford virtuosi (the early scientists) were responsible for establishing what Brian Cowan calls 'a distinctive style of coffeehouse sociability that became a sort of template upon which the later, and much more numerous, coffeehouses of the Restoration era modelled themselves'.[6] Men like Thomas Willis and Christopher Wren, who were involved in the Anne Greene case discussed in chapter 3, were frequenters of the earliest coffeehouses in Oxford. Indeed, as Cowan points out, the coffeehouse provided a space in which the new 'scientific' ideas could be freely discussed and tried out:

> The coffeehouse was a place for like-minded scholars to congregate, to read, as well as to learn from and to debate with each other, but it was emphatically *not* a university institution, and the discourse there was of a far different order than any university tutorial. The coffeehouse thus occupied a social space distinct from those older centers of learning which were constrained by their dependence on church or state patronage as well as their stubborn 'scholastic' refusal to accept the methods and supplements offered by Bacon's 'new learning' which were so dear to the virtuosi.[7]

Some of the virtuosi, such as Thomas Willis, expounded not only the virtues of the coffeehouses, but also the virtues of coffee; some, such as Robert Hooke, were exceptionally enthusiastic frequenters of coffeehouses, using them to form networks of like-minded scholars, to learn what others were doing and to promote their own work.[8] Even though some well-known virtuosi, such as Robert Boyle, remained aloof from coffeehouse culture, coffeehouses and the new experimental method were linked from their very beginnings. Every now and then, we have a glimpse of what we might expect to have been the case – that these miracle cases, and the debates about miracles, were discussed by the virtuosi and others in the coffeehouses: for example, George Rust reported to Joseph Glanvill that Valentine Greatrakes was the constant topic of conversation in the London coffeehouses in 1666, when Greatrakes was in town performing his cures.[9] William Molyneux, an Irish intellectual and Fellow of the Royal Society, complained that John Toland – who is later discussed in chapter 7 – talked about his heterodox religious ideas too freely in coffeehouses.[10] The coffeehouse was therefore one area of the public sphere where a certain, educated section of society with an interest in a broad range of ideas (those of a high church sensibility did not much like coffeehouses, not least because they were seen as beyond the control of church and state), would have discussed at least some of these miracle cases. Coffeehouses were also outlets for the selling of pamphlets and other publications, and sometimes the sites for the display of curiosities and rarities; the unusual was witnessed, discussed and read about in the coffeehouse environment.[11]

There has been some considerable debate about whether and how women participated in coffeehouse culture.[12] Women were involved in many of these miracle stories, and the likelihood is that, within the coffeehouses at least, those women were more discussed than discussing. This does not mean that women did not have their own social networks through which news and gossip were spread. Female sociability, not only in the home but also in the street, the marketplace, at church and with neighbours, provided opportunities for conversation about, and comment on, the latest events.[13] The events surrounding Martha Taylor's prodigious fast in the 1660s, discussed in chapter 5, give some sense of how village culture approached and talked about these apparently miraculous events, and how central women were to the 'watches' set up to test Taylor's fasting. The 'copycat' cases of healings (Elizabeth Savage, Lydia Hills and Susannah Arch), which followed the news of Marie Maillard's cure while reading the Bible, in the early 1690s in London, indicate the ways in which knowledge was circulated through nonconformist and other informal networks in London, and how quickly news spread by word of mouth. Robert Shoemaker has argued that in this period, women were especially visible in the metropolis, and enjoyed a relative freedom of movement in public life.[14]

What was absolutely vital in the public discussion of these stories was print. A shared print culture was central to the public narration of the miracle stories: each miracle event made an impact through its telling and retelling; each telling and retelling contributed to the public debate about the miracle's meaning. Undoubtedly, print culture and its influence increased in the later seventeenth century. As Adam Fox puts it, 'After the Restoration, evidence for the influence of print on the information which people received and the opinions which they expressed becomes even more plentiful.'[15] For this reason, the bulk of the primary sources guiding this book's narrative are printed materials, supplemented sometimes by diaries and letters when these add to the range of opinions on a particular miracle claim, especially if the ideas expressed in them were shared with others in a semi-public group (as, for example in the correspondence between members of the Royal Society and their friends, about the case of Valentine Greatrakes).

The miracle stories found their way into very different sorts of print culture. They were narrated in some distinctive, early modern forms of cheap print culture that combined a religious message with entertainment, such as the godly ballad, pamphlets and chapbooks, as well as in anthologies of cautionary tales, which had tended to emphasise the providential, and which in turn, in the early seventeenth century, had been intended to replace Roman Catholic miracle stories and stories of saints. In that sense, this later seventeenth-century miracle pamphlet literature was the flipside of the genre of cautionary tales and providential literature which had been an earlier generation's attempt to replace Roman Catholic printed material about saints and miracles with something soundly Protestant.[16] They were the 'flipside' in that they emphasised rewards for piety rather than punishments for irreligious and bad behaviour. But, as Ian Green has pointed out, early modern cheap Protestant print of this sort was often subtly subversive of more official doctrinal lines, stressing good works and leaning 'towards the obstinate popular semi-Pelagianism of which parish clergy from different camps complained'.[17] It is not a surprise, then, to find these older print genres being easily harnessed to the telling of Protestant miracle tales that frequently emphasised piety and good works. In that sense, print culture played an important part in 'Protestantising' miracles, and this can be seen especially in the cases discussed in chapter 6.

Sermons were another important medium through which the miracle claims were interpreted and debated, and were significant components in the discussions that took place about almost all of the miracle cases discussed in this book. For some people, the pulpit would have remained the main medium through which they heard about public events. As Tony Claydon has suggested, sermons should be taken seriously as part of any late Stuart 'public sphere'; before 1689, attendance at a Church of England service was required by all members of the population; after 1689, if individuals did not attend Anglican services, they had to go to services at a licensed dissenting place of worship. This meant that everyone (at least theoretically) had to listen to sermons, but there was also a great trade in printed sermons, which were cheap and easy to produce.[18] Edmund Hickergill commented, in 1681, 'I know very well that every book-sellers stall groans under the burthen of sermons, sermons; – sermons as common (and as commonly cried about the streets) as ballads.'[19] The pulpit and the published sermon were still vital ingredients in stimulating public debate.

New forms of print culture also emerged in this period, most notably, the learned periodicals that were associated with the rise of experimental philosophy, and related pamphlets; for, as we shall see throughout this book, but especially in chapter 4, the virtuosi were concerned to create authoritative knowledge about the natural world, by which, for example, they could test the probability of miracles in their own day. Print culture was essential to their whole enterprise, but also raised questions of authority and credibility. As Adrian Johns puts it, 'In experimental philosophy, the issues of credit associated with the printed realm became acute. Experimental knowledge rested substantially on the accreditation of communiqués about experience. These documents, whether printed or handwritten, had to be read and trusted across wide distances and in very different cultural settings.'[20] In their relation and discussion of the miracle cases, the natural philosophers who became interested in them, faced – as with other knowledge – the question of credibility and attestation, as we shall see.

A shared print culture across a wide social spectrum presupposes greater literacy, and literacy was certainly on the rise,[21] though statistics for the number of people who could read in this period (as opposed to being able to sign their name) are notoriously hard to compile. The fastest period of growth in literacy seems to have been from 1600 to 1675, though this statistic is for men. It is much harder to get reliable statistics for women's literacy because the evidence is so scarce. (Many literacy statistics are based on a person's ability to sign his or her name and most women did not need to sign any documents until Lord Hardwicke's Marriage Act of 1753.) Nevertheless, the women who were at the centre of many of the stories discussed in this book could often read, and they could sometimes write; indeed, in some cases their cures depended on reading the Bible, and in almost all instances, their reputations as believable and respectable 'subjects' were established by their literate piety. Furthermore, shared reading practices – reading out loud in church, the home, schools, and even in the alehouse – meant that not everyone had to be able to read in order to know what news was circulating or to offer an opinion on it; here the boundaries between oral and literature culture were rather fluid. Almost everyone had contact with, and was influenced by, print culture.[22]

These miracle stories and their (often multiple) narrations therefore also reveal how many different sorts of people – of varying social status – engaged with theological ideas, whether in their writings or their practices. For this reason, I avoid the use of the term 'popular religion' with all the resonances that has, from an older historiographical tradition, of the *survival* of older forms of religious belief and practice at a time when it is asserted, there was an increasing division of elite and popular, as the elite were enlightened and the masses either followed suit, in pale imitation of their elders, or retained their old 'superstitious' ideas.[23] The evidence in these miracle cases points rather to the engagement of ordinary people in the re-crafting of practices surrounding miracle claims and the theological re-thinking of the place of miracles within Protestantism, as well as to discussion among, and sometimes fierce contestation between, all sorts of people – if not always face to face, then certainly in print culture about the meanings of miracles. Instead of 'popular religion', I use the term *lived religion*, a concept borrowed from historians of American religion such as David Hall and Robert Orsi.[24] The study of lived religion begins with *practice* in the dynamic sense and proceeds to draw out the theological (and other) meanings of that practice within a specific context. Looking at the details of particular religious practices can reveal how those practices shift, change and are challenged; in what ways they are context-specific; and how the individual or group associated with the practices enacts or disrupts prevailing doctrines. Doctrine is therefore understood to emerge from and, in turn, inform particular religious practices. This is especially pertinent for this period when the emphasis was on a practical Christianity: attending church regularly; adhering to a work ethic; integrating the ethical lessons of the gospels into daily life; observing fast days; and reading the Bible regularly. Right living was an expression of right doctrine, and it permeated all levels of society. Miraculous happenings were often seen to occur as a result of the daily routine of Christian practice, such as reading the Bible as a part of one's daily devotion. Conversely, providential disasters were seen to befall people who strayed off the regular tracks of piety.

There were, however, distinctive groups that became interested in miracles for their different reasons: Interregnum independents and radicals who wanted to follow scripture to the letter or believed that the working of miracles was a sign that they were the true church; conformist 'Latitudinarian' Anglicans who were interested in the boundaries between reason and revelation, the natural and the supernatural; and some, such as the Presbyterians, who rigorously disavowed the possibility of miracles on theological grounds (as we see in chapter 5). This is to reinforce M. J. Ingram's point that there was not a single 'popular religion' opposed to an official or elite religion, but a range of overlapping and interacting 'religious cultures', not necessarily related to social divisions, and in complex interaction with official doctrine and precepts. Interest in and engagement with miracle claims varied widely across these overlapping groups.[25]

Making the miracle cases the primary foci of this book, I examine a number of developments: the articulation of a new theology of the miraculous in a Protestant context, over and against the official Protestant doctrine of the cessation of miracles; the intra-Protestant disagreements about miracles; the particular context which made it possible for people to claim that miracles had occurred; and the responses and debates that the miracle stories generated. By looking at what the miracles meant to those most closely involved, it is possible to create a picture of a multi-textured debate that reveals the *circulation* of ideas amongst different religious and social groups, not simply the handing down of ideas from the elite to the masses. Beginning with lived religion and moving to theology and philosophy provides a route into the ways in which a diverse group of people – much more diverse and from a broader social range than has usually been suggested – was involved in that broad intellectual and cultural movement known as the Enlightenment.[26]

In taking ordinary people as agents in the shaping of Enlightenment religion, the historian has to take careful account of the assumptions and fears of the participants themselves:[27] the elite feared the 'enthusiasm' and 'superstition' of the 'vulgar'. 'Enthusiasm' was 'nothing else but a conceit of being inspired' wrote Henry More, the Cambridge Platonist, in 1656, or 'a vain belief of private revelation' as Dr Johnson defined it in his dictionary some hundred years later.[28] It was associated with the sectarian groups of the civil war period and, later, with some of the dissenters – that is, with those who were seen to base their beliefs on their own direct inspiration from God. This sense of individual religious authority had, of course, led to the proliferation of religions sects in the 1640s and 1650s – a matter of grave concern for the Church of England. Superstition, on the other hand, was associated with Roman Catholicism and the power of the priests who were thought to do untold damage by leading the ignorant astray. David Hume, writing in 1741, described superstition as 'an enemy to civil liberty' for it 'steals in gradually and insensibly; renders men tame and submissive; is acceptable to the magistrate, and seems inoffensive to the people: till at last the priest, having firmly established his authority, becomes the tyrant and disturber of human society, by his endless contentions, persecutions and religious wars'.[29] These religious stereotypes were founded in real fears: the memory of Protestant interconfessional strife in the civil war; the fear of Roman Catholic absolute monarchy with James II's ascent to the throne in 1685, the year that Louis XIV revoked the Edict of Nantes, and the ongoing fear of Roman Catholic Jacobitism which persisted until the middle of the eighteenth century. But they were, in the end, still religious stereotypes, gaining ground in the eighteenth century in a culture that loved ridicule and satire, and witnessed the progress of politeness: 'educated incredulity at the credulousness of the uneducated' was, as much as anything, a rhetorical stance taken to show that one belonged to polite society.[30] At a time when courtesy books emphasised restraint and control, and taught a person to spit in their handkerchief rather than on the floor, and indeed to refrain from spitting too often, the sight of the French Prophets shrieking, whirling, burping and shaking as they uttered their prophecies and made outrageous claims of miracles performed or promised, made the 'polite' (and all those who aspired to that status) shudder.[31]

These stereotypes pointed to another fear, however: the fear of imposture, a perennial worry about what was false and what was true religion. In the wake of the civil war, in a period in which religious contestation remained a vibrant part of the culture, questions about imposture were shot through almost all talk about religion, and necessarily affected the debates and discussions about miracles. Was a miracle truly the work of God? Was it a fake, the result of overweening 'enthusiasm' or cunning 'superstition'? Was it, even, diabolical? And how might one tell? In the second half of the seventeenth century, new tools were being developed which promised an answer, or at least a method that would lead to an answer: the new philosophy or the beginnings of modern 'science'.[32]

Miracle claims were revived and indeed increased at just the moment that the new philosophy and the experimental method were developing;[33] though it may seem counter-intuitive to the usual historical story, the evidence suggests that miracles and science 'grew' together in the second half of the seventeenth century. As Robert Boyle and others in the Royal Society were constructing the new technologies for their experimental philosophy, it was natural that they should investigate those miracle claims. This they did, most notably, in the case of Valentine Greatrakes in 1665–6; their methods were copied by gentleman amateur scholars and local gentry in the provinces (for example, in the case of Martha Taylor, discussed in chapter 5) and by succeeding generations (as illustrated in the examinations and analyses of the case of Marie Maillard in London, in the mid 1690s, discussed in chapter 6). Indeed, the miraculous bodies (the women and men who were healed, for example) provided *bodies of evidence* for the new experimental method. In investigating those claims, the fellows of the Royal Society and Anglican clergymen (and it has been calculated that about eight per cent of the Society's fellows were Anglican clergymen in its early years),[34] largely orthodox in their outlook, realised that to deny altogether that these events might be miracles would be to go down the route towards atheism. Miracles had to be accounted *plausible*; and, if the evidence were great enough, *probable*. This required proper testimony about what had happened and a proper understanding of the natural world such that it was clear whether the event could be explained naturally or not. Thus a vital new ingredient was added to the debate about miracles – natural philosophy; the promise of knowledge about the natural world so that a judgement could be made about whether an event claimed as miraculous was 'above' nature or not. What was also promised, or at least hoped for, was a reduction in ignorance and impostures.

What, then, was the relationship between all of this activity – the miracle claims and the investigations and debates they provoked – in the second half of the seventeenth century and the philosophical debate about miracles in the first half of the eighteenth century? To ask this question is to provoke two broader questions. First, what was the relationship between lived religion and what has, for so long, been thought of as a turning point in the West's attitude to religious belief and practice, what Paul Hazard (working, however, from a French model), called 'the crisis of the European mind'? For Hazard, this was the moment when 'The most widely accepted notions, such as deriving proof of God's existence from universal consent, the historical basis of miracles, were openly called in question. The Divine was relegated to a vague and impenetrable heaven somewhere up in the skies. Man and man alone was the standard by which all things were measured.'[35] Such a judgement – and it has been widespread, deeply influential and endlessly discussed – is based on the reading of a narrow band of philosophical texts, mostly sceptical in tone; indeed, the traditional conception of the Enlightenment has most often been associated with a particular philosophical canon. A second question is, therefore: what is the relationship between experience – including lived religion – and philosophy?

Neither intellectual historians nor philosophers tend to spend much time considering this relationship. Nevertheless, the particularity of people's experiences always provokes the philosopher's questions – if it were not for horrendous events, why else would philosophers write about the problem of evil, for example? – but the philosopher usually ignores those particular experiences. Indeed, the philosopher, whose task is necessarily to generalise, does not usually take into account individual experiences precisely because they disrupt the generalisations that are the bread and butter of philosophical method. There are, then, concrete and specific circumstances for which the philosopher cannot account. But in making sense of lived religion and their own religious experiences, people find it necessary to turn to philosophical questions as well as to questions of evidence. While individuals claim that they have experienced and witnessed particular miracles in specific historical circumstances, it is the philosopher's task to ask whether and how miracles *can* occur. It is no surprise, then, that a half-century of miracle claims and the debates that they generated, in the latter part of the seventeenth century, should be followed by a philosophical debate about miracles.[36] What is surprising about that philosophical debate is how often concrete examples of contemporary miracle cases were discussed by the philosophers, though this has not been drawn out by commentators. Chapter 7 looks specifically at the philosophical debate's relationship to particular miracle claims of the late seventeenth and early eighteenth centuries. This is not, of course, the context in which the eighteenth-century philosophical debate has usually been set, not least because discussions of that debate have been confined to intellectual history.

Taking account of the lived religion which preceded the philosophical debate thereby gives a different motor of change – a different cause of that debate. This is not what historians and philosophers have usually argued. An older historiographical tradition presumed that it was the sceptical thinkers, such as the deists, who wished to remove all mystery and revelation from Christian doctrine, who had provoked the Enlightenment philosophical debate about miracles. In 1876, the agnostic Leslie Stephen published his *History of English Thought in the Eighteenth Century*; in this influential work Stephen assumed that the protagonists in the debate were the deists, and thus it had been up to the orthodox or apologists to put up a rigorous defence. He argued that they did this, but the deists were not confuted, merely driven to bolder ground. In short, rationalism attacked, and Christianity had to defend itself.

R. M. Burns in his book of 1981, *The Great Debate on Miracles from Joseph Glanvill to David Hume*, challenged this view, arguing that it was the opponents of the deists, the advocates of belief in miracles, 'who began the debate by stressing the importance of miracles to a greater degree than ever before in the history of Christianity'. Thus, he turned Stephen's argument on its head stating that 'the attack on miracles began as a defensive reaction to this development'. More generally, Burns challenges the presumption behind Stephen's argument that one will find 'scepticism concerning miracles growing in direct proportion to the adoption of scientific attitudes' and that 'those who emphasised the miraculous were motivated by religious traditionalism' while those who attacked miracles were 'a few "advanced" spirits . . . influenced . . . by the development of modern scientific attitudes in late seventeenth-century England'. Rather, Burns suggested, those who wrote in support of miracles 'may more plausibly be regarded as the advanced thinkers of their age, most in touch with the scientific spirit'.[37] Burns therefore looks at these 'advanced thinkers', men of Restoration science and religion such as Robert Boyle, Joseph Glanvill and other members of the Royal Society as well as influential Anglican divines (whom he calls proponents of a 'liberal' Anglican theology), demonstrating their interest and even belief in miracles, as evidenced in their writings.

Burns' reinterpretation is quite right: there was a renewed interest in miracles amongst members of the Royal Society and 'moderate' Anglican divines; many of them wrote in support of miracles, and employed their reading in the new philosophy to support their case. But why did 'the advocates of belief in miracles' jumpstart the debate? Why did they stress 'the importance of miracles to a greater degree than ever before in the history of Christianity', as Burns (with a certain degree of hyperbole) puts it? Burns asks the question, 'why did a debate of such unparalleled intensity occur at precisely this juncture in history, and in England?' but his answers are vague: toleration allowed free debate (especially after the freedom of the press was established in 1694); the civil war period was a stimulus to free thinking and led to widespread alienation from traditional forms of belief. He admits these are 'remote and general factors'[38] but his fuller explanation still does not answer the question entirely: 'the debate on miracles was but one specific aspect of a more wide-ranging controversy between those who were spokesmen for the established religion of England by the end of the seventeenth century, and who we can therefore excusably term "orthodox", although they were certainly not orthodox in every sense of the term, and a certain group of radical critics who are generally referred to as "Deists"'.[39] This gives a hint of the religious controversies that dogged Enlightenment England and certainly points to the 1690s as a significant turning point, but it still does not reveal why there was a renewed interest in miracles not only amongst certain Protestant groups but also amongst some of the Fellows of the Royal Society and moderate Anglican divines in the second half of the seventeenth century. I suspect the answer is simple: the interest was there because miracle claims were being made. Burns, writing as an intellectual historian, did not take lived religion into account and therefore could not fully answer his own question. I argue in this book that those Royal Society fellows, clergymen and theologians displayed a renewed interest in, and stress upon the importance of, miracles in this period precisely because so many people were making claims that they had experienced miracles or were able to work them. They therefore felt compelled to investigate, assess and discuss them.

This, then, was one link between the miracle claims and debates of the second half of the seventeenth century and the philosophical debate on miracles in the first half of the eighteenth century. Lived religion prepared the ground. This was true not only in general terms, but also rather more specifically in relation to the setting of the *terms* of the philosophical debate. Many of the participants in the seventeenth-century debate, faced with cures that could not always be explained naturally, for example, drew on the methods of the new philosophy and suggested that evidence and testimony were the vital components in assessing the credibility of a miracle claim. Miracles were therefore considered plausible upon very great and well-attested evidence. This 'middle way' position of the Anglican apologists was well established by the beginning of the eighteenth century. It was therefore the point which the deists and sceptics like Hume had to refute; evidence had to be proven unreliable, however plentiful and however well attested. In order to do that, they referred not only to the biblical miracles but also to recent examples of miracle claims, especially those of the French Prophets in the first few years of the eighteenth century. Thus in the eighteenth-century philosophical debate, examples of miracle claims and stories were frequently invoked by all sides. My discussion of the philosophical debate in chapter 7 does not set out to analyse the whole debate – this would be quite beyond the scope of this book – but rather looks at how cases of contemporary miracles, miracle stories that could be remembered from within a generation or two, were used to support or refute specific arguments in the overall debate.

If, therefore, as I am suggesting, a broader Enlightenment discussion on miracles began much earlier than the deist intervention in the 1690s, then not only are new participants, practices and texts included in the debate, but the 'parameters' of the Enlightenment may also be stretched.[40] Over and against an older historiographical tradition which saw the Enlightenment in a distinctly 'French' mode and as a secularising phenomenon which occurred largely in the eighteenth century,[41] this book fits into a more recent body of work which argues that there was an English Enlightenment and that it – or at least its first impulses – happened earlier rather than later. Roy Porter, for example, calls this pre-1750 phase 'the first Enlightenment' in England.[42] Porter saw the English Enlightenment as distinctive: not necessarily intellectually coherent, and certainly not a monolithic movement, but rather a set of sensibilities which had particular and practical outcomes that made England the birthplace of 'the modern'. This new emphasis on the English Enlightenment has emerged from a body of scholarship that has sought to be more precise about all the national contexts of that broad cultural and intellectual movement we call the Enlightenment.[43] This has led, in the work of historians such as J. G. A. Pocock, to the idea that there was a proliferation of enlightenments, numerous intellectual and cultural movements, each shaped by their specific context.[44] In particular, the English Enlightenment has been regarded as occurring rather early (at least in its first phase); as influential upon the French *philosophes*, and as distinctly *religious* in character.[45]

This book is also about how Protestant concerns shaped particular Enlightenment ideas in England and as such it relates to a number of strands in recent historical scholarship. First of all, the revival and indeed increase in miracle claims, and increased belief in miracles, in the second half of the seventeenth century challenges easy assumptions about the decline of religious belief in this period. Such assumptions were inherited from Victorian historians who, for their own purposes, wished to represent the eighteenth-century Church as one in decline.[46] However, a significant sea change has occurred in this area of scholarship in recent years. J. C. D. Clark in his *English Society, 1688–1832* of 1985 argued that England was a 'confessional state' until the repeal of the Test and Corporation Acts in 1828 and Catholic Emancipation in 1829, and thereby suggested that the Church of England was integral to the fabric of society – though he did not illustrate how this was the case 'on the ground'.[47] Ecclesiastical historians have since been engaged in that research 'on the ground', in parish and diocesan archives, and have shown this to be a period not necessarily marked by church decline but often by considerable activity, with lively parishes, pastoral attentiveness from many clergy, and successful parish-level teaching of the rudiments of the Christian faith.[48] Secondly, in suggesting that the roots of the eighteenth-century philosophical debate lie in Protestant ideas about practices concerning miracles in the preceding half-century, this book relates to a number of books (primarily in the field of intellectual history) that give religious roots to Enlightenment ideas. Amos Funkenstein, for example, located the metaphysical roots of the scientific revolution in medieval scholasticism, and argued that science and theology merged into one idiom in the seventeenth century.[49] Historians such as Michael Buckley and Alan Kors have argued that orthodox theology opened the way to scepticism and even atheism: their work has been about France where Enlightenment thought about religion can more generally be equated with such scepticism. Nevertheless, their research – focused on the 'rational' preoccupations of Roman Catholic theologians in early modern France – reinforces the idea (commonly found amongst both historians and sociologists) that rational religion necessarily leads to secularisation.[50] In the English context, contemporaries certainly feared that was the case – as the events and debates discussed in chapter 6, about the 1690s, especially illustrate – but it was not necessarily so. For example, Justin Champion has suggested that the deists – those stalwart defenders of the primacy of reason in all matters – were not so much anti-religious generally, but anti-clerical, their attack focused upon the perceived injustice of the distribution of authority in society rather than on religion per se.[51] Rational religion might therefore be thought of as just one more choice amongst many possibilities in the articulation of a Christian faith: we cannot assume an inevitable and universal march towards rational religion. More recently, Jonathan Sheehan, writing about England and Germany, has posited that 'the Enlightenment Bible grew out of the soil of the Protestant Reformation', arguing that the Bible was re-made in a new image (through the work of translators and cultural commentators) in the Enlightenment.[52]

In short, religion was shaped anew in the Enlightenment, and it was central to the whole project of modernity. This sort of approach challenges the idea, promoted by older views of the relationship between religion and the Enlightenment, as well as by the presuppositions of the secularisation thesis, that religion in the Enlightenment period (especially those religious beliefs and practices dubbed 'irrational') should be viewed only as the tenacious survival of earlier belief systems and rituals. And if religion was constantly made 'anew' in the Enlightenment, then perhaps secularisation – or a decline in religious belief and practice – correspondingly ebbed and flowed. The sociologist, David Martin, one of a number of historians and sociologists at present re-thinking the secularisation thesis, writes, 'instead of regarding secularization as a once-for-all unilateral process, one might think rather in terms of successive Christianizations followed or accompanied by recoils'.[53]

My own view, in relationship to the specific case of miracles, is that religious belief and practice were made anew in this period; miracles were reconceptualised and re-made in new images – a Protestant image, a scientific image, a rational image, a political image, a prophetic image – by several different Protestant groups, as well as particular individuals. They were certainly not merely survivals of an earlier belief system, and they were not only Protestant miracles, they were also genuinely 'Enlightenment miracles'. These various different Protestant and Enlightenment notions of a miracle both formed and informed the foundational strands of the eighteenth-century philosophical debate on miracles. A key intellectual position that emerged in early Enlightenment culture of England was the belief in the possibility of miracles occurring in one's own day; Robert Boyle subscribed to it, as did many of the orthodox Anglicans who contributed to the eighteenth-century debate. At the same time, given that some of the other interlocutors in that debate questioned the idea that God would perform miracles at all, we can see another aspect of Enlightenment religion at play here – a more sceptical position which did, indeed, have its roots in the work of those Protestant theologians who proposed the doctrine of the cessation of miracles but did not, themselves, contemplate taking the next step to question whether God would perform miracles at all. As historians, we have to be careful not to take the next false step, by presuming that the more sceptical position was the only position representative of English Enlightenment religious thought and practice.

* * * * *

The overall shape and scope of the book therefore look something like this. Protestant miracles emerged in Interregnum England, in the wake of the bloodshed and conflict of the civil war, when numerous religious groups and individuals claimed divine inspiration and religious authority. In the 1650s, groups led by the spirit, proclaiming no need for a hierarchically structured or clerically led church – Quakers, Ranters, Muggletonians, Seekers, Diggers, Fifth Monarchists and others – manifested themselves and coalesced, vying for converts with the independent churches who had emerged earlier in the century, such as Presbyterians (who formed the official religion under Cromwell) and General and Particular Baptists. In this context, miracle claims were made as being properly scriptural or 'apostolic'. The response to Baptists who claimed they had experienced divine healing and Quakers who proclaimed they could perform miracles was therefore largely one of intra-Protestant disagreement. Had miracles ceased in the early church or not?

There was competition too: what authority did these groups have to make their miraculous claims? These intra-Protestant doctrinal disagreements about miracles continued after the Restoration, as exemplified by the case of Martha Taylor in the late 1660s, when the Presbyterians who commented on the case challenged any – including imagined – definitions of the case as a 'miracle'. But already in the 1650s, another line of thinking was emerging which would prove influential in the following decades. The cacophony and chaos of the religious sects, and the bloodshed of the civil war as a whole, caused fear and alarm. Some men therefore, even at this stage, while Oliver Cromwell was still alive, looked to the future and wondered how they could mould a 'middle way'. Such an intellectual, religious and political position therefore began to develop amongst Anglicans, in religious exile in their own country, who wished to find a rational underpinning to all Christian faith, a theological and epistemological foundation upon which different sorts of Christians could co-exist peaceably. This emerged as a prevalent concern in the Restoration and was bound up with the emergence of the new philosophy. By the mid-1660s, when Valentine Greatrakes was performing his cures publicly, a new approach to miracles began to emerge out of that middle way – what is often called 'latitudinarianism' in the Church of England – and the work of the individuals and institutions of the world of Restoration science, with which it was profoundly intertwined. This led to a different approach to miracles: to the investigation of them, but also to a belief amongst orthodox Anglicans that miracles might indeed be plausible, as long as they were fully tested. This investigative mode, shaped primarily by moderate Anglicanism and early science, lasted at least until the end of the seventeenth century. Debate and discussion were facilitated by the increase in print culture and the numerous public opportunities for debate in coffeehouses and clubs, as well as pamphlets, popular journals, more learned papers and sermons. At the turn of the century, however, a new mode or approach emerged: scepticism. As early eighteenth-century England began its progress towards politeness, this scepticism was combined with the literary trademarks of the day, ridicule and spoof, to form a rather different cultural context, in which miracle claims could be more easily dismissed. The extravagant miracle claims and promises of the French Prophets, in the first couple of decades of the new century, did nothing to lessen either the scepticism or the ridicule; Anglican apologists had to respond accordingly. Many did this by becoming more and more 'evidentialist' in their approach, especially with regard to the biblical miracles. These, then, were the changing contexts in which miracles, and attitudes to miracles, were 'made anew' in the century from 1650 to 1750.

This book, while focusing especially on the early Enlightenment, looks at how miracles and attitudes to miracles were forged over that hundred-year span. It begins in the 1650s when in Oxford a group of men were having some of the first conversations about the new philosophy and were conducting the first 'modern scientific' experiments, while all around the country Quakers were claiming to perform miracles and Baptists were engaged in divine healing. It ends in 1748 when Hume made his (in)famous and highly sceptical contribution to the philosophical debate on miracles and an old woman named Bridget Bostock healed (with fasting spittle and prayer) the hundreds of people who came to her hovel in Cheshire every day in search of a cure for their ills.

CHAPTER 2

Protestantism and Miracles

I. The Cessation of Miracles?

Holy places and objects, and the rituals associated with those material manifestations of the divine, were vital to late medieval piety. Medieval England was a sacred landscape filled with pilgrimage sites and shrines: the tombs of famous saints such as Thomas Becket at Canterbury; the shrines of local saints, such as Frideswide in Oxford; and sites of other relics, such as that of the 'true blood' at the Cistercian Abbey in Hailes, Gloucestershire. The shrines at all these and many other places such as Westminster, Canterbury and St Albans were places of pilgrimage to which the sick went to be healed, hoping for a miracle.[1] At the shrine of St Thomas Becket in Canterbury Cathedral, over seven hundred miracles were officially recorded in the fifteen years after Thomas' death in 1170. The water of Thomas – into which, it was said, some of Thomas' blood had been infused – was the most important of the relics for healing miracles at his shrine.[2] Important too were the many holy wells across the country; frequently associated with a particular saint – such as those connected to St Frideswide in Oxford and Our Lady of Walsingham in Norfolk – they were often also linked to an older folk tradition of sacred or 'magical' places, and represented the Church's 'christianisation' of 'unacceptable' sources of supernatural power to its own ends.[3] For the medieval Christian, the pilgrimage itself and the rituals upon reaching the shrine – venerating the relics, drinking holy water or washing parts of the body in it – were central components of a religious tradition in which miracles, especially miracles of healing, were experienced in relation to holy place, ritual and sacred object.

The belief system that undergirded this set of religious practices was challenged and many of its material manifestations destroyed at the Protestant Reformation. For many of the sixteenth-century reformers and their Protestant heirs, miracles had ceased with biblical times. Miracles were to be viewed with suspicion precisely because they were associated with intermediary figures and objects – saints, relics and holy places – and all the ritualistic trappings of Roman Catholicism. Most Protestants came to think it wrong to claim that a human institution had the power to work miracles: saints and relics were unnecessary, interrupting the newly privileged relationship between God and the individual, and therefore challenging God's omnipotence. To rely on anything but this relationship with God was, for the strictest of Protestants, blasphemous. Even petitionary prayer was seen as suspicious by some: a person should not tempt providence for the impossible. Only scripture was to be the bedrock of faith. Signs and wonders were to be discarded for the promises made by God in his Word.

Some of the Protestant reformers in the sixteenth century therefore began to teach the doctrine of the cessation of miracles. This doctrine held that miracles had ceased after the Church had become established – that is, when they were no longer needed – and this cessation was usually (though not always) dated at the establishment of Christendom in the fourth century. A reading of Luther and Calvin, the two major magisterial sixteenth-century Protestant reformers, suggests that there are two key features of their writing on miracles. First, the reformers were clear that the truth of their teachings was not based in or proven by new miracles, though they were often asked for miracles as proof of the truth of Protestant claims by the Roman Catholics, as Calvin noted in his prefatory address to King Francis, in his *Institutes*. The attackers of reformed Christianity, he said, 'do not cease to assail our doctrine and to reproach and defame it with names that render it hated or suspect. They call it "new" and "of recent birth". They reproach it as "doubtful and uncertain". They ask what miracles have confirmed it.' In addressing this challenge, Calvin wrote: 'In demanding miracles of us, they act dishonestly. For we are not forging some new gospel but are retaining that very gospel whose truth all the miracles that Jesus Christ and his disciples ever wrought serve to confirm.' He warned that scripture is primary, and that scripture itself warns us that miracles merely *confirm* right doctrine.[4] What caused anxiety here, for Calvin, was the call to produce miracles. His refutation of miracles in his own age came out of that context; and yet even that refutation had its ambivalences. He wrote, 'God's name ought to be always and everywhere hallowed, whether by miracles or by the natural order of things' and 'we are not entirely lacking in miracles, and these are very certain and not subject to mockery'.[5]

What was vital for both Luther and Calvin, and they repeated this constantly, was that miracles should always point to, and lead people to, the Word. Luther, for example, wrote that, 'it is an absurd procedure on the part of all men to regard works with more admiration than that with which they regard the Word of God'. 'Therefore,' he continued, 'the Word of God must be given consideration first of all; and if someone were to perform all sorts of miracles, yes, even to raise the dead, and comes without the Word, he must be repudiated. All the apostles and prophets have given this warning.' And, in typical style, he could not resist a dig at the papacy: 'the pope has established his tyranny without the Word by miracles of that sort'.[6] Calvin, in his commentary on chapter 20 of the Gospel of John, wrote a defence of miracles, so long as they were mere additions to the Word.

> It may seem absurd, however, that faith is founded on miracles, when it ought to be devoted exclusively to God's promises and Word. I reply: No other use is given to miracles than to be aids and supports to faith. They serve to prepare men's minds so that they might give greater reverence to the Word of God. . . . Therefore although faith properly rests on the Word of God, and looks to the Word as its only object, the addition of miracles is not superfluous, so long as they are also related to the Word and direct faith to it.[7]

A second feature of the major Protestant reformers' writing on miracles was that it did not consist of endless tracts on the subject. Rather, it was largely in the course of preaching sermons and writing commentaries on the miracle stories in the gospels and the Book of Acts, and in the Old Testament, that the reformers developed the doctrine of the cessation of the miracles. Furthermore, what they preached and wrote in these sermons and commentaries was always in dialogue with the issues of the day which they faced – primarily, the Roman Catholic claims that miracles were the sign of a true faith, and their fear that the gullibility of ordinary people would lead them to turn to signs and wonders rather than the trustworthy Word.

The doctrine of the cessation of miracles therefore developed not so much from some abstract distaste for, or even hatred of, miracles but rather out of the particular context of the sixteenth-century conflict between Protestants and Roman Catholics, a conflict that was about who was teaching the truth and where authority resided. While Roman Catholics challenged Protestants to produce miracles in order to prove the truth of their message, the Protestants in turn tried to discredit Roman Catholicism by pointing to the potentially false or even evil origin of their miracles. Luther, in a piece of typical anti-popish rhetoric, interpreted many of the Roman Catholic rituals associated with miracles and healing as the work of Satan:

> at times the devil also takes possession of a person and then lets himself be cast out by adjuration, blessing etc. All this he does for the purpose of

confirming his lies and deceptions and of impressing the people, so that because of these apparently great miracles they are seduced into idolatry. This he has accomplished to date with pilgrimages and the idolatrous adoration of saints, at one place with the Sacred Blood, at another with this or that Mary.

Preaching on the miracle stories in the gospels, Luther had an eye to stories that must have been doing the rounds, which he wanted to refute, such as the following:

> Yes, the devil can contrive to make a person who has been wounded, shot or injured in some other way appear to be dead; he can render a person insensate for a while, with the result that everybody believes he is really dead. Later on, however, this person regains consciousness, and the people say that he has been brought back to life through the power of this or that saint. I have heard of a lad who had been lying submerged in water for two days; but when his parents took him and pledged him to St Anne, he was restored to life. Are these not miracles and signs? No, for surely these people were not actually dead. The devil so befuddled people's senses that they thought them dead until he let them regain consciousness.[8]

Similarly, Calvin wrote in his *Institutes*,

> And we may also fitly remember that Satan has his miracles, which, though they are deceitful tricks rather than true powers, are of such sort as to mislead the simple-minded and untutored [cf. II Thess. 2: 9–10]. Magicians and enchanters have always been noted for miracles. Idolatry has been nourished by wonderful miracles, yet these are not sufficient to sanction for us the superstition either of magicians or idolaters.
>
> The Donatists of old overwhelmed the simplicity of the multitude with this battering-ram: that they were mighty in miracles. We, therefore, now answer our adversaries as Augustine then answered the Donatists: the Lord made us wary of these miracle workers when he predicted that false prophets with lying signs and prodigies would come to draw even the elect (if possible) into error.[9]

In the first volume of his *Commentary on the Acts of the Apostles* of 1552, he wrote about this again, putting the emphasis not on Satan but on human beings, arguing that 'Satan's illusions are far different from the power of God.' If human beings cannot tell the difference between the power of God and 'lying wonders' then 'this error proceeds only from our own defects (because we are so dull and unobservant). For God shows his own power clearly enough.' In arguing this, Calvin seemed to suggest that miracles could occur in his day: 'Therefore in the miracles which God displays there is sure enough corroboration both of the doctrine and of the ministry if only our eyes are open to see.' His emphasis here – regarding the truth of the miracle or not – is on the perceiver (a theme later echoed in John Locke's *Discourse on Miracles* of 1701/2), in a theology which, typically for Calvin, pitches the reprobate against the elect, and seems to suggest, in contrast with his comments in the *Institutes* quoted above, that the elect could not be led astray. 'If the proofs are not strong enough for the wicked so that they are often deceived by the false miracles of Satan, the cause must be their own blindness. But whoever has a pure heart perceives God with the purity of inward vision as often as He shows Himself. Nor can Satan deceive us except when through the wicked-ness of our hearts our judgment is corrupted and our eyes blinded or glazed by our own dullness of vision.'[10] This notion that Satan might be the origin of miracles persisted throughout the Reformation period and into the seven-teenth century: discerning the truth of a miracle (or for that matter, of any claimed divine revelation, such as a vision) was therefore in part about whether it was the product of good or evil forces.

As the church was reformed in England, this 'anti-miracle' position was expressed initially not in a theological debate but in the condemnation and destruction of relics and holy sites for healing: these were easy targets in the broader Protestant attack on Roman Catholicism. With the dissolution of the monasteries in the 1530s there occurred the destruction of many of the shrines and relics that had been housed in monasteries, abbeys and cathedrals. Saints' bones – such as those of Thomas Becket at Canterbury – were broken and scattered, and relics were declared hoaxes. Former miracles and the apparatus by which they were effected were reinterpreted as fraudulent; the medieval past was rewritten by the Protestant Reformation propagandists to discredit Roman Catholicism. The holy blood at Hailes was described as an unctuous gum, which had been coloured and was later declared to be drake's blood. On 24 November 1538, at Paul's Cross, Bishop Hilsey preached against it as a 'feigned relic', and on Christmas Eve 1539, the Cistercian monastery at Hailes was dissolved.[11] Holy wells were filled in or locked up and sealed over, such as that of St Anne at Buxton in 1538, so that people could no longer come for the healing waters. Such actions were part of a larger campaign against popery and superstition, embodied in the Royal Injunctions against 'monuments of idolatry and suspicion' not only of 1538, but also of 1547 and 1559.

This led some leading church figures to teach the doctrine of the cessation of miracles in the course of defending the Protestant faith. John Hooper,

Bishop of Gloucester and then Worcester in Edward VI's reign (martyred under Mary), wrote *A Brief and Clear Confession of the Christian Faith* in 1550, containing 100 articles of faith.[12] The fifty-seventh article clearly stated the doctrine of the cessation of miracles:

> I believe that this holy doctrine of the gospel in the very time by God appointed was confirmed & approved by heavenly miracles, as well by Jesus Christ himself, the prophets and apostles, as by other good and faithful ministers of the same Gospel; and that after such a sort, that for the confirming thereof, there is now no more need of new miracles; but rather we must content ourselves with that is done, and simply and plainly believe only the holy scripture without seeking any further to be taught; watching and still taking heed to ourselves that we be not beguiled and deceived with the false miracles of Anti Christ, wherewith the world at this day is stuffed; which miracles are wrought by the working of Satan, to confirm all kinds of idolatry, errors, abuses, and iniquities.[13]

A doctrinal debate on the cessation of miracles emerged more fully in the latter part of the sixteenth century in England, largely prompted by the continuing conflict between Roman Catholics and Protestants in the era of Counter-Reformation missionary activity. D. P. Walker argues that the doctrine did not merely reflect developing Protestant theology but was also used to discredit Roman Catholic miracles – and to respond to the Roman Catholic use of miracles in anti-Protestant propaganda – both in England and on the Continent. Dating the fuller development of this doctrine at the turn of the century, he suggests that 'the greatest boost to the Protestant interest in and anxiety about miracles was given by Justus Lipsius's two trea- tises, published in 1604 and 1605 . . . about miracles performed at two shrines of the Virgin Mary . . . in the Catholic Netherlands'.[14] These miracles were presented by Lipsius as signs that the Roman Catholic Church was the true church. (Lipsius was a humanist scholar, who had taught for thirteen years at a Protestant university and who seems to have converted back to – or always covertly to have remained within – Roman Catholicism.) The treatises provoked a great deal of polemical literature on both sides. The Protestant argument in this literature was that God only needed miracles to establish the new religion of Christianity in the first instance; any contemporary miracles were accounted for as the work of Satan; the true church is founded on scrip- ture alone. The Roman Catholics responded by admitting that there were perhaps fewer miracles in these days, but precisely because fewer were needed. However, they argued, miracles were still necessary for three reasons: first, because this was a time of atheism and heresy; secondly, because miracles were marks of the true church; and thirdly, to convert the many existing 'heathen'. Lipsius in his treatise also suggested that miracles were no longer necessary to prove the divinity of Christ – a doctrine now generally accepted by all Christians, he thought – but that they were needed to show the continued importance of the saints, relics and other cults and practices that had been attacked by the Protestants.[15]

Miracles were also deployed in Roman Catholic mission activity in England; Alexandra Walsham suggests that when Jesuits were sent across the Channel after 1574, 'they found miracles, visions, and exorcisms very effective as prosletyzing tools'.[16] Late sixteenth- and early seventeenth-century England therefore witnessed many claims of miracles, including healing – especially associated with the new relics of recent Roman Catholic martyrs – as well as dramatic Roman Catholic exorcisms, such as that performed by the Jesuit William Weston in 1585–6, in the households of Sir George Peckham at Denham in Buckinghamshire and Lord Vaux at Hackney.[17] Some Jesuits also wrote tracts arguing against Protestant claims that miracles had ceased, such as Thomas Stapleton (an Englishman exiled in Louvain), who made the familiar case that miracles verified the Roman religion, and the lack of miracles amongst Protestants showed them to be upstarts who had no such tokens of apostleship.[18]

When English Protestants wrote polemical and even vicious tracts against miracles in this period, they therefore did so in the context of this (now treasonable) activity of Jesuit missionaries, faced with Roman Catholic claims that their version of the Christian faith was true precisely because it was veri-fied by the occurrence of miracles. Walker has argued in his book *Unclean Spirits* that the doctrine of the cessation of miracles, held as a firm principle, was a fairly recent and distinctively English invention.[19] He suggests that this was, in part, because of the lack of a 'party line' on miracles amongst the early continental Protestant reformers, and was also in part a product of the English Protestant context.

Exorcisms, which were sometimes discussed in relation to miracles and were generally associated with Roman Catholicism, provided an interesting test case for the role of the supernatural amongst Protestants at the end of the sixteenth century when it was clear that Roman Catholics were not the only ones performing dramatic and public exorcisms. In the 1590s, a number of controversies arose out of Puritan exorcisms, and triggered attempts by those at the centre of the Church – described as 'Anglican' by Walker – to suppress them.[20] Many of the more radical Calvinist Protestants in England, the 'Godly', scorned the Roman Catholics for use of exorcism. For these Godly, before any attempt was made to remove the affliction (that is, by exorcism), God's purpose in that affliction should first be discovered, and repentance made. Only then could they seek to remove the affliction through prayer and fasting. Nevertheless, while many Puritans criticised the Roman Catholics for their dramatic ceremonies of exorcism, their own rituals of prayer and fasting could be highly performative, with the minister commanding demonic spirits to leave a person's body. This, in turn, led some to conduct highly dramatic exorcisms. Such events were well-publicised, in particular by John Foxe in the sixteenth century. John Darrell, a Cambridge graduate and preaching minister who never held a living (having a small personal income), was one of the most well-known – and ultimately infamous – of the Elizabeth Puritan exorcists. In the late 1580s and 1590s, he conducted a number of spectacular cures of people who were said to be possessed. After his final case, in Nottingham in 1597, Darrell was convicted in 1598 by the court of High Commission for counterfeit for his practices of exorcism. Historians agree the trial was badly conducted and the verdict unjust. It was in part inspired by the desire of conformist Anglicans, most notably Archbishop Whitgift and Bishop (later Archbishop) Bancroft, to suppress Puritanism within the church. One outcome was that canon 72 of the Church Canons of 1604 forbade any minister 'without such Licence to attempt upon any pretence whatsoever whether of possession or obsession, by fasting or prayer, to cast out any devill or devils, under paine of the imputation of Imposture, or Cozenage, and Deposition from the Ministerie'.[21] In short, a minister had to have the express permission of his bishop to attempt an exorcism. As David Harley points out, as no such licences were issued, beneficed clergyman could not use such methods publicly except during the civil war and Interregnum.[22] Walsham suggests that amongst Roman Catholics 'Demand for this rite grew against the backdrop of the Anglican campaign against John Darrell and other puritan exorcists and particularly after the canons of 1604 made it effectively illegal within the framework of the Church of England.'[23]

In discussing the ensuing debate about the supernatural between these different parties, Walker rather optimistically argues that there was agreement on at least one thing: the doctrine of the cessation of miracles. Thus, says Walker, 'this doctrine, especially in its Anglican [sic] form ... makes it possible for a pious Christian to live in a world entirely devoid of any super-natural occurrences: the miracles in the Bible truly happened, but they happen no more; divine providence still rules this world, but only through normal, natural means'.[24] As we shall see, such agreement was by no means universal.

In late sixteenth-century and early seventeenth-century England, protago-nists in this debate on cessation included John Jewel, apologist for the Church of England, who declared that miracles were no longer 'proofs' of the true church. Jewel wrote that 'Neither are we bound of necessity to believe all such miracles whatsoever without exception.' He too wanted to refute the claims of the Roman Catholics: 'Sometime even in the church the people is shamefully deceived with feigned miracles, wrought either by the priests, or else by their companions, for lucre's sake.' And in a clear statement of the relationship between true doctrine and miracles in his own day he declared: 'Miracles be not evermore undoubted proofs of true doctrine.'[25] There were others who explicitly refuted Roman Catholic miracles, such as Richard Sheldon, a convert from Roman Catholicism and former Jesuit, who, in his *A Survey of the Miracles of the Church of Rome, proving them to be anti Christian* (1616) aimed to show that Roman Catholic miracles were either fakes or diabolical, the product of the anti-Christ.[26]

Some Protestants, as we have seen in the cases of Luther, Calvin and Bishop Hooper, came to believe that God sometimes allowed Satan to perform miracles. For some later writers, the only way of discerning the veracity of a miracle was by assessing the miracle-performer's doctrine, to see if it was 'sound'. This position was often considered problematic because it involved admitting the possibility of a miracle-performer (an intermediary figure) but it was developed by figures such as Increase Mather, the American Puritan, in his much circulated and influential collection of wonder tales, *An Essay for the Recording of Illustrious Providences* of 1684. The Enlightenment debate on miracles came to question this possibility that Satan could perform miracles. The Anglican divine, William Fleetwood, in his important defence of miracles published in 1701, claimed that only God could perform miracles.[27] By that time, Fleetwood was only articulating what, in practice, had been thought for several decades amongst Protestants, especially Latitudinarians like him. While it was always good rhetoric to accuse Roman Catholic miracles of being 'diabolical', the issue of adjudication for many Protestants, in miracle cases, came to be one of distinguishing true from false (or hoax) miracles – not true from 'diabolical' – as well as discerning whether miracle claims (such as healings) could be explained by natural laws, or whether they were 'above nature'.

The English Reformation therefore saw the beginning of an intellectual debate on the cessation of miracles that stretched into the Enlightenment period and beyond. It stemmed from a particular context: the refusal on the part of many Protestants to affirm the truth of their beliefs by the display of miracles, and an accompanying suspicion of the practices surrounding Roman Catholic belief in miracles. At the root of this was the importance for Protestants of scripture over sign or wonder in proving sound doctrine, and the Protestant emphasis on a person's direct relationship with God without the intermediary role of the 'wonderworker' priest. However, just because some members of the established church argued that miracles had ceased did not mean that instances of the miraculous stopped occurring. Here was the clash between doctrine and lived religion, with the formulation of doctrine emerging from a very particular context of events.

The age of miracles may have been declared over by some Protestant reformers, including key figures of the later English Reformation period, but signs and wonders, events and objects which were beyond naturalistic explanations, continued to cause widespread comment and interest in post-Reformation England, and Protestants strongly believed in the intervention of God in the world. Thus for many Protestants – especially for the stricter Protestants for whom any talk of the miraculous was dubious at best, dangerous at worst, the wondrous and unnatural came to be explained in terms of God's omnipotence and judgement in the world: they employed the doctrine of Providence, whereby all events and 'signs' in a person's, a community's or a nation's life were interpreted in terms of God's purpose. It was Calvin who had brought a new emphasis to the doctrine of Providence in his insistence on the complete sovereignty of God, drawing on Stoic ideas (revived in the Renaissance), though rejecting the Stoics' determinism, and rejecting, too, the role of chance or fortune in understanding the unpredictability of human affairs. The doctrine of Providence did not mean, at least for Calvin, that human beings would understand God's purpose – that remained largely incomprehensible, even to believers. It did mean, however, that human beings could rest in the comforting knowledge that the universe was ordered by God's sovereignty and power and that all of life, however hard, had a divine purpose.[28]

For the Calvinists who came to dominate many aspects of the later English Reformation, providence was an acceptable alternative to miracles. Every detail of life was interpreted in terms of God's purpose and judgement, from storms, floods and earthquakes right down to the minutiae of a person's daily life. Protestant ministers frequently preached sermons on the meaning of a recent fire or storm – such events were usually interpreted as calls to repentance, in the tradition of the Hebrew Prophets – and in doing so, they also catalogued the lucky escapes of the Godly during those times. Protestant autobiographies were filled with similar interpretations of a person's life. Walsham has argued rightly that it was not only the 'hotter sort' of Protestants (those often called the Puritans) who made Providence a central component of their theology and lived religion: 'Providentialism was not a marginal feature of the religious culture of early modern England, but part of the mainstream, a cluster of presuppositions which enjoyed near universal acceptance. It was a set of ideological spectacles through which individuals of all social levels and from all positions on the confessional spectrum were apt to view their universe.'[29]

For some Protestants, the difference between interpreting a sign or event as a miracle or an act of providence was vital; the trial of Anne Hutchinson in the Massachusetts Bay Colony in America in 1637 provides a vivid example of Puritan vigilance about this distinction. Those trying Hutchinson attempted to trap her by asking her if she expected to be delivered by a miracle as Daniel had been. She replied, carefully, that she hoped the Lord would deliver her by His providence. The Revd John Cotton of Boston said, 'If she doth expect a deliverance in the way of Providence, I cannot deny it .... If it be by way of miracle, then I would suspect it.'[30]

The fact that this occurred in a trial is perhaps significant with regard to the theological distinction between a miracle and an act of providence. Providence implied God's judgement, a notion that was central to Calvinist theology; a miracle, on the other hand, might have nothing to do with God's judgement or a person's moral character. A miracle was an act of God simply designed to indicate (albeit sometimes by extraordinary and even spectacular means) God's existence and works in the world. When an intervention in the world, a shift in the nature of things, was interpreted as a providential act of God, it implied that the intervention resulted from God's judgement, be it punishment or reward, of a person's, a community's, or a nation's behaviour. For those who were so influenced by a theology of providence, the notion of a miracle (which might be interpreted as a free gift from God) could be hard to tolerate.

Protestants in the sixteenth century had inherited the medieval definition of a miracle, such as that formulated by the eleventh-century theologian Anselm, for whom miracles were acts of God that directly intervened in the natural world and the everyday life of humankind. The focus was therefore on God's activity in the world. This had marked a shift from the patristic position: for Augustine in the fourth century, all wonders were potentially miraculous, and the focus was on what provoked wonder in the human person.[31] The Protestant Reformation theologians inherited the medieval interest in miracles as acts of God and retained the distinction between *miranda* (wonder) and *miracula* or *mirabilia* (that is, an event caused by the direct intervention of God in the natural world). Providential events were seen as *miranda*, preternatural events (not above or beyond nature).

And yet, focusing on these sorts of clear definitions as propounded by keen Calvinists, and in the intellectual debate on the cessation of miracles, will lead us to draw the distinction too sharply for the majority of ordinary church-going people in England. Certainly, for many Protestants, especially Calvinists such as the Presbyterians, miracles were safely relegated to the early church, and wonders could only be interpreted as providential, not miraculous (as we shall see in the case of Martha Taylor, discussed in chapter 5). For others, a belief in miracles continued, even in the sixteenth century; and the practices surrounding them remained, albeit often changed in shape or focus.

Teaching and preaching on the cessation of miracles, and royal injunctions against 'monuments of idolatry and superstition', did not necessarily, at all times and in all places, affect local belief and practice – at least, not in the ways in which churchmen and royal officials expected or desired.

It has been suggested by Alexandra Walsham that, in the case of holy wells, wholesale destruction did not occur but, rather, the pilgrimage tradition was 'allowed to linger on the margins and fringes of scattered country parishes'. People were going to holy wells for healing as late as the nineteenth century: cases of this were recorded by folklorists of the time, who assumed that such practices represented the remnant of an older folk tradition. Such folklorists did not account for the ways in which customs at holy wells may have been adapted to suit Protestant belief, that is, there was an appropriation of a medieval tradition of pilgrimage and healing, in which rituals were shorn of their 'overtly "popish" components'. This tradition of healing through water was, in turn, adapted in places such as Bath, Buxton and Harrogate to develop the culture of spas and 'taking the waters'.[32]

Another sixteenth-century case illustrating Protestant ambiguity about miracles is found in John Foxe's *Book of Martyrs*. Martyrs have, since the early church, been associated with miracle working, not least through their relics, but also in the heroic tales of their superhuman and miraculous endeavours, as narrated in martyrdom accounts written after their deaths. What happened to these miraculous elements when Protestants were martyred, as occurred in Mary Tudor's reign in England? It seems that echoes of medieval miracle stories remained even in Protestant martyrdom accounts, as for example in Foxe's declaration that Thomas Cranmer's heart was 'found in the midst of the fire whole, without any blemish'. Significantly, Cranmer had spoken the dying words of the first-century martyr, Stephen, as he had gone to the stake.[33] Foxe's attitude towards miracles was, perhaps, rather more ambiguous than historians and editors of his work have previously thought, and Thomas Freeman has shown that Foxe altered later editions of his Book to remove the allusions to the miraculous to meet the requirements of his readers.[34]

It is also the case that for many in the sixteenth and seventeenth centuries – and, for that matter, the eighteenth century – the distinction between miracles and providence was, and remained, blurred. While Reformation theologians, scholars and the 'hotter sorts' of Protestants may have been scrupulous in distinguishing between providence and miracle, in practice the vast majority of people did not make always make clear distinctions between providence, miracle, wonder and prodigy.[35] This is clearly illustrated by the titles of the 'wonder literature' of the seventeenth and eighteenth centuries, the period with which this book is most closely concerned, which used the terms 'miraculous' and 'miracle' very loosely: this literature ranged from pamphlets such as *The Miraculous Child or, Wonderfull news from Manchester* (1679) which gave an account of a three-year-old child who could speak Latin, Greek and Hebrew, despite never having been taught those languages, to collections such as Nathaniel Crouch's *Surprizing Miracles of Nature and Art* (1729). Clearly the terms 'miracle' or 'miraculous' could stand in for 'wonder' and 'wondrous'. There also existed a certain looseness about the distinction between a miracle and special providence, in which God demonstrated a particular concern for a specific person or community – as opposed to general providence, which suggested God's general concern for and judgement of the world. Furthermore, as discussed in chapter 1, publishers and writers adapted the safely Protestant genres of Providence literature – cautionary tales, godly ballads, chapbooks and biographies of exemplars – and transformed them into Protestant miracle literature.

The claims made by some Protestants in the sixteenth and seventeenth centuries that miracles continued in their day suggests that while official condemnation of miracles occurred and theologians proposed the doctrine of the cessation of miracles, other Protestants nevertheless reincorporated a belief in the occurrence of miracles in their day into their theology and practice. In short, there existed a real diversity of belief and practice about miracles amongst Protestants. Looking at both doctrine and lived religion allows us to see the ways in which theology was a genuine concern for ordinary people as demonstrated in and by their religious practices. This raises questions about *how* people claimed to experience miracles or divine healing when the medieval apparatus for miracles, especially healing miracles, had been questioned, discredited or even destroyed. If miracles, especially healing miracles, had been understood as occurring through sacred place, object and ritual in the late middle ages, then how did Protestants reconfigure miracles within the parameters of their practice of piety, in which sacred place and object were replaced by the Word, and ritual was often quite minimalist? How could Protestants experience and, more importantly, legitimate a miracle without seeming dangerously 'popish'? What was a Protestant miracle? These questions will run throughout this book, but will be addressed specifically in this chapter through an examination of the practices of divine healing amongst Baptists, which emerged in the mid seventeenth century, and continued through into the early eighteenth century.

II. Baptists and Healing Miracles

In 1646, the Baptist Vavasour Powell, a Welsh evangelist who spent two years (1644–6) in Dartford, Kent, where he survived the plague, fell ill with 'a very dangerous fever and ague' just before returning to Wales. He wrote in his autobiography that it was thought he would die: 'in so much as I was in the eyes of all my friends, and in the judgement of Physicians, also hopeless as to life'. And yet he was healed. 'God gave me faith to be healed by that means prescribed, James 5. And I sent unto some Godly preachers in London, desiring them to come unto me, and perform that duty of anointing me with oyl.' After some brief doubts as to whether he would be healed, he came to have faith 'that God would recover me and accordingly, after a suddain and strange trance which I fell into, and continued in for about six hours, wherein I did sweat abundantly, yet discerned not at all, during that time, how it was with me, or what was done with me, my sickness presently abated'.[36]

Powell wrote this account many years later, in 1671, but his narrative was representative of many of the stories of divine healing which began to be circulated in the mid-seventeenth century. During the civil war and Interregnum, claims of divine healing and even miracles began to arise in a particularly public way in England amongst several of the independent churches and sects, most notably the Baptists and Quakers.[37] These claims, and the practices upon which they were based, continued into the eighteenth century. This practice of healing with oil, rooted in the scriptural injunction in chapter 5 of the Letter of James even became a way in which opponents could identify certain 'sectarians'. The Presbyterian Thomas Edwards writing in his first volume of *Gangraena*, listed the 180 errors of the sectarians: numbers 145 and 146 dealt with the sectarians' belief in miracles and healing by anointing with oil.

145.   That the gift of miracles is not ceased in these times, but that some of the Sectaries have wrought miracles, and miracles have accompanied them in their Baptisme, & c. and the people of God shall have the power of miracles shortly.
146.   That anointing the sick with oil by the Elders praying over them, with laying on of hands, is a church ordinance for church members that are sick, for their recovery.[38]

Edwards went on to relate several incidents of Baptists engaged in healing practices, particularly the use of healing oil as commanded in James 5:14–15 ('Is any sick among you? Let him call for the elders of the church; and let them pray over him, anointing him with oil in the name of the Lord; and the prayer of faith shall save the sick, and the Lord shall raise him up; and if he have committed sins they shall be forgiven him.')

Edwards gave two examples of William Kiffin's healing practices. Kiffin was a prominent and wealthy Baptist in seventeenth-century London who was converted to Baptist principles in about 1642 and was minister of a congregation in Swan Alley, off Coleman Street, from 1644 to his death in 1701. The first story involved a visit by Kiffin and his co-pastor, Thomas Patient, to one of their members who was ill, a woman named Palmer who lived in Smithfield. They laid hands upon her and anointed her with oil. The woman recovered and testified to Kiffin's congregation: 'That physicians left her as they found her, but Brother Kiffin and Patience Anointing her, she suddenly recovered; for which in that place, she desired thanks might be put up; which Kiffin did also relate, and did according to the woman's desire (return thanks).'[39] In the second incident related by Edwards, Kiffin was again involved. He visited a sick woman, this time alone; he anointed her with oil on her breast and stomach and prayed, but this time without success, 'yet she did not mend upon it; whereupon she sent for him again'. At this point, Kiffin remembered that, according to scripture, there should be more than one elder to conduct the anointing and realised that his solo visit may have been the reason for the failure: he remembered 'the words of the Apostle, That it was the Elders of the Church, he took with him his Brother Patience; and so they prayed with her and Anointed her with Oyle, and she was raised up, and desired that thanks might be given unto God for it'.[40]

Edwards relates a third story, of an attempt by various prominent Baptist ministers, including 'Master Knowls and Master Jesse' (Hanserd Knollys and Henry Jessey)[41] and others in a meeting in Aldgate, London, to restore the sight of a blind woman 'by anointing her with oyle in the name of the Lord'. The incident was described thus:

> the old blind woman was set in the midst of the Roome, and she first prayed aloud (all the company joyning with her) to this effect, that God would bless his own ordinance and Institution for the restoring of her sight; after she had done praying, Master Knowls prayed for some space of time, to the same effect for a blessing upon this anointing with oile, and after prayer she was anointed with oyle, these words being uttered by him who anointed her as to this effect, the Lord Jesus give, or restore thee thy sight.

Edwards did not record whether she was healed; or maybe his witnesses ('a godly minister' and his wife who was 'much inclined to the sectaries') failed to tell him.[42] Edwards is, of course, a hostile source, and his language against the sectarians was often inflammatory. But this in itself is relevant for it suggests that Baptists may have come to be identified by others – especially their enemies – in part by their practices of religious healing.

However, we should not forget that the Church of England – and therefore the population at large – was familiar with the concept of religious healing: the Book of Common Prayer had always had an order of service for the Visitation of the Sick, consisting of general prayers for healing, suitable readings from scripture and confession and absolution (which also served to prepare the sick person for death). The nature and 'extent' of this bedside rite was, nevertheless, the subject of some debate. Anthony Sparrow was a high churchman (he was ejected from his Fellowship at Cambridge in 1644 for his Royalist sympathies but after the Restoration he became first Bishop of Exeter and then Bishop of Norwich), who wrote an influential commentary on the Prayer Book, *A Rationale or Practical Exposition of the Book of Common Prayer*, first published in 1657 and much reprinted. In the section of his *Rationale*, 'Of the Communion of the Sick', he suggested that people had got out of the habit of calling a priest for the sick, despite a canon commanding all physicians to do so. As Sparrow put it,

> That which chiefly occasioned the making of this good law was the supine carelessness of some sick persons, who never used to call the physician of the soul till the physician of the body had given them over. And if the physician did, as his duty was, timely admonish them to provide for their soul's health, they took it for a sentence of death and despaired of remedy, which hastened their end and hindered both the bodily physician from working any cure upon their body and the ghostly physician from applying any effectual means to their soul's health.

Sparrow went on to quote James 5.14, even suggesting that by 'the ghostly offices of the priest . . . we may possibly save the body without the physician'.[43] However, there were those in the Church of England who feared this smacked too much of the Roman Catholic sacrament of extreme unction. John Gilbert, incumbent of a church in Peterborough, writing nearly thirty years later, also turned to James 5, and its two themes: the remission of sins and the recovering of the sick. He argued that the forgiving of sins could be retained because it was 'perpetual and common to the church in all ages' but the healing of the sick, promised in James 5, was no longer plausible because it was merely 'temporary while God empowered it [the church] to work such effects'. This is simply a variation on the argument that miracles ceased once the church was established. Thus, Gilbert argued that the church 'not being assured nor having any promise to assure it that its ministry shall be effectual to the recovery of bodily health, it does not warrant it to her children, and therefore does not think fit to use the ceremony of the anointing of the sick with oil, which was then used as a sign effective of their recovery'.[44] Gilbert's stance was shaped by the political context in which he was writing; he was responding to the work of the influential French bishop, Bossuet, a year after Louis XIV revoked the Edict of Nantes (which had given toleration to

Protestants) and in the second year of the Roman Catholic James II's troubled reign in England, and therefore with a heightened sense of antipathy towards the Roman Catholic faith. The very future of the Church of England, and therefore of freedom, was seen to be at stake.

While the Church of England debated the meaning and extent of James 5 in its own context, the Baptists, by contrast, quite simply saw religious healing as a thoroughly biblical practice. In taking *all* components of James 5 seriously, the role of faith, the forgiving of sins and the healing of bodily illness, Baptists were aiming to live by the Word. Their precise following of the injunctions in James 5 was, therefore, something which marked them out. Such 'marking out' was significant. At a time when the identities of the various religious sects remained unstable, with no clear-cut denominational lines, one way in which the independent churches could be identified, not least from each other, was by their controversial religious practices, and in the post-Reformation world of seventeenth-century England, religious healing with its implication of miracles was controversial. Thomas Edwards, a Presbyterian and therefore a Calvinist and, in the Interregnum years, part of the ruling religious group troubled by the proliferation of sectarian groups, in relating such healing practices in William Kiffin's congregation and amongst Baptist ministers such as Knollys and Jessey, was particularly hostile to them.

Of course, the Baptists, who emerged in the early seventeenth century under the guidance of John Smyth and Thomas Helwys were identified, both by themselves and by their opponents, most obviously by their rejection of infant baptism and subsequent adoption of believers' baptism. This was central to their theology and their ecclesiology, creating *voluntary* communities of believers set apart from the established church. By the mid-seventeenth century, these congregations had multiplied and grown considerably, and a form of self-identification had occurred in the division between General (Helwys) and Particular (Smyth) Baptists, the latter being Calvinist in their theology. By 1641 there were seven Particular Baptist churches in London alone, and in 1643, they issued a joint Confession of Faith in order to distinguish themselves from various other emerging independent congregations.[45]

But to the outsider, such distinctions might easily go unnoticed or seem irrelevant, and in practice Baptist congregations were not always clear-cut about their identities, to such an extent that many can only be ascribed the title 'independent' rather than given a 'denominational tag' until the latter part of the seventeenth century when the Restoration settlement forced such self-identification upon all dissenters. The practice of religious healing was therefore something tangible, potentially flamboyant and frequently controversial, which marked out Baptist church communities to outsiders. In fact, such practices of religious healing occurred initially and primarily amongst the

Particular Baptist churches of London but outsiders would not have made such distinctions. The success of such practices led to claims of divine healing, though the Baptists themselves often stopped short of describing their cures as miracles.

Baptists continued their healing practices after the Restoration and, again, some commentators saw them as attempting miracles. One Thomas Morris, of London, in 1666/7 wrote to Samuel Jeake (senior), town clerk of Rye in Sussex (a nonconformist who fancied himself a bit of an expert in religious matters): 'There are some among us that doe pretend to miracles, as for instance in a society called the Baptists that I know now dwelling in Southwarke'.[46] Hanserd Knollys, (formerly an Anglican clergyman), who, after baptism in 1645, had proceeded to gather around him one of the first Calvinistic Baptist churches in London and worked closely with Kiffin for over forty years, was engaged in healing practices, as Edwards' third story illustrated. In his autobiography, he wrote of his own healing by anointing with oil and prayer. Soon after he had been released from prison in 1670, 'God made me his Prisoner by a sharp and painful Distemper in my Bowels, called the Griping of the Guts, and he brought me near to the Grave. But in time of my greatest Extremity, God remembered Mercy, forgave mine Iniquity, healed my Disease, and Restored my Life from Death.'[47] Knollys saw the time while he was ill as a period of trial, with 'Satan . . . very busy during this time of Sickness': one of his grandchildren died, another had the smallpox, while yet another was stillborn; two sons died; and, finally, his wife became sick (she died on 30th April of the following year).

Faith – itself given by God – was essential during this period, and, as commanded in James 5, for his own healing. In giving Knollys faith, God also 'brought my will unto a free submission, Subjection and Resignation, to his most wise and holy will'. While he was ill, Knollys was daily visited by 'two learned, well-practised and judicious Doctors of Physick'. They could not cure him, though he was persuaded they did 'what possibly they could to effect a cure'. Therefore:

I resolved to take no more physic, but would apply to that holy ordinance of God appointed by Jesus Christ, the great physician of value, James 5.14–15. And I got Mr. Kiffin and Mr. Vavasour Powell, who prayed over me, and anointed me with oyl in the name of the Lord: And the Lord did hear the Prayer and heal me.

Faith, submission to the Lord's will, and prayers from the Godly were all vital ingredients in his cure:

there were very many Godly ministers and gracious Saints, that prayed day and night for me (with submission to the will of God) that the Lord would spare my life and heal me, and make me more useful and serviceable to the Lord, to the Church and to the Saints; whose Prayers God heard, and as an Answer of their Prayers, I was perfectly healed, but remained weak long after.[48]

The Baptists participated in this form of religious healing because for them it was a solidly biblical practice. In their specific practices, they followed the precise injunction in James 5, with elders of the church anointing the sick with oil and all the faithful praying. It is interesting that most of the Baptists engaged in these healings were Particular Baptists and therefore Calvinists, for Calvin himself had written explicitly against the use of James 5 for healing practices, in the course of his denial of extreme unction as a sacrament, in a larger discussion about the means of grace in the *Institutes*. He described this laying on of hands as 'merely playacting, by which, without reason and without benefit, they [the Roman Catholics] wish to resemble the apostles'. This was not an instrument of healing, argued Calvin, 'but only a symbol, by which the unschooled in their ignorance might be made aware of the source of such great power, that they might not give the credit of it to the apostles'.[49] For Calvin, the emphasis was always upon the omnipotence of God. Responding to the potential Roman Catholic challenge that extreme unction was commanded by James (i.e. scriptural), Calvin touches on the cessation of miracles, adding a new twist – that miracles ceased not so much because they were no longer needed for the spread of the gospel (the usual explanation) but rather because human beings were ungrateful:

James spoke for that same time when the Church still enjoyed such a blessing of God. Indeed they [the Roman Catholics] affirm that the same force is still in their anointing, but we experience otherwise. Let no one now marvel how with such great boldness they have mocked souls, whom they know to be senseless and blind when deprived of the Word of God, which is life and light; for they are not ashamed to wish to deceive the living and feeling senses of the body. Therefore they make themselves ridiculous when they boast that they are endowed with the gift of healing. The Lord is indeed present with his people in every age; and he heals their weaknesses as often as necessary, no less than of old; still he does not put forth these manifest powers, nor dispense miracles through the apostles' hands. For that was a temporary gift, and also quickly perished partly on account of men's ungratefulness.[50]

The Baptist individuals and congregations that practised religious healing did not leave any evidence of whether any of them had read that section of the *Institutes* (or, for that matter, *any* part of the *Institutes*). Nevertheless, it is revealing that, while they followed the injunctions of James 5 to the letter, they tended not to speak or write explicitly of the cures wrought in their circles as *miracles* (although their critics, such as Thomas Edwards, did), though they were at pains to emphasise that the power to heal came from God.

Not surprisingly, the debate as to whether miracles could occur in their own age was never far from the surface so long as healings occurred amongst their members. Thomas Grantham, a General Baptist minister of Lincolnshire, wrote in 1678 that, 'The gift of healing is not wholly taken away, if we dare beleive [sic] our Eyes, or the persons restored to health very suddenly, at the earnest Prayer of Faithful Men, and often times in the use of that ordinance James 5:14.' Indeed, he believed that if more people followed that ordinance, then more such healings might occur: 'Would the Lords people wisely and holily observe this precept, they should doubtless see more than yet they have seen of his power and goodness to his Church in the use of this ordinance, for the precept being perpetual, and a gracious promise annexed thereto; There wants only judgement and faith on our part, to render it effectual, for he is faithful that hath promised.' His description of such sudden restorations to health as miracles was cautious and ultimately ambivalent:

> Howbeit the truth is that Miracles are rarely found, yet from what mine Eyes have seen, and from what I have heard by report from some, whom charity will not suffer me to think would affirm an untruth I may not say (as some) they are not at all to be found. It is enough to me that God hath no where said he will not work them, but on the contrary hath laid a bar against our forbidding them.[51]

Placing these healing practices in a broader cultural context, we should not lose sight of the fact that religion and medicine were intimately connected in seventeenth-century English society, as recent scholarship has illustrated.[52] Ministers were often also physicians, and for some Independent ministers who were ejected from their livings at the Restoration, medicine became their primary means of making a living.[53] Prominent amongst the Baptists as a practitioner of both 'physic' and prayer was Henry Jessey, a Particular Baptist minister and Fifth Monarchist (that is, a member of one of the radical groups of the civil war period) who had studied medicine in the 1620s while working as a tutor in Suffolk, after leaving Cambridge.[54] In 1647, Jessey wrote *The Exceeding Riches of Grace Advanced by the Spirit of God* about Sarah Wight, a member of his congregation and a prophet for whom fasting was central to her ability to prophesy. Wight fasted for seventy days, eating nothing and drinking very little, during which time she prophesied but was also seriously ill. She was therefore visited by a wide array of people: religious radicals, ministers and doctors, as well as those who sought her counsel and advice, and the simply curious. Some of the doctors present tried to encourage Wight to eat,[55] but Jessey saw her spiritual growth and her physical recovery as more intimately connected, and they applied prayer. In his Preface to the book, Jessey wrote of Wight's recovery in June 1647 as the Lord working a miracle, for she had not been likely to live. He wrote, 'she then not being likely to live, unlesse the Lord work a Miracle: he raised her wonderfully, by faith in his Son, without any meanes (when she could use none) and that by degrees: first, to EATE and to ARISE. . . . Then (on Midsummer Day) to WALK.' He then went on to expound his theology of salvation and healing, inviting the reader to 'pray for despairing soules (here now being many of them) and for the more exalting of Jesus Christ, in the pouring out of his Spirit upon his sons and daughters that beleeve, by stretching out his hand to heal, (soules and bodies) and that Signes and Wonders may be done in his Name'.[56]

Christopher Blackwood, a Particular Baptist, made the connection between physical healing and spiritual healing explicit when he was writing about Jesus' healing miracles in his commentary of 1659, on the first ten chapters of Matthew. 'The diseases of our body . . . flow from sin; . . . The end why Christ cured the bodily diseases of persons, as Matthew 9.2, was that they might seek to him for the healing of their souls, as in the blinde man, John 9. 5, 6.' He argued that Christ 'had no sin and therefore no sickness'. His understanding of the relationship between spiritual and physical sickness is thus related to his theology of salvation: 'Christ took not our sins by taking them upon him, but out of compassion he took them away and restored the sick to health.'[57]

As well as seeking divine healing through prayer and anointing with oil, based on James 5, some Baptists also took on other means of spiritual healing or 'spiritual physic'. Knollys' description of the ways in which his physical illness was bound up with a time of trial and testing in his faith and Jessey's emphasis on the healing of both 'soules and bodies' indicate the ways in which, for Protestants, physical and spiritual health were specifically related. As we have seen, the more radical Calvinist Protestants began to practise spiritual physic, especially by keeping fasts and prayer days, and a number of prominent Puritan divines, such as William Perkins, saw themselves as physicians of the soul. A mental affliction (which might also be called possession) was treated spiritually, with the belief that sin was at its root. Sufferers were enjoined to consider their sins, repent and convert by being born anew, in

order to be made mentally (and physically) well. These 'Godly' saw their practice as thoroughly biblical, pointing to the story of Jesus' healing of a boy with
a spirit which had made him dumb, in Mark 9:14–29.[58] Jesus rebuked the
unclean spirit and commanded it out. The disciples had already tried to rid
the boy of the demonic spirit, and when they asked Jesus why they had failed,
he replied: 'This kind can come out only through prayer and fasting.'[59]

However, as we have already seen, this ritualised prayer and fasting could
easily look like or even become a form of exorcism, and although the late
sixteenth-century case of John Darrell caused much controversy and triggered
a canon of the Church of England forbidding it, the practice continued
amongst the separatists and their dissenting heirs – for whom a canon of the
Church of England had no authority – throughout the seventeenth century
and into the eighteenth century. The records of Broadmead Baptist Church
provide examples of the ways in which such days of prayer and fasting (or
exorcisms) occurred in Baptist congregations. On 23rd February 1673, 'A Sad
Providence fell out to this Congregation, which was This: – Our Br. John Fry,
a Bachelor, fell distracted.' Formerly a 'very sober, Practicall Christian', Fry
first began to despair that he was 'Lost and Damned; then he brake out in bad
language to all ye brethren that came near him, calling them very bad names,
and immodest Expressions to some women, raveing and strikeing them that
came near to hold him'. Members of the church were forced to bind him on
the bed, and he spat and swore at them, and made blasphemous statements
against God. They concluded that he was 'thus sorely Assaulted and pressed
by ye Devill, (as all that beheld and heard him could not otherwise Judge)'.
Physical means alone were tried, to cure him, but without success, so that
'some of ye Brethren desired ye Church might seeke ye Lord, by fasting and
and Prayer (to ye Lord) to heale and deliver him'. They kept a day of prayer
for Fry in his room on 28 February and though his raging was so great they
thought they could not stand to stay in the same room as him, by the Lord's
assistance they stayed and the Lord answered their prayer so that 'ye Spirit of
Rage left him'. Another day of prayer was held on 5 March for the 'Spirit of
Fear' which remained in Fry, and by the end of that day this observably left
him so 'that he was not soe much in horror and frightfull apprehensions as he
had been'.

Nevertheless spiritual means of healing were mixed with medical: 'meanes
were used Physically for his recovery, as Bloodying, Purgeing, and Leeching,
to Draw ye Distemper from his head'. Such methods were used because
'according to our Prayers, that if ye Lord pleased to have us use Outward
means, that he would Direct to it, and blessed ye meanes: which he
Compassionately answered'. Although Fry's fits ceased, he could not return to
faith and prayer (indeed, an aversion to prayer was seen as a classic symptom

of possession) and was in despair for what he had said against God during his fits. Therefore the Church appointed another day of prayer for him, on 9 April, 'To seeke ye Lord, (as it were to Perfect ye worke of his Recovery,) To take ye Spirit of Shame from him.' The spirit of shame was indeed removed and the very next day he 'was embouldened to goe forth about his businesse in ye City, as he did formerly'. The record of these events was written three years later, at which point the Lord had 'kept him in his former gracious frame of Spirit; and he usually Exercises in prayer, in ye Congregation, on fast days, as formerly, and hath been very well Ever since in his body'.[60] A second example of exorcism in the same church occurred on an occasion when Henry Jessey was visiting. A member of the congregation had a daughter 'that was bewitched, (as termed)'; that is, 'the child was very much changed, and had strange fitts, and as it were haunted by an Evill Spirit'. Thus the whole church 'put aparte a day for it, to seek ye Lord by fasting and prayer, when Br. Jessey was here, and ye child was restored well as before and to this day'.[61]

In the political-religious climate of the late seventeenth century, the nonconformists' use of fasting and prayer to exorcise demons could bring them into conflict with the established church, as in the case of Richard Dugdale, the 'Surey Demoniack' in Lancashire (in an area of Lancashire in which only about half of the population had an allegiance to the Church of England). In April 1689, Dugdale, a nineteen-year-old gardener, approached an Independent minister, Thomas Jolley, claiming that he was possessed by an evil spirit. Jolley, along with a number of other Independent ministers, readily engaged in the practice of fasting and prayer for Dugdale over a number of months, Dugdale's symptoms continuing unabated until February 1690. Dugdale's dramatic displays of possession and the ministers' performative rituals of prayer and fasting drew huge crowds, and the case became famous, prompting a pamphlet war later in the decade. Jolley and his supporters claimed they had succeeded in exorcising Dugdale by fasting and prayer. By contrast, the Tory Anglican Zachary Taylor, curate of Wigan and one of the King's six preachers for Lancashire, claimed that Dugdale's afflictions had been wholly natural in the first place. M. F. Snape's detailed analysis of the case illustrates the ways in which churchmen of different affiliations understood Dugdale's symptoms either as possession, and therefore within a religious framework, or as epilepsy, and therefore in naturalistic terms, provoking a serious debate. Snape suggests that the debate was brought to a decisive conclusion by the publication of a pamphlet in 1698 by an anonymous author, who was probably Presbyterian, who suggested that the Independent ministers were deceived by Dugdale, though he berated the high churchmen for their ill-treatment of the nonconformists. Despite being rebuked by the author of this pamphlet for his intolerance and intemperance with regard to the dissenters, the Anglican, Zachary Taylor, still saw the victory as his and wrote another combative pamphlet to say so.[62] Keith Thomas sees the case and the ensuing debate, occurring at the very end of the seventeenth century, as triggering a greater spread of scepticism amongst the educated classes.[63] But this is to presume that secularisation occurred and was inevitable. As Snape notes: 'for the countryfolk of eighteenth-century east Lancashire, it would seem that Taylor's victory was largely lost upon them, for it in no way seems to have diminished their traditional belief in the relevance and efficacy of formal exorcism'.[64] Thomas's assessment also ignores the fact that people of varying denominations had been split about cases of 'possession' for some time, even in those denominations which practised prayer and fasting.

Ultimately, we can point to a variety of beliefs, indicating the ways in which Protestants held a range of complex and sometimes paradoxical ideas about the miraculous from the sixteenth century onwards. Miracles and the practices associated with them were the topic of continuing conversation and debate. Some correspondence between one Thomas Morris of London and Samuel Jeake Senior, the nonconformist minister and lawyer of Rye, in November 1666, gives us a glimpse of this ongoing conversation amongst the 'middling sorts'. Morris reported to Jeake that Baptists in Southwark 'both printed and published to the world (one Mr Clayton beeing their teacher) their casting out of devills, or several uncleane spirits, out of a youth that was possest'. Morris himself spoke with the youth's father a short time after the youth had been 'dispossest' and 'he did affirme it to be really true'. Morris was writing to Jeake to ask his opinion of the miracles claimed by some in their own day. The nonconformist Jeake's reply to this particular point (in a very lengthy response) was that, 'Daemoniaks, whether really possesst with devills, or rather infest with a raving insomnia of ye worst kind as some thinke it matters not greatly, be it as you will'.[65] For the latter opinion, he made reference to the Particular Baptist, Christopher Blackwood, who, in his *Expositions and Sermons on Matthew*, gave a naturalistic explanation of the story of Jesus casting out devils from those possessed in chapter 5, verse 16: 'When the even was come, they brought unto him many that were possessed by devils, and he cast out the spirits with his Word, and healed all that were sick.' Blackwood wrote of this: 'Now if you ask what these persons that were possessed with devils were? Answ. It was in likelihood no other but madness. John 10.20 He hath a devil and is mad; so that these persons labored not of simple dotage, but of raving madness.'[66] Blackwood therefore placed the emphasis on Christ as healer rather than exorcist.

There was considerable disagreement amongst Baptists about practices such as fasting and prayer, and the use of holy oil for healing, as well as the larger question of whether miracles could occur in their day. Continuing his reply to Morris's letter of November 1666, Jeake went on to note that not all Baptists agreed that miracles could happen in the present age – 'seeing one of the best of that profession, in print hath boldly affirmed, upon the authority of Chrysostome, there hath beene no miracle done these 13 hundred yeares'.[67] Jeake was again quoting Blackwood but he took Blackwood's words rather out of context. The specific question for Blackwood was whether 'the doing of miracles is essential to a dispenser of Baptisme'. His answer was no. But Blackwood was addressing here a particular concern related to the role of an intermediary figure. He was concerned that people should understand that Christ was the only mediator:

> It darkens and derogates from Christ's mediatorship, to whom it belongs to intercede for his People, which they blasphemously ascribe to Saints, especially to the Virgin Mary. Now Christ alone conveys the things that are Gods to us, and ministers the things that are ours to God. Now we are commanded to come in our Wants, not to Saints departed or Angels, but to this Mediator. Heb. 4.14, 15, 16.[68]

Baptists who practised healing by anointing with oil were sometimes criticised for it by members of other churches, as the story of Richard Davis, the Baptist Independent Minister at Rowell in Northamptonshire, illustrates. Soon after he was appointed minister in 1690, he came under severe attack from a group of local Presbyterian ministers who were jealous of his popularity as a preacher and disliked the fact that he and his lay brothers had poached members of their own congregations. These local dissenting ministers went about the area collecting bad reports about him. In 1692 they called him to be examined before the 'United Brethren' at Kettering. One of the charges brought against him was that 'he anoints the sick with oil [and this] is confessed both by himself and his friends'. Davis acknowledged this and asserted that it was his right to retain his private judgement on the matter.[69] Davis was also disliked by some of the other local dissenting ministers for the fact that 'at his ordination the imposition of hands was made by the Elders of the Church'. It was reported by one Mr Maurice that 'this gave great umbrage to many of the neighbouring ministers who were present, several of whom abruptly withdrew, saying that "here was no business for them"'.[70] Disagreement about the practice of religious healing was sometimes related to the contentious subject of the laying on of hands at ordination, about which there was much dispute in the General Baptist churches especially, in the seventeenth and eighteenth centuries.[71] The question at stake in both cases was whether such rituals of the early Christians – 'primitive ceremonies' – still had validity or relevance in the seventeenth century.

There could even be disagreement *within* Baptist congregations about such practices. Such was the case at a Baptist church in Colchester in the early eighteenth century. In 1705, a member of the Colchester church went to Tiverton in Devon where he was called to be minister; he then wrote to the church in Colchester to ask whether it was necessary to have the laying on of hands at ordination. The pastor in Colchester was away at the time, so a member of the church and an assistant in the ministry, William Rawlings, wrote a reply saying that 'Laying on of hands being an insignificant thing only to denote the person ordained, it having no power to convey any ministerial gifts to the person ordained, so we rather judge it to be a primitive ceremony, such as the anointing of the sick and the washing of the feet, which ceased with the lives of the apostles and with the extraordinary gifts of healing.' The letter was brought to the church for approval (for authority lay in the congregation, as a whole, under the rule of Christ; not merely with the minister) but many members rejected it replying 'that they believed anointing with oil, and also laying on of hands were ordinances in the church, and ought still to be practised'.[72]

The story did not end there. Rawlings entered a period of 'great darkness of the soul', and for the following two months kept many days of fasting and prayer. While in Bury St Edmunds one day in December, he was praying earnestly and asked God why his soul was in darkness: 'I was immediately answered by thought of mind, that I had denied his ordinances.' Thus he was 'convinced, that the ordinance of the laying on of hands, and anointing with oil were continued in the church; and that if I practised them, the Lord would own them'. Returning to Colchester, he approached one Mary Munnings, a widow in his church who kept a milliner's shop, who had a fifteen-year-old crippled daughter. He told her that he had been convinced of the ordinance of anointing with oil, and she was surprised, knowing he had opposed it before. She thought it was a fancy on his part, and asked him whether he had any faith in the application of healing to her daughter, who was a cripple, to which he replied that he did, and he asked her if she had faith in that – which she said she did. Then he looked into the room where the daughter sat and said:

Child! Do you believe that the Lord can make you whole? She reply'd, the Lord's hand is not shortened that it cannot save, neither is his ear heavy that it cannot hear. Well, I replyed, if you believe his ability, I believe his willingness; then her mother asked me, whether I would please to administer the ordinance to her?

Rawlings returned the following week to anoint Anne Munnings. With a pennyworth of oil already procured by the maid, he prepared for the healing by studying the Bible for three hours, not simply to find the injunction to heal with oil in the Letter of James, but also to find stories of Jesus' healing for inspiration:

> desiring a Bible, I desired not to be interrupted, and searched from one end to the other, for the space of three hours, viz. from nine to twelve, in which time I had collected most parts of the Scripture for the ordinance and for the encouragement of faith, as James V.14, Mark VI.13, Mark XI.24, which last I called a seal to my commission.

After this he said a series of prayers and blessed the oil. 'Then I anointed her in the name of the Lord Jesus of Nazareth, on the place grieved, three times, according to the number of persons of the Trinity.' After further prayers and having received an ecstatic vision of Christ at God's right hand presenting a petition, Rawlings declared that Anne should be made whole again, and he received a reply from God, *I will, she shall be whole.* He thus declared twice, that Anne was indeed made whole, after which she got up and said: 'What shall I render to the Lord for all his benefits! For while you pronounced me whole the second time, my bones snapt without the least pain, and are come into their places.' And, so, Rawlings reported, 'to our astonishment we beheld her straight and whole, and a full hand's breadth taller than before. So she put forth her foot, showed us her ankle, and all was well.'[73]

This story reveals a great deal about the complex and sometimes paradoxical ways in which Protestants adapted the means and meanings of miracles to their own theology and practice. This form of divine healing, anointing with oil, was seen by many Baptists as thoroughly biblical, though not by all; indeed, as we have seen, Rawlings had not believed in it initially but later came to do so, after, he claimed, he received a message directly from God. He came to believe that he had wrongly denied the biblical basis of this ordinance – and, importantly, had been given a direct message from God in order that he might believe in it. The Protestant emphasis on both the centrality of the Word and the direct relationship between God and the believer were therefore retained and, indeed, reiterated. There is also a distinctly Protestant element to this story in terms of *place*, that is, where the miracle happens: the home. With the advent of Protestantism, the focus of piety had shifted, at least in part, from the church to the home: a new importance was given to household prayers and reading the Bible in private or in small, household circles. So too the site of the miracle shifted. Miracles were no longer linked to a particular sacred place as they had been in the middle ages. For Anne Munnings her divine healing occurred, in good Protestant fashion, in her house. Similarly, the various cases of divine healing explored earlier in this chapter happened in the home or in the small gathered churches of the Independents and Baptists, buildings which had no particular sense of sacred place, and little or nothing in the way of visual aids to piety or ritual, but were simply meeting places for godly fellowship.

However, the story of William Rawlings and Anne Munnings raises another more complex question about miracles and Protestantism, regarding the role of the intermediary figure. What was Rawlings' role in the healing? As the narrative progresses, Rawlings becomes an increasingly dramatic figure, so that he, not Anne, nor her faith, is at the centre of the action. After anointing her, he began to see how very crippled she was: 'her hip-bone was out of socket, and fleshly matter had filled the cup, and the hip-bone was sprung up under her arm; her leg was crooked, and her ankle sprung out of its place, so that on the inside none was to be seen; her left foot in the form of a stump, besides her other bodily infirmities for the want of her limbs'. Thus he began to despair about the project he had undertaken. Rawlings decided that it was his faith, rather than Anne's, that would heal her. He was to be the intermediary figure between God and Anne, effecting the miracle. This part of the narrative is worth quoting at length:

> When I saw her leg so deformed, for I never saw it before, my countenance fell, and I said within myself, Sure I am worse than a mad man; can crooked bones be made straight? And with that such a trembling seized me, that I could not stay my hand (but with the help of the other) to anoint her: and while I was in this confusion, this text dropt into my mind. *Though you believe not, yet he abides faithful, and cannot deny himself.* So as soon as I had anointed her, I fell on my knees, as it were in an agony, and said these words: Lord, I leave the work in thy hands to be accomplished. And while I was thus saying, I fell as it were into an extacy, and beheld as it were the heavens open, and Christ at the Father's right hand presenting a petition. Then I cried out, Lord, that is our petition, and we wait for an answer. The mother and sisters [of Anne] wondered at the expression; but as soon as I had said so, I had these words brought to me; *Be it unto you according to your faith;* I replyed, I believe she shall be made whole. And then, before I came off my knees, I praised God for making her whole; and when I had concluded, I got up and walked some turns around the room; and then sat down, and fixing my eyes upon her, said, Child, the Lord hath made thee whole.[74]

We get a vision of Rawlings pacing, praying, sighing, struggling with his faith; Anne is the passive recipient of all of this. Her bones 'snapt' and she was cured when Rawlings told her she would be well because the Lord had made her whole.

Anne Munnings' story is markedly different from the many other instances of divine healing discussed in this chapter, in which the *healed person's* faith was at least as important as (if not more important than) the actions of those engaged in the ritual of anointing with oil.[75] When, for example, Hanserd Knollys called his fellow Baptist ministers, William Kiffin and Vavasour Powell, to anoint him with oil when he was ill with a distemper in his bowels in 1670, his own faith and submission to God's will were central components of his healing. By contrast, in the case of Anne Munnings, Rawlings functions as an intermediary figure, a miracle-worker, whose faith, Bible reading and anointing with oil are the central actions in the cure. There is a further complexity in the turn of events as recounted by Rawlings: in his moment of 'extacy' in which, in his vision of heaven, he interceded for Anne with Christ and saw Christ present their petition to God for Anne's healing. Baptists who engaged in practices of divine healing were always at pains to emphasise that healing power came from God, and that the one true mediator with God was Christ, as Christopher Blackwood was so keen to make clear. Rawlings was therefore treading a fine line between being an intermediary figure, who might cause suspicion by placing himself at the centre of events, and a faithful Protestant throwing himself on Christ's mercy.[76]

Baptist theology emphasised that everything was done through Christ. The Baptist Church at Broadmead in Bristol, after the exorcism of John Fry, wrote in their record book,

> Oh, ye Condescendtion, Mercy, grace, favour, and faithfulnesse of ye God and father of our Lord Jesus Christ, that he should answer prayer, and heare such poor, vile, and unworthy ones as we were! Oh, nothing in us, nothing in us! Not for our sakes did he do this wonderfull thing in our day, But for his owne name's sake: having engaged himself to do for us what-ever we ask in ye name of our Lord Jesus Christ. *Laus Deo.* SOLA DEO GLORIA.[77]

Such theology echoed an early Protestant distaste for intermediary figures, on the grounds that such figures rendered Christ, the real mediator, useless. For Baptists, each individual congregation was governed by Christ.

III. Conclusion

The doctrine of the cessation of miracles did not, perhaps, become as fixed in the sixteenth and seventeenth centuries as historians have often presumed.

Certainly, miracles were a matter of intellectual debate, but such debate usually occurred as a result of practices and events, not least the conflicts between Roman Catholics and Protestants and the ensuing demands for proof of the truth of their message. In short, the argument for the cessation of miracles was often made precisely because people claimed that they were experiencing miracles. Doctrine, and its formulation and development, were profoundly linked to practice. Later in the seventeenth and eighteenth centuries, especially in the philosophical debate on miracles, writers came to refer to the cessation of miracles as a more fixed doctrine than it perhaps was for many of the Protestants of the earlier period.

The *practice* of healing according to biblical injunctions saw a revival in the civil war years of the mid-seventeenth century and continued into the eighteenth century. Thus there occurred new claims of divine healing, most especially amongst the Particular Baptists, though they were often cautious in describing such healings as miracles. This practice contributed to the Baptists' self-identification as an emerging, independent church for whom scripture was the ultimate authority, and for whom Christ – who had the power to heal – was the head of each congregation. They had, of course, self-consciously overthrown the rituals of the established church in England (and necessarily rejected Roman Catholic liturgical practices): this was the key to their worshipping and political identity. But, in following a specific biblical injunction to heal, they (unintentionally) created new liturgical practices, in which place and object were important in different ways. The *ritual* was rigorously based on a scriptural text – James 5; *place* was the home or the location of a small gathered fellowship of true believers; *object* was the holy oil used or the Word itself, in the form of the English Bible. Miracles were re-made in a Protestant image.

CHAPTER 3

Miracle Workers and Healers

The Protestant reformers who argued for a limited age of miracles did not deny the possibility of miracles but, rather, placed them in a specific context – the early church, when it had been necessary for the evidence for the truth of Christianity to be marshalled. They were sceptical of miracles in the sense that they opposed the whole Roman Catholic apparatus that mediated them, that is, which placed the church between God and the believer. Miracle-workers – intermediary figures – were therefore thought to have no place in a Protestant church. In reality, as we have seen, such chariness about miracles was by no means thoroughgoing, and as people read scripture with their own authority, forms of miracle-working re-emerged in the mid-seventeenth century. Some religious figures even claimed to be performing miracles themselves. This chapter looks at two arenas where this was the case. First, it looks at the examples of miracle-working claimed by members of the Society of Friends, the most significant of the sectarian groups which emerged in the 1650s. Affected by the Seekers who joined their ranks, they perceived the capacity to perform miracles as a sign of their true apostolic authority. Secondly, it examines the monarch's claim to heal by touch; that is, healing scrofula (or the King's Evil) by touch in a particular ceremony. This act, grounded in medieval ideas of kingship, had had a problematic status after Henry VIII's reign: Elizabeth had 'cleansed the ritual'; James I had been reluctant to practise it; but it was reasserted as part of the Restoration settlement, with its delicate relationship to Catholicism and its interest in asserting the divine origin of kingship. By the eighteenth century the practice had gone out of favour, but it continued to be associated with the Jacobites and crypto-Catholic royal figures.

I. Miracles amongst Friends

While the Baptists were sometimes criticised for their practices of divine healing, the Quakers were far more frequently taunted and harassed for their claims of experiencing and working healing miracles. George Fox and other Friends, in contrast with the Baptists, did not hesitate to proclaim that such cures were miraculous, and in making these claims, they often invited criticism. While many of the cures that they claimed as miracles were done very simply with the laying on of hands or quiet words spoken to the sick person, it was in itself controversial that Quakers were acting as healers and workers of miracles; furthermore, they could sometimes be flamboyant in their performance of divine healings, thereby attracting attention. The first Quaker record of a miracle appears to have been made in 1652, in a letter to James Nayler from Richard Farnsworth, dated 6 July:

> . . . the presence of the Lord went along with me, and in Derbyshire at a great market town called Chesterfield, his power was much manifested through me among some of their greatest professors. I was at a stand for hearing them. They have a new gathered church as they call it. But there was one of them that lay under the doctors hand of a fever and I was made instrumental by the Lord, and she was made well.[1]

Stories of healings, mostly healings performed by individuals through the laying on of hands, abounded amongst the Quakers in the mid-seventeenth century. George Fox, the Quaker leader, was attributed with the performing of one hundred and fifty miraculous cures in all, many of which became famous, by word of mouth or letter. He voraciously collected stories of such miracles as he travelled about the country visiting the sick, and as he corresponded with other Friends, and noted them in his journal. He related one hundred and seventy-one episodes of miraculous events in his *Book of Miracles*, which he compiled in the late 1680s just before he died and which, he hoped, would be published after his death for the edification of the Friends. In fact, no version of it was published until the twentieth century; the Quakers' desire for respectability in the late seventeenth century meant that the manuscript was buried. The *Book* was published with an introduction and notes in 1948: in 1932, Henry Cadbury found in the Friends House in London a comprehensive catalogue of papers and works written by George Fox, which included reference to the *Book of Miracles*. The *Book* was lost but the catalogue cited the beginning and ending word of the account of each miracle, and from that – through use of Fox's journal and other sources – Cadbury reconstructed the *Book of Miracles*. One of the problems with this document is that most of the miracles Fox describes are not corroborated by any other evidence; there is, however, other evidence, from supporters and opponents alike, that the Quakers claimed they could perform miracles and that such claims were – at least in parts of the country – a feature of Quaker identity in the 1650s.

George Fox made notes in his journal, while on his travels around the country, about the many people he believed had been miraculously cured, and the wide range of physical and mental complaints from which they had been suffering: a withered arm, lameness, kidney stones, a broken neck, 'crooked-ness', 'distraction'. It was Fox's intention that these cases would be included in the *Book of Miracles* when it was published. These healings took place outside or in the home, and quite often during a Meeting of the Friends – and of course Meetings were held in people's homes. An early case recorded by Fox (which occurred probably in 1653) took place in Hawkshead in Cumberland where he was travelling with Margaret Fell and William Caton. They came to rest at a Friend's house and saw 'a boy lying in the cradle . . . about eleven years old, and he was grown almost double'. Fox described the boy as 'crooked' and 'scabbed'. Fox instructed the servant to wash the boy, for he was dirty, to get him up and bring him to him. 'Then I was moved of the Lord God to lay my hands upon him and speak to him, and so bid the lass take him again and put on his clothes, and after we passed away.' Some time later they called at the house again and the mother, who had been out at the time that George Fox had laid healing hands on her son, declared they must have a Meeting while he was there 'for all the country is convinced by the great miracle that was done by thee upon my son'. The doctors of Bath and Wells whom they had visited had given up on him; the parents feared he would die, but after Fox's visit, they had come home 'and found our son playing in the streets'.[2]

Sometimes Fox was moved to heal people in the middle of a Friends' Meeting, as in Arnside in Westmoreland, when he asked a man named Richard Myers, with a lame arm, to stand up. Fox said, 'Prophet Myers, stand upon thy legs'. Fox continues: 'And he stood up and stretched out his arm which had been lame a long time, and said, "be it known unto you all people and to all nations that this day I am healed."' After the meeting was over, his parents could hardly believe it until he took off his doublet and they saw it was true. 'And he came to the Swarthmore meeting and there declared how the Lord had healed him.'[3]

Fox also recorded his cures of those who were mentally afflicted or 'distracted' – the healing took place not by dramatic exorcism, as with the Puritans and even some Baptists, but by quiet words. Two different stories indicate how Fox approached such cases. The first took place in Nottinghamshire:

And coming to Mansfield Wodehouse there was a distracted woman under a doctor's hand, with her hair loose all about her ears; and he was about to let her blood, she being first bound, and many people being about her, holding her by violence, but he could get no blood from her. And I desired them to unbind her and let her alone, for they could not touch the spirit in her by which she was tormented. So they did unbind her. And I was moved to speak to her and in the name of the Lord to bid her be quiet and still. And she was so. And the Lord's power settled into her mind and she mended; And afterwards she received the Truth and continued in it to her death. And the Lord's name was honoured to whom the glory of all his works belong.[4]

The second case occurred in Cumberland where 'a man's wife was distracted and very desperate, attempting to kill her children and her husband. But I was moved of the Lord God to speak to her, and she kneeled down of her bare knees and cried and said she would walk of her bare knees if she might go with me. And the Lord's power wrought through her and she went home well.'[5]

These examples show the characteristics of Fox's healing stories as he related them in his journal. They tended to be relatively simple, achieved by the laying on of hands or by quiet words spoken; those healed were Friends – who often then testified within the Friends' Meeting as to their miraculous cure – and others whom he met on his travels, who sometimes joined the Friends as a result of their cure. Many of the features of these Quaker healings are quite different from those that occurred in Baptist circles. There is little of the questioning, struggle and agony that the Baptists experienced and articulated in their approach to divine healing (think of William Kiffin's concern to follow the scriptural injunction in James 5 absolutely to the letter, or William Rawlings' agonised revision of his views on the laying on of hands). Fox had no doubts about *performing* cures but he also made it clear that it was 'the Lord's power' doing the healing; healing was not done in response to James 5, and as we read Fox's journals and witness the itinerant Fox, travelling about healing, we cannot help but be struck by the similarities in style with Jesus' own healing ministry. The theological differences between the Baptists and Quakers are important in explaining their different attitudes to divine healing. The Baptists saw their healing activities as a direct response to a scriptural injunction, God's Word, to be obeyed in the context of their local churches, each of which was under the rule of Christ. The Friends had a more mystical approach, relying more intuitively on being led by God, via the 'inner light of Christ'; as one Quaker historian put it, 'they believed that they were being led as God guides the bird, along a trackless way'.[6] This meant that Fox and others were open not only to performing miraculous healings but also to visions, prophecies, 'sights' and other psychic experiences, in themselves and others, all of which Fox documented in his journal as he experienced or encountered them.

The Quakers compared George Fox and other Friends who performed cures to Jesus the healer, but they regarded this comparison as neither accidental nor blasphemous. The precursors to the Quakers were the Seekers, who had rejected the bickering between different sectarian groups as they emerged and later flourished in early and mid-seventeenth-century England, by rejecting all organised religion. They believed in an invisible church made up of scattered believers, as they waited for someone with apostolic authority who would restore the primitive church of apostolic times. They believed that such a person would prove his apostolic power by 'signs', including miracles. They had their roots in radical figures of the sixteenth-century Protestant Reformation, such as Sebastian Franck and Dirck Coornhert who both taught such an idea, either implicitly or explicitly, and Galenus Abrahams (leader of the Amsterdam congregation of the Dutch Collegiants) who wrote, 'Nobody nowadays can be accepted as a messenger of God unless he confirms his doctrine by miracles.' William Allen, an English Seeker, wrote in 1655 that one would be raised up in whom God will attest to his authority 'with visible signs of His presence, by gifts of the Holy Ghost, and divers miracles as at the erection of the Gospel Churches'.[7] In the ferment of 1650s England, there were many who were awaiting such an apostolic leader, and it is not surprising that in the early days of the Friends, Seekers came to make up much of the membership of that Society. In 1652, an early significant group of Friends at Balby, near Doncaster, consisted largely of a group of Seekers, and the acceptance of Fox and his message by the community of Seekers in Preston Patrick ensured the spread of Quaker ideas into Westmoreland and North Lancashire.[8]

This apostolic expectation also meant that there was an *ethical* dimension to these cases of divine healing amongst the Quakers; far from being dismissive or suspicious of the role of the healer – as other Protestants were – they saw the success of such healing powers as a sign of the spiritual fitness of the healer. Those who performed miracles were deserving of being able to do it: no one exemplified this more than the Quaker leader, George Fox. As a result of such apostolic expectations, no healing was thought impossible. In Shrewsbury, a Friend named John Jay or John Gay was thrown by his horse which then, as Fox recorded in his Journal 'cast him on his head and broke his neck, as they say' and 'people took him for dead', and even Fox 'saw that he was dead' and 'took him by the hair of his head and his head turned like a cloth, it was so loose'.[9] But Fox was not daunted: 'I put my hand under his chin and behind his head and raised his head two or three times with all my strength and brought it in, and I did perceive his neck begin to be stiff. And then he began to rattle and after to breathe.' The people around were 'amazed', took him into a house and sat him by the fire and then put him to bed. 'So after he had been in the house for a while he began to speak and did not know where he had been. And the next day we passed, and he with us pretty well, about 16 miles to a meeting in Middletown, and many hundreds of miles afterwards.'[10]

Stories of raising people from the dead were the miracle claims that provoked the most controversy (and, not surprisingly, the most frequent disappointment), as an infamous case associated with James Nayler illustrates. A rival with Fox for the leadership of the Friends and thus for the position as the one who came with apostolic power, proving his role with signs and miracles, Nayler was a Yorkshireman, about eight years older than George Fox, a yeoman who had served in the parliamentary army. He had been a member of an Independent Church until January 1653 when he had had a powerful religious experience and joined the Quakers with whom he went on to have a remarkable and dramatic career. He was a brilliant preacher, skilful at handling discussions with enemies and winning new adherents to the Quaker cause. In 1656, in an infamous incident, he rode into Bristol on a donkey and his companions sang 'Holy, holy, holy' to him; shortly afterwards, as he and other Quakers were travelling into Devon, they were arrested and thrown into an Exeter prison. It was while there that he believed he could raise to life from death a woman named Dorcas Erbury (daughter of the Seeker William Erbury), by laying his hands upon her. He laid his hands on her head and cried, 'Dorcas, arise.' She duly arose, and the case excited division within the ranks of the Friends, especially when people began to address Nayler in their correspondence to him as 'the everlasting Son of Righteousness', 'only begotten Son of God' or even Jesus.[11] When cross-examined by magistrates, Nayler was asked: 'Was Dorcas Erbury dead two days in Exeter, and didst thou raise her?' He replied:

I can do nothing of myself: the Scripture beareth witness to the power in me which is everlasting; it is the same power we read of in the Scripture. The Lord hath made me a signe of his coming: and that honour that belongeth to Jesus Christ, in whom I am revealed, may be given to him, as when on earth at Jerusalem, according to the measure.[12]

When Dorcas Erbury was questioned, she was bold in her claims about Nayler's identity:

Q. Dost thou own him that rode on horseback to be the Holy One of Israel?
A. Yea, I do; and with my blood will seal it.
Q. And dost thou own him for the Son of God.
A. He is the onely begotten Son of God.

She went on to testify that she believed he had raised her from the dead:

Q. Christ raised those that had been dead: So did not he.
A. He raised me.
Q. In what manner?
A. He laid his hand on my head, after I had been dead two days, and said *Dorcas arise*: and I arose, and live as thou seest.
Q. Where did he do this?
A. At the Gaol in Exeter.
Q. What witness has thou for this?
A. My mother, who was present.[13]

A little less than a year later, on 28 February 1657, Susanna Pearson, another Friend, promised to raise from the dead William Pool (a Quaker who had committed suicide) near Worcester, but she met with no success. This had involved taking his corpse out of the grave and seeking to raise it to life by copying the action of Elisha when he raised the son of the Shunammite woman (in 2 Kings 4: 32–7), and then praying. As the Quakers thought they were living in new 'apostolic times', so the mimicking of scripture in this way was given theological warrant. However, as she had no success, the corpse was re-buried. Enemies of the Quakers soon used the case to criticise them, as Thomas William noted in his account of the event to Margaret Fox (George's wife): 'And so she and another woman went to the grave and took him forth, and nothing prevailing they buried him again and so the enemy got the advantage.' George Fox wrote by this account, 'mad whimsy'.[14]

While such attempts and claims had a certain extravagance about them, the notion of being brought back from death and near-death experiences were not completely alien to the culture in which the Friends were operating. Some other examples of well-publicised cases will serve to illustrate the context in which they were operating. In 1651, the story of Anne Greene was circulated in two pamphlets: Greene had been executed on 14 December 1650, but afterwards was revived by four physicians. The first pamphlet, *A Declaration from Oxford, of Anne Greene*, described the events in supernatural terms:

A young woman that was lately, and unjustly hanged in the castle-yard; but since recovered, her neck strait, and her eyes fixed orderly and firmly in her head again: with her speech touching four angels that appeared to her when she was dead; and their strange expressions, Apparitions and passages happened thereupon, the like never heard of before.

Interestingly, the woman herself is reported as describing the event in terms of providence and not miracles – which, she assumed, had ceased: here is an interesting case of an ordinary person accepting official Protestant teaching on this subject. When she was recovering in bed she said, 'Behold Gods providence, and his wonder of wonders, which indeed, is a deliverance so remarkable, since the ceasing of miracles, that it cannot be parallel'd in all Ages, for the space of three hundred years.'[15] Divine intervention to save her life was interpreted as a clear sign of innocence (she had been hanged for infanticide). The second account was written by 'a scholler in Oxford for the satisfaction of a friend, who desired to be informed concerning the truth of the businesse' and included poems written by fellows and scholars of Oxford colleges, including Christopher Wren. This was intended to be a sober and accurate account, narrating the care of the physicians in Anne Greene's recovery, but it too invoked God's providence by way of explanation:

There happened lately in this City a very rare and remarkable accident, which being variously and falsely reported amongst the vulgar (as in such cases it is usuall) to the end that none may be deceived, and that so signall an account of God's mercy and providence may never be forgotten, I have here faithfully recorded it, according to the information I have received from those that were the Chief Instruments in bringing this great wake to perfection.[16]

The 'schollers' involved in this case were none other than the physicians Thomas Willis (1621–75) and William Petty (1623–87), both leading figures amongst the Oxford virtuosi who met together and collaborated in the 1650s, and who were hoping to perform an autopsy on her body. (Willis was to become a leading figure in anatomy.) But when the coffin arrived and as they were about to begin their work, they realised that her body was showing signs of life; they, along with physicians Ralph Bathurst (a Fellow of Trinity College) and Henry Clerke (a Fellow of Magdalen College), revived her and, when the justices wanted to hang her again, pleaded with them for her life to be spared, which it was. Willis and Petty made something of the story, proud of their involvement in it: although both went on to become wealthy and renowned figures, and in the late 1640s and 1650s were much involved in some of the most innovative experimental work being done in Oxford, at this stage they were keen to establish their reputation as doctors, having turned to that profession in the civil war. Willis, for example, eventually (according to his contemporaries) became the most financially successful medical practitioner in the country, but in 1650 he was still practising medicine in his rooms at Christ Church and as an itinerant practitioner in the villages around Oxford. Indeed, his and Petty's medical reputations were enhanced by this event and, in the competitive marketplace of medicine, this in turn boosted the success of their practices.[17] That the story lived on, and became a part of Willis's and Petty's reputations, is evidenced by John Evelyn's account of dinner with Thomas Petty in March 1675, by which time he had become Sir Thomas:

I supped at Sir William Pettys, with The Bish: of Salisbury, & divers honourable persons: we had a noble entertainement, in a house gloriously furnished; The Master and Mistris of it extraordinary Persons: Sir Will: being the sonn of a meane man some where in Sussex, was sent from Schole to Oxon: where he studied Philos: but was most eminent in mathematics and Mechanics, proceeded Doctor of Physick, & was growne famous for his Learning, so for his recovering a poor wench that had ben hanged for felonie, the body being beged (as custome is) for the Anatomie lecture, he let bloud, put to bed to a warme woman, & with spirits & other meanes recovered her to life; The Young Scholars joyn'd & made her a little portion, married her to a Man who had severall children by her, living 15 years after, as I have been assured.[18]

The story of Anna Atherton in the next decade gives an interesting example of a near-death, rather than a 'resurrection' experience. In 1669, Atherton fell sick and by February of the following year was presumed dead. The women who came to prepare her body for burial found it to be still warm, and her mother commanded that it be left 'uncoffin'd'; after seven days, Anna came out of her trance and reported her near-death experience to her mother. She said that she had been to heaven and had been told by the angel who led her there that she could not be admitted now, but must go back to earth, take leave of her friends, and return to be admitted later. 'So he [the angel] brought me thither again, and is now standing at the Beds-feet; Mother! You must needs see him; he is all in white.' Her mother told her, 'It was but a Dream or Fancy'. For proof of her experience she

told them [her mother and brother] of Three or Four Persons that were dead, since she was deprived of her Senses, and named each Person, (one of whom was dead, and they knew not of it before they sent to enquire:) she said, she saw them passing by her while they stood at the Gate. One whom she named was reputed a Vicious Person, came as far as the Gate, but was sent back again another way. All the Persons she named, dyed in the time she lay in the trance.

Anna died two years later, 'in great Assurance of her Salvation; speaking comfortable words and giving wholesome Instructions to all who came to visit her'. This account was written by her brother, a doctor, and published as a two-page pamphlet (with illustrations of Anna in her trance).[19] The purpose of publishing the pamphlet is best indicated by the work's title: *A Miraculous Proof of the Resurrection: Or, The Life to Come Illustrated. Being a Strange Relation of What Hapned to Mris Anna Atherton*. The incident seems to have been used as a miraculous proof of Christian beliefs about the Resurrection. But it was also published as 'an Invitation to an Holy Life in Maidens' in a generation described as 'Adulterous and Atheistical' and therefore fits into a genre of literature that we shall encounter again in chapter 6. (The publication of the story in pamphlet form may also simply represent the Atherton family's desire for a moment of fame and some small earnings from the selling of the story.)

The afterlife of this account tells us of a continued fascination with brushes with death. The narrative was reprinted by William Turner, for the purposes of illustrating, by concrete example, the rightness of Christian doctrines on the Resurrection, in his *Compleat History of the Most Remarkable Providences* (1697) under the chapter heading, 'Person's reviving after a supposed death'. Other stories of the (apparently) dead coming back to life without the aid of any human beings as indications of the remarkable or miraculous were also included in the chapter, such as the case of Mrs Lydia Dunton (wife of a rector in Huntingdonshire) who 'was laid out for dead several Days, yet came to life again, to the great Admiration of all that saw her in that condition'.[20] Turner also included the story of Anne Greene, and another woman hanged in Oxford who came back to life in 1658, one Elizabeth, servant of a Mrs Cope of Magdalen parish in Oxford.

These brief examples illustrate that extraordinary events, not only claims of miraculous cures but also the coming back to life of the dead (even if only briefly in Anna Atherton's case), were not therefore dismissed out of hand in mid- and late seventeenth-century culture. What marked out Fox and a few other Quakers as unusual and controversial was their role as miracle-workers. In pursuing this role, they believed that they were recovering the authenticity of the primitive church. It was the claim that *they* were healing the sick and even raising the dead by the power of Christ that caused theological offence and provoked suspicion and ridicule. In 1660, Thomas Underhill catalogued 'the blasphemies and errors of the Quakers which they have published in their printed books' and documented their claim 'that the same gift that worketh miracles is among them, as was among the Apostles'.[21] The Protestant writers at the Reformation had tried to emphasise that such figures were no longer needed; as one writer had put it, in 1554, 'For, if ye may make at your pleasure such things to drive devils away and to heal both body and soul, what need have ye of Christ, of his Death, of his Resurrection, in whyche consist our whole salvation.'[22] There were, therefore, plenty of criticisms of the Quakers' claims to work miracles in the mid-seventeenth century, and not a little scepticism. Richard Blome in 1660 ridiculed the claims of a man he thought a Quaker, named Nicholas Kate, who said, 'that when the fullness of time was come he should work miracles'.[23] In the fifth edition of Ephraim Pagett's *Heresiographie* (1654), the miracle-working activities of the Quakers and Ranters were described thus: 'in their private Conventicles they pretend to acting of Miracles, as turning water into wine, dispossessing of divels &c'.[24] In the broader culture, miracle-workers were still firmly associated with Roman Catholicism: the Puritan Richard Baxter wrote of the Seeker Clement Wrighter, with whom he was engaged in a pamphlet war: 'a Seeker he professed to be, but I easily perceived that he was a juggling Papist, or an infidel. His assertion to me was that no man is bound to believe in Christ that doth not see confirming miracles with his own eyes.'[25] Jonathan Clapham, minister at Wramplingham in Norfolk, in a tract of 1656 refuting 'the wicked and damnable doctrines of the Quakers', included a section titled 'The Quakers pretend to miracles'. But, in expressing his scepticism about a Quaker healing which had taken place in his own town, he seems (ironically) to have been surprised by the *lack* of performance in the healing, and the failure of the Quaker healer, Richard Hubberthorn (a mild-mannered yeoman who had been one of the leading figures in the community of Westmoreland Seekers who became Quakers), to mimic the first-century apostles in the mode or manner of the healing:

> In this town it was reported to me (as neer as I can remember) in these very words. Was it not a miracle for T.C. that had been brought so low by a Quartane Ague to be so suddenly recovered? I answered it was a merciful providence, but not miracle; and further demanded by what means he was cured? It was replyed, that Richard Hubberthorn, did but go to his door and speak to him, and presently he recovered but afterwards enquiring of the man himself, what Hubberthorn said to him, he told me, he said nothing, but bade him look to the light in him, he did not rebuke his

distemper, nor command him in the name of Christ to arise and walk, and since that time this man hath continued in a languishing condition.[26]

Clapham believed that the Quakers' miracles were 'feigned things' and likened them to the miracle claims of the Papists. But just in case anyone was tempted to believe in the Quakers' claims of miracles, he reminded his readers that the scriptures warn that in the last days 'this power of working miracles is to be in the hands of false prophets and deceivers' and he gave his own spin to the idea that miracles had ceased in his own age:

> Whilst we hold fast the Doctrine of Christ and the Apostles, all the miracles which they wrought are ours, for they were wrought to confirme the faith which we now professe; nor let any expect a continuance of them in all ages, for if they should be so ordinary they would not be deemed miracles.[27]

Critics of the Quakers sometimes asked them to produce miracles on demand, thereby mocking the Friends' employment of miracles to legitimate their religious claims. In 1655, George Whitehead, a Quaker who was being pursued by an angry mob, found himself at the house of Lady Hubbard in Norwich. Lady Hubbard's chaplain, one Dr Collins, heard the noise and came out to see what was happening; there he saw George Whitehead, and, understanding that he was a Quaker, began to question him, the mob remaining quiet for a while behind them. The chaplain asked him if he had the same spirit that the Apostles of Christ had had, and Whitehead replied that he had, though to a lesser degree. The chaplain then challenged him to 'demonstrate or prove it by some sign or Miracle as the Apostles did'. Whitehead replied, quoting Paul in 1 Corinthians 13, that different people have different gifts – 'to one is given the Word of Wisdom; to another the Word of Knowledge; to another Faith; to another working of Miracles; to another Prophecy; to another diverse kinds of Tongue; to another Interpretation of Tongues, &c. but all by the Same Spirit, i.e. the Spirit and Power of Christ'.[28] For Whitehead, some had the gift of working miracles in that age, but not all; in claiming the revival of first-century apostolic power, it was a matter of correct interpretation of the scriptures. Correct biblical interpretation was vital in a fraught situation, with a hostile chaplain quizzing him theologically, and his persecutors standing silent in a ring around him, ready to attack when the questioning was over and no miracle had been produced. It was a tense moment, typical of many such moments endured by the Quakers for whom, 'in those days Prisons and Gaols were made Sanctuaries and Places of Refuge and Safety to us, from the Fury of the Tumultuous mob'. In the end,

Whitehead was rescued by a sympathetic soldier who commanded the mob to stand off and make way, and escorted him to the safety of another Friend's house in the city. The soldier went on to become a Friend.[29]

Other sectarians demanded miracles of the Quakers, often in a competitive rather than critical spirit. For there was indeed competition between the different religious groups that emerged in the civil war and Interregnum periods: whose version of Christianity was authentic? Miracles were counted (at least by some) as one sign of the restoration of primitive – and therefore genuine – Christianity. There was also the reality that miracles could function as a missionary tool, just as they had in the early church, attracting new adherents and legitimating the group's claims.[30] Samuel Eaton, an Independent minister in Cheshire, wrote that, as the Quakers claimed the Spirit came into them (and their quaking was a sign of that), then 'let such persons confirm Gods speaking or the Spirits speaking to them by signes and wonders and by diversitie of Miracles as Christ and the Apostles did . . . else they must of necessity be accounted Impostors and Deceivers of the People'.[31] The Quakers replied immediately and anonymously of themselves: 'And wonders and miracles and signs are amongst them but your adulterous generation could never believe.'[32] In 1659, George Fox wrote in defence of the Quakers' refusal to produce miracles on demand: 'Many prayed by the spirit and spake by the spirit, that did not show miracles at the tempter's command, though among believers there are miracles in the spirit which are signs and wonders to the world as Isaiah saith.'[33] His point was that those who pray and speak by the Spirit do not produce miracles when tempters demand them, as was also the case amongst the earliest Christians, as shown in the Acts of the Apostles.

T. L. Underwood notes the place of miracles in the long-running dispute between the Baptists and Quakers in the mid-seventeenth century. Fox made the argument that groups that did not experience miracles – that is, the power of the apostles – were not the true church. He asked, 'Whether you Baptisers cast out Devils, and Drink any deadly thing, and it not Hurt you, and whether ye house was ever shaken when you met and where did He give ye Holy Ghost?' It was of course a rhetorical question; Fox presumed the answer was no, and went on to conclude, 'This was to show that you are not beleevers, nor in the power yt the Apostles was in.' In turn, the Baptists demanded proof of the Quakers' claim that they had the teaching of the Spirit amongst them. In 1656, the Baptist Jeremiah Ives, in a dispute with Nayler, asked, 'Whether ever any was immediately sent of God to preach the Gospel, but either God did bear witness to them from heaven, or else he did enable them to work Miracles, by which they might evince the truth of their authority upon earth?'

Nayler wrote a letter to Fox reporting that the London Baptists were asking him 'to prove my Call by a miracle there'.[34]

Claims that miracles could be worked – indeed were being worked in that very age – were therefore bound up with the rivalry between the various sectarian groups of the period to prove that they were the true church. Miracles were a sign of apostolic authority at work and ultimately held the promise that the New Jerusalem would be ushered in. Such beliefs and signs would bring in new adherents, and, in the case of the Quakers, there is evidence that the working or claims of miracles attracted the Seekers – waiting for such signs – into the group, swelling the ranks, especially in northwest England. These internecine feuds about the working of miracles are, however, only a part of the story. In the mid-seventeenth century, new cultural, intellectual and political forces were at work, and were brought to bear on the question of miracles.

In healing by touch there was also a political challenge at a time when the King had been executed and the world had been turned upside down. For the one person who could legitimately heal by touch was the monarch. The belief that the monarch could heal scrofula – a collection of symptoms, including 'an itch and tumour in the glands, joints and other tissues' eventually developing into ulcers, a condition that was also known as the King's Evil[35] – was, of course, intimately connected to claims for the divine right of kings and, more generally, to debates about the nature of the monarchy. Charles I's use of the royal touch was interpreted by his opponents as one of the ways in which he was justifying his claims to absolute rule and acting as a representative of God, and it came to be resented. When the sectarians in the civil war and Interregnum period – along with others, after the Restoration – made claims to heal by touch, they were therefore challenging the notion that the only person who could do this was the king. When George Fox healed a girl of the King's Evil by laying hands on her and praying, as he did for example in Coleshill in Warwickshire, it was not a politically neutral act for the leader of a group that did not see any need to doff their hats to their social 'betters' or observe the other niceties that kept the social hierarchy in place.[36] Healing by touch – but especially healing scrofula by touch – was therefore a politically charged act. It is to the monarch's claim to heal by touch that we now, therefore, turn.

II. After the Restoration: Touching for the King's Evil

With the restoration of the monarchy in 1660, Charles II quickly made it clear that he would be continuing the practice of touching for the King's Evil, a practice that had been initiated by Edward the Confessor, and formalised into a written liturgy in the reign of Henry VII. Indeed, Charles II touched for the King's Evil even before he arrived in England, asserting his kingly authority before stepping foot on English soil again. From 17 April to 23 May – the day he set sail for England to resume the throne as Charles II – while in Breda in Holland 'he touched two hundred and fifty'. Sir William Lower reported:

> the English assure, that not only was it not without success, since it was the experience that drew thither every day, a great number of those diseased, even from the most remote Provinces of Germany, but also that there was no person healed so perfectly, who was not infected again with the same disease, if he were so unfortunate to lose, through negligence, or otherwise, the medal, which the king hands on his neck, after he hath touched him; without any hope to be cured of it, if he be not touched again, and have another Angel about his neck.[37]

This was a key period for Charles to demonstrate his kingship; the English Parliament opened on 25 April; the House of Lords declared on 1 May that government should be by king, Lords and Commons, and a week later the Commons agreed. In June, within weeks of arriving in England to resume the throne, Charles began touching for the King's Evil. That this practice proved popular is indicated by the issuing, just two years later in 1662, of a proclamation, to be published in every market place, 'for the *better ordering* of those who repair to court for their cure of the disease called the kings evil' (my italics). It declared that Charles II was 'as ready and willing as any king or queen of this Realm ever was in anything to relieve the distresses and necessities of his good subjects' but was setting aside special days for the people to come to court for such healing. The days set aside were the week before Christmas and the month before Easter, 'being times more convenient both for the temperature of the season, and in respect of any contagion which may happen in this near access to his majesties sacred person'. People could not present themselves for such healing by the king more than once, and they were thus to bring certificates from 'parson, vicar or minister' of their parish 'testifying according to the truth, that they have not any time before been Touched by the king, to the intent to be healed of that Disease'.[38] Furthermore, those who wished to be touched by the king for scrofula had to be examined by the king's surgeon who would check that they did in fact have that disease. This was crowd control, for Charles allowed far greater numbers to come for healing than had his predecessors, touching in all about 90,000 for the King's Evil during his reign;[39] it was also a sign of the bureaucratisation of the process as Charles used it to establish and display his royal authority.[40]

The elements of the ceremony had been consolidated in the late fifteenth century by the first Tudor monarch, Henry VII, who needed, like Charles II two hundred years later, to establish his authority through such rituals. Charles used and developed these rituals to the full. As Harold M. Weber puts it in his work on Charles II's relationship with, and use of, the media, 'Even more than his father, Charles exploited the political aspects of his healing office, organizing a massive deployment of state machinery to literalize, as it were, the metaphoric resonance of the monarch's identity as the nation's physician.'[40] The ceremony was designed to display kingship: the king was placed on 'a great chair', which was in 'a place somewhat distant from the people', as Sir William Lower described it, and the sick came to the king in his grand seat so that he might lay hands on their cheeks. The juxtaposition of the royal person in his throne and the disfigured subjects with their running sores, tumours and swellings kneeling before him could only emphasise the monarch's authority, as well as the king's extraordinary benevolence in mixing so closely with the sick. A passage from scripture was read (Mark 16:14–17) and the line 'They shall lay their hands on the Sick, and they shall be healed' (in verse 17 of that passage) was read out each time the king touched a sick person. The ceremony continued with a further reading from scripture (John 1:1–14); when the chaplain came to verse 9 of that reading ('That light was the true light, which lighteth every man which cometh into the world'), he repeated it as the king gave to each person who had come for healing a gold token (which Charles changed from the traditional gold angel to a medal, in 1665). Then the reading from John was concluded, prayers were said, the king washed his hands and left.[41] The royalist John Browne thought the very ceremony was its own justification for the practice:

He [the king] takes leave of the people, and they joyfully and thankfully do every one return home, praising God and their good King; and when this method is apparent to all men, and carries in it the greatest truth imaginable, what man of Sense, Reason or Honesty can there be, which shall dare to deny the truth and efficacy thereof, being both glorious and praiseworthy? Considering that the Liturgy used therein is holy, the simplicity and reverence of the Ceremonies thereof being performed with all decency, the person who performs this being hitherto constituted by a Divine permission, performing it without any appearance of superstition, the Author of the whole work being the Holy Spirit, and this Gift arising hence with both its use and fruit.

Browne was defending the ritual against the charge of superstition: 'In the whole there is nothing but God Worshipped, Christ venerated and poor Christians cured.'[42]

Royalist commentators jumped in to demonstrate that the ways in which Charles' touching for the King's Evil was a sign of his divine authority as king. Thomas Allen, in his book *Cheirexoke: The Excellency or Handy-work of The Royal Hand* of 1665, wrote that 'Monarchy is the most secure and most preserving form of Government upon Earth' and that 'he that rebels against his lawful prince, rebels against God'.[43] This divinely appointed king was the physician of the nation, or as John Browne put it, nearly twenty years later, in 1684:

Unto whom shall we most likely resemble, or presume to compare our Dread Soveraign King Charles the Second . . . who sits as the great Moderator of our English Isle: The great Parent of our Health and Safety, and the Royal Well-wisher of our Lives and Fortunes as to our Prosperity and plentiful enjoyment, who hath as far excelled his Predecessors in this sanative Faculty, . . . who as he was given to us for our health, and the health of our nation, so in this Curative Faculty he outshines all the World.[44]

Curing scrofula by miraculous touch was a sign of the monarch's God-given authority. Not surprisingly, Thomas Allen evoked some of the cures wrought by Charles II's father, the deposed and beheaded Charles I, summing up 'And should I go to particulars, and summe up all those Miracles (for I dare not call them lesse) that have been wrought by that Pattern of true Piety; A Prince whereof the world was not worthy; the best of all Christian kings, now undoubtedly in Heaven, their number would be as admirable as their nature.'[45]

But much had changed since Charles I's reign, and the claims of the Quakers and others that they could heal by touch was a matter of considerable concern to writers like Allen. How could the king be re-established as the sole person in the kingdom endowed with God's gift of healing by touch? The opening sentence of Thomas Allen's work betrayed his nervousness:

I cannot but take notice, that for several years last past, divers Persons, taking the advantage of there being no king in Israel, have hugg'd themselves too much, with the vain hopes of having Fortune to be their mistress, whom they more courted for Success, than the Deity, boasting themselves the Seventh Sons, Stroakers, and what not, have become great Undertakers, promising by their manual touch, the perfect Cure of those Swellings, commonly called by the name of the Kings Evil.

These 'new lights' as he called them, who claimed that they received miraculous powers directly from God, were a threat: 'That which God doth bestow upon Kings should be that, which both for the Rarenesse and Singularity of the Priviledge, might more manifest his Glory; which would not be, if he should attribute the same thing, and that by right of birth to any other.'[46] There were other threats too: Allen mentioned the 'seventh sons' or – even better – seventh sons of seventh sons who, it was thought, could cure scrofula by touch just like the monarch by virtue of their peculiar genealogy. Interestingly, this belief seems only to have emerged in the sixteenth century.[47] The question of who could heal by touch was important in political terms at a time when the monarchy was so newly re-established. Because the sectarian leaders of the Interregnum period had claimed that they had the authority to heal – and their theology maintained that God inspired individuals in that way, whatever their station in life – there were political challenges to the king's claim to be the only miraculous healer, with powers bestowed upon him (and him alone) by God. The window for debate about the nature of the king's authority had been opened.

Of course, there had been doctrinal challenges to the idea that the king was in possession of some sort of miraculous power since the Protestant Reformation in the sixteenth century. The king's healing power derived from his sacred character, and this was established in the ceremony of anointing – a rite of the ancient religion. Furthermore, the Reformers distrusted the miracles attributed to saints, and the king's healings were suspiciously similar to these. James I is recorded (by a papal spy, admittedly) to have been reluctant to perform the royal touch, because 'he could not see how he could heal the sick without a miracle; but miracles had ceased – they no longer happened'.[48] Marc Bloch, who has written one of the major histories of touching for the King's Evil, sees an inevitability in the reformers' denial of the royal miracle as they entered a clearer appreciation of their own ideas: 'They came to see it as one of the ingredients in the system of practices and beliefs they rejected as the sacrilegious innovation of idolatrous ages; in a word, they considered it . . . "a superstition" which must be rooted out from the faith.'[49]

The English kings enjoyed an additional healing ability to their French counterparts with their 'cramp rings', thought to cure epilepsy and associated illnesses such as rheumatism and muscular spasms, which were rubbed by the monarch, blessed in holy water and distributed to be worn by the sufferers. Addressing Edward VI's court in 1547, the reformist preacher Nicholas Ridley denounced a number of idolatrous practices, and many in his audience concluded he was attacking the blessing of the cramp rings – their sprinkling with holy water was a ritual action that was deemed too close to exorcism for comfort. Edward rewarded Ridley with a bishopric, but the practice was nonetheless continued to the end of his reign. Mary zealously continued all the earlier practices, but the cramp rings tradition was ended when Elizabeth became queen. Though she maintained the scrofula touch, albeit with the ritual translated into English and the sections about the Blessed Mary and the saints cut out, the cramp rings tradition was evidently considered too difficult to maintain in a Reformed atmosphere.

Doctrinal challenge mixed with political challenge in the civil war and Interregnum. The privileges of royalty were questioned and attacked, and miraculous healing was one such privilege. More extreme Protestants added to their original doctrinal hostility to the healing a further antipathy to it by their hatred of absolute monarchy and all practices, such as the healing, which might be considered manifestations of this absolutism. But as some thought miraculous healing unsuitable for monarchs, so it was taken up, as we have seen, by others claiming apostolic power.

Claims from others that they had the power to heal by touch led to the raising of questions about just why and how the monarch could cure the King's Evil. As John Aubrey put it, in 1696, 'The Curing of the King's Evil by the Touch of the King, does much puzzel our Philosophers.'[50] Further confusions were added as others, in a different, post-Restoration political climate, made claims that they could heal by touch; or people sometimes made the claim for them. For example, in the early 1680s, claims were made that the Duke of Monmouth – Charles II's illegitimate son by Lucy Walter, and rival for the throne to the Duke of York, later James II – had the power to cure by touch. Henry Clark, an Anglican minister, wrote a pamphlet (published by the Whig Benjamin Harris) relating that a twenty-year-old woman, named Elizabeth Parcet, was cured of the King's Evil, by the touch of the Duke of Monmouth, having been directed by 'God, the Great Physitian . . . to go and touch the Duke of Monmouth' which she did, despite the disapproval of her mother. She went with several of her neighbours to Henton Park, where the duke was staying, and 'she prest in among a Crowd of people and caught him by the hand, his Glove being on, and she had a Glove likewise to cover her wounds'. But she was not satisfied with this, 'her mind was, she must touch some part of his bare skin'. Thus she persisted and when she heard that the duke was coming along again, she tore off her gloves; 'the Duke's Glove, as Providence would have it, the upper part being hung down, so that his hand-wrest was bare; she prest one and caught him by the bare hand-wrest with her running hand; (saying, God bless your Greatness; and the Duke said God bless you)'. On returning home, her mother was angry and threatened to beat her, but 'she cryed out, O Mother, I shall be well again', and within several days, her sores dried up and the eye that was given up for lost was restored to sight.[51] There were also stories, put about in response to the claims for the Duke of Monmouth, and therefore as satire by Tories, that Mrs Fanshawe, the sister of the Duke of Monmouth, had cured an Apple-woman's son of the King's Evil by the stroke of her hand. Some responded to that story by saying it was a papist rumour, put about to upset the Protestant cause.[52] The story that the Duke of Monmouth had cured people of the King's Evil was re-told in several publications at the time, including *The Protestant (Domestick) Intelligence* and *A Choice Collection of Wonderful Miracles, Ghosts and Visions* (1681). John Aubrey included it in his *Miscellanies* of 1696, along with stories of cures by seventh sons of seventh sons and the following extraordinary story – told to him by Elias Ashmole – which suggested that healing could happen in random ways by all sorts of royals, even dead ones. One William Backhouse of Swallowfield in Berkshire had an ugly scab on the middle of his forehead. Backhouse dreamt of a church and a hearse (memorial tomb), and was told in the dream to take the drops of mois-ture on the marble and put them on his scab. The next day he went to a church, saw the very same hearse made of black marble, which was the tomb of Queen Catherine, wife of Henry VIII, and put the drops from the marble onto his scab, which was perfectly cured in seven days.[53]

Could *any* royals heal by touch? What gave monarchs their healing power? The question continued to be asked in the eighteenth century, even though Anne was the last of the monarchs to touch for the King's Evil and the Hanovers wanted nothing to do with the practice, dubbing it 'superstitious' in the age of politeness, and reluctant to risk raising questions about their own succession to the English throne when a Stuart heir was still alive. Nevertheless, commentators continued to write about touching for the King's Evil, which was a politically hot issue especially in relation to the Jacobites. Samuel Werenfels was inspired, at least in part, to write his *Dissertation Upon Superstition in Natural Things* in 1749, by the following story about a Bristol labourer named Christopher Lovel:

> an Instance is just now produced, of a Cure performed by a Prince never anointed at all; and a curious example it is. Christopher Lovel, afflicted by the King's Evil, set out from England in Quest of Relief. He applied to a certain, nameless, Hereditary, unanointed Prince. He succeeded in his wishes; was miraculously healed; returned Home; relaps'd; and died of the Struma at last. Q.E.D.[54]

On the basis of this story, Werenfels suggested it was the unction a monarch received during the Coronation that gave him (or her) the power to cure, though others refuted that. The prince was, of course, Charles Edward Stuart, the Young Pretender, and the Jacobites got their own back with a story they circulated in 1751 of a Birmingham box-maker named David West, who was allegedly cured of the King's Evil after an encounter with 'the most comely person he had ever beheld', an apparition identified as Charles Edward Stuart. This person or apparition touched West to heal him, and recited a Latin prayer, afterwards saying, 'I touch, but God healeth' and then instructed West not to tell anyone about this encounter for twelve months. The Jacobite Press emphasised the fact that this had happened on Restoration Day (in 1749).[55]

Touching for the King's Evil became increasingly associated with Roman Catholicism, with which Jacobitism was primarily associated. William III's aversion to the royal touch was based on his association of it with Roman Catholic beliefs and rituals. This is hardly surprising for his predecessor, James II, during his short period as king, had begun to enlist the services of Roman Catholic clergy when he touched for the King's Evil, and had replaced the liturgy which his brother, father and grandfather had used, and taken up the liturgy used by Henry VII, complete with Latin prayers, the invocation of the Virgin Mary and the saints, and the sign of the cross. As Bloch puts it, this return to the Roman Catholic past, 'only served to discredit the royal miracle among a section of the Protestants'.[56] In exile, James continue to touch for the King's Evil, in Ireland and in St Germain in the 1690s; after his death his spirit was credited with the performance of several miracles, and there was an unsuccessful attempt to have him canonised.[57]

The proliferation of figures touching for the King's Evil – and curing other illnesses by touch – in the seventeenth and eighteenth centuries led to new, or at least renewed, questions about the efficacy of the royal practice, and the grounds on which it worked. For even if the monarch did successfully heal scrofula by touch, the fact that others did too (the religious radicals and Stuart princes, as we have seen, and Valentine Greatrakes, to whom we will turn in the next chapter) raised questions. These questions were not necessarily about the plausibility of miracles but rather about how such healings occurred, given that they were no longer unique to the king, and therefore traditional answers that bound together divine right with healing gift no longer held. This sometimes led people to reject any explanation of the king's cures as miraculous but it was not necessarily scepticism (of a Humean sort) that provoked their initial questions.

William Beckett, a Whig, a surgeon and a Fellow of the Royal Society, writing about the King's Evil in 1722, agreed that such cures occurred at the touch of the king, but did not believe they were miracles, and he did not know how they worked. He therefore sought another explanation. He proposed and rejected several of the usual explanations: for example, the hereditary right of succession – like John Aubrey, he pointed out that that had been broken over the past three hundred years; the ceremonies – he noted that they had been changed within the last two hundred years; the gold given at the touching – he observed Charles I had not always been able to use gold because of his financial troubles, and had had to resort to silver. Noting also the reported successes of the Duke of Monmouth, Beckett therefore arrived at his own conclusion that such cures worked by 'the power of imagination and the biological effects that puts into motion'. He believed that in people suffering from scrofula, 'we observe the Blood to be impoverish'd, and to have a very languid Motion; the Chyle is thrown into it in a very dispirited state'. Such sufferers therefore needed a powerful force in the imagination to quicken the blood, and thus effect a cure:

> Can it be otherwise supposed, than that when a poor and miserable Creature, prepossess'd with the most eager Thoughts of Relief, shall see the Royal Majesty condescend to apply his Hands for the Cure of the Sores and Swellings he is diseas'd with, but that it must procure a fresh Turn to the Blood and Spirits, give the effete and languid Nerves fresh vigour, excite the intestine Agitation of the Particles of the Blood, and produce an agreeable Alteration in the Whole Constitution?

Beckett's explanation of the cures is written entirely in terms of the body's agency: 'For an Animal Body is not a meer aggregate of Flesh, Bones, Blood-vessels & c. but an exquisitely contriv'd and very sensible machine, whose Parts are easily set at work, by proper tho' minute Agents, which may by their Action upon one another, perform far greater things than could be expected from the bare energy of the Principles that first put them in motion.'[58]

The increase in such mechanistic explanations may easily lead to the assumption that the medical came to supersede the supernatural; Harold M. Weber certainly arrives at that conclusion.[59] This increasing professionalisation of medicine occurred alongside a new scepticism about miracles amongst some philosophers in the eighteenth century. Indeed, the philosophical debate about miracles reached its peak at about the same time that the monarch finally stopped touching for the King's Evil. It is tempting to link these various strands and conclude that the decline in the royal touch was an inevitable result of the 'modernising' forces of the Enlightenment, as Harold Weber does; but Paul Monod, in his important study of Jacobitism, warns against that temptation, highlighting the political reasons for the end of the royal touch. He writes that belief in the royal touch was killed 'not by the spread of rationalism after 1688, but by political necessity. It was hard to uphold the sanctity of a royal succession that had been altered by Parliamentary manipulation, and monarchs whose legitimacy was so easily challenged could not afford to take the risk of trying to perform miracles. Although every English ruler claimed to be sacred, and Queen Anne went so far as to act the part, they were highly vulnerable to Jacobite competition. Williamite and Hanoverian supporters, therefore, were obliged to heap scorn on the royal touch as "superstitious" and ineffectual.'[60]

However, it cannot be denied that by the early eighteenth century, a change had occurred in the ways in which cures claimed as miracles – and other miraculous claims – were investigated and explained. In the next chapter, we turn to the most famous healer by touch of the late seventeenth century, whose activities sparked an epistemological shift: Valentine Greatrakes. The mid-seventeenth century witnessed not only the revival of an intra-Protestant debate about whether miracles had ceased or not, based on the claims of certain groups to be able to work them and to have experienced them in their own age, but also the beginnings of an interaction between those claims and the new practices and theories that were emerging, aimed at investigating, understanding and explaining the natural world – that is, what historians used to call the 'Scientific Revolution'.[61] Miracle-workers, and others who made claims that miracles had occurred, opened up the question of whether miracles had ceased with the end of the apostolic age or could yet still occur; they had their own theological and political agenda in the posing of that question; others had different agenda and different intellectual perspectives, and lost no time in bringing them to bear on the miracle 'cases' that emerged and contributing to the ensuing debate. Or to put it another way: the 'Enlightenment' had arrived.

CHAPTER 4

Valentine Greatrakes and the New Philosophy

In this chapter, the celebrated case of Valentine Greatrakes is discussed: Greatrakes was a healer who emerged in Ireland in the 1660s, and visited England in 1666 where his powers to heal came under a new sort of scrutiny. He attracted the attention of many of the great churchmen and philosophers of the day, including some of the virtuosi of the recently formed Royal Society, and his case represents a turning point in attitudes towards such miracle claims. Debate about him went beyond the doctrinal (although doctrinal questions about the occurrence of miracles in that age continued to be asked) and entered the domain of natural philosophy: the elite witnesses of Greatrakes' healing work asked on what grounds and with what results his (often successful) cures could be tested, in order to see whether they were miraculous or could be explained in natural or mechanistic terms. While the cases of miracles amongst Baptists and Quakers certainly provoked theological discussion about the possibility of miracles in their age, this case can be seen as the beginning of a particular Enlightenment debate in England about the *plausibility* of miracles, and hence a turning point in the overall narrative of this book.

* * * * *

In 1654, a healer named Matthew Coker, of Lincoln's Inn, came to public attention in London. He claimed he had the gift of healing from God, and was said to have cured a lame leper named Henry Flemming, restored sight to the blind and caused the lame to walk. Many of the cures he effected in a local hospital, and all by touch. One man in the hospital, for example, had 'legs benumbed towards the feet, & was well restored; as also a hand with the fingers grasped inward, and long time useless & dead (or withered, as perhaps it may be the more proper term) and he found life and quickness entring [*sic*] into them more & more, as my hand continued on them'. Even the 'hard of belief' were cured; to one, Coker said, 'Lay aside thy crutches, and walk' and he 'walked without them many steps: but not believing, he did it with the more fear and astonishment'. Coker said he did all of these cures 'by the Finger of God; which any Christian may easily judge, it being beyond the work of Satan to give the least of such good gifts'.[1]

Coker's claims were accepted by Robert Gell, D. D., Rector of St Mary Aldermary, who wrote to the philosopher Lady Conway in May 1654, telling her about Coker, and relating that the Earl of Pembroke was also entirely convinced since he had benefited from the laying on of hands himself and had witnessed the cure of a mad person.[2] Henry More, the Cambridge Platonist, also became interested in Coker and initially, at least, urged his friend Lady Conway, who suffered from terrible headaches and was always in search of a cure (she had sought the medical advice of the most prominent physicians, including Thomas Willis), to let Coker try his healing skills on her head; as far as we know, she never saw Coker. Over ten years later, Lady Conway was informed of the healing work of an Irishman named Valentine Greatrakes;[3] this time, she agreed to see the healer, and thus it was that Anne Conway's headaches were the cause of Greatrakes' celebrated visit to England in 1666 though, ironically, she remained one of the people he failed to heal.

With the arrival of Greatrakes, known as the 'Irish Stroker', the debate about miracles took a new turn. It went beyond the intra-Protestant disagreements – which had greeted the Baptist and Quaker claims – about whether miracles had ceased in apostolic times or not, as those interested in natural philosophy began to ask different questions about the plausibility of miracles, sometimes offering mechanistic or naturalistic explanations for Greatrakes' cures. Henry More was a member of the Royal Society and his interest in Greatrakes was not untypical of that membership. The Royal Society had, just several years before, been given its royal charter and its members – philosophers, churchmen and others – met regularly; this was exactly the kind of case that fascinated them. Several of them had been tracking Greatrakes' activities even before he arrived in England. For example, Henry Oldenburg, Secretary of the Royal Society, had written to Robert Boyle about Greatrakes in the autumn of 1665 when Greatrakes was becoming known for his cures in Ireland; Oldenburg had heard about Greatrakes from John Beale, Rector of Yeovil in Somerset (also a Fellow of the Royal Society since 1663 and correspondent of Oldenburg, Boyle and others in that circle).[4]

Greatrakes attracted their interest because his cures were not designed to make a point about the validity or apostolicity of a certain religious group (as with the Quakers), or the need to follow a passage of scripture to the letter (as with the Baptists). His primary purpose was, simply, to heal suffering bodies. He therefore raised some questions for the virtuosi: if he did not use any medicinal aids, what was the source of his healing power? Did he cure by natural or supernatural means? How could their newly developed experimental method help to answer this question? They began with the supposition that certain knowledge belonged to God only; God's knowledge and omniscience transcended human reason, which was in itself a God-given gift. In this sense, these early scientists were heirs of some of the thinking of the Great Tew Circle, and most of them shared the Latitudinarian sensibility that was beginning to prevail in the Church of England.[5] The Society's experimental method was therefore based not on dogmatic certainties (as it was in European science) but on the accrual of evidence and a gradual progress towards truth, which would result in probability judgements.[6] Any phenomenon should be observed and tested rather than ruled out *a priori*; if the evidence for it was great enough, and well enough attested, it should be regarded as probable or even *morally* certain. The Society members had a positive attitude to the testimony of others (unlike the sceptics), though not an uncritical attitude, as we shall see in the investigation of Greatrakes, and this was reflected in the *shared sense* of investigation that lay at the heart of the Society's conceptualisation of its project.

It was natural that these men should apply their method to events claimed as miracles, for they were dealing with empirically observable phenomena: the curing of a limb, the healing of a disease. If upon investigation, the evidence for a miracle was great enough, and well-enough testified, the possibility of a miracle should not be dismissed. In short, it was more important to establish whether phenomena existed, via the experimental method, than to dismiss any phenomena (even miracles or spirits or ghosts) according to *a priori* criteria (which their more dogmatic counterparts would have done). The result was that the doctrine of the cessation of miracles was now questioned on new grounds.

Some prominent members of the Royal Society therefore argued that miracles were still possible – but only upon very great evidence. Robert Boyle, one of the most prominent members of the Royal Society and one of the most well known of the experimentalists and natural philosophers in the 1660s, declared at a key moment in the discussion about Greatrakes that, 'I remember not, that I have hitherto met with . . . any, at least cogent, Proofe that Miracles were to cease with the Age of the Apostles'.[7] Boyle was a pious man whose primary intellectual concern was the relationship between God's power, God's creation (the natural world) and human understanding of that creation. He was therefore interested in well-attested accounts of supernatural phenomena, because they might well be or provide evidence of God's power in the creation. As a tolerant Anglican of broad churchmanship, he counted amongst his friends and colleagues both Roman Catholics and dissenters, but was nevertheless hostile to all views of the world that belittled God's power in it, attacking both Aristotelian and Hobbesian (materialist) views of creation, considering them irreligious or atheistic threats. His study of nature was therefore in part a theological pursuit, as much a part of his religious agenda as was his expertise in biblical languages or his support of missionary projects in New England.[8] He was also interested in others' investigations of unusual cures. He reported to Henry Stubbe that the physician William Harvey had experimented with curing tumours by stroking them with the hand of a man dead of a 'lingring disease', and had had some success with this method of healing.[9]

Joseph Glanvill, an Anglican clergyman, who went on to become one of the leading defenders of the Royal Society, had an interest in the miraculous; although he was not an 'experimentalist' like Boyle, he was concerned to find evidence for the existence of spirits, believing this would confirm the truth of Christianity. He was not personally involved in the investigation of Greatrakes, as others such as Boyle were, but his interest in the case should not be of any surprise, even though he devoted the greater part of his intellectual attention to investigating ghosts, spirits, demons, witchcraft and other similar manifestations of the supernatural, on the grounds that to deny such a spirit world was to promote atheism. He was supported in his work by Henry More, one of the first of the Royal Society members to greet Greatrakes in England, in 1665. More contributed to Glanvill's most important defence of the supernatural, *Sadducismus Triumphatus*, which was published in 1681 (just after Glanvill's death). In that text, Glanvill asserted that:

> Matters of fact well proved ought not to be denied, because we cannot conceive how they are performed. Nor is it a reasonable method of inference, first to presume the thing impossible, and thence to conclude, that the fact cannot be proved. On the contrary, we should judge the action by the evidence, and not the evidence by our fancies about the action. This is proudly to exalt our own opinions above the clearest testimonies, and most sensible demonstrations of fact.[10]

According to men such as Boyle, More, Glanvill and others involved in the Greatrakes case, the same method could and should be applied to miracles.

Anne Conway, the woman whose illness initially prompted Greatrakes' visit to England, believed in the possibility of miracles occurring in her own day, though she sometimes doubted the credibility of the alleged miracle-worker, as Robert Gell affirmed in his letter to her about Coker, in 1654:

There are 2 things questionable, and really questioned by some at this tyme. The one whether there be any such gifts of healing in the Church at this day, as were in the Apostles tymes. The other, whether Mr Coker have those gifts (for the Apostles name in them in the plural) or onely pretend unto them, as the Wiseman speaks of some who boast a false gift. Your Ladiship seemed not to question the former, nor indeed is there reason for that loud cry, That miracles and gifts of healing are ceased in the Church, Since the arm of the Lord is not shorten'd, nor doth he anywhere in His word say, that they shall cease. And the necessities of mankinde are the same. And greater glory is promised to the Church in these later dayes, than in the former. And our Lord hath lefet a speciall promise to believers of that kinde. Job 14.12.

But your Ladiships doubt is rather touching the person, whether he have that gift.[11]

Conway, like More (her friend and tutor in philosophy) and Glanvill had read Descartes (whose work had been published in England in the 1650s) and rejected his mechanical reductionism. She, too, was concerned to refute the materialism of Hobbes and Spinoza, and did so in her own philosophical work, *The Principles of the Most Ancient and Modern Philosophy* (published posthumously in London in 1692), in which she argued that because God is essentially good, so is his creation. She was willing to entertain the possibility of miracles being a part of that good creation, and a result of God's power in that creation, even though she did not receive such a miracle herself. Interestingly, towards the end of her life, she joined those one-time miracle-workers, the Quakers, finding their mystical quality appealing.

The role of Greatrakes' *practice* of healing the sick is significant in understanding the investigation of his healings as a key turning point in the intellectual path that forged the English Enlightenment approach to miracle claims, precisely because it illustrates that this was not a de-contextualised debate about miracles. R. M. Burns in his book on the Enlightenment debate on miracles is right to highlight the work of such Royal Society members as Boyle, who proposed a method by which miracles could be considered plausible or even probable, in a longer trajectory of the 'great debate' on miracles; but he discusses that intellectual development without considering the context in which it occurred – namely, the investigations of miracle claims that were actually occurring in the 1650s and 1660s and beyond, as experimental philosophy was being developed. Peter Dear, an historian of science, argues that, 'the absence of miracles in everyday life in England (formularised in the Anglican doctrine of the cessation of miracles) corresponded to a set of ... inferential practices that granted the singular experience a foundational rather than incidental relation to authentic knowledge of nature'. He contrasts this with the French context in which he maintains 'the handling of miracles in everyday French life involved a set of inferential practices that privileged universalised experiences of precisely the sort found in the mixed mathematical sciences over the singular experiences found at the heart of English experimental philosophy'. Dear makes this point as a part of his broader argument about the contrasting ways in which the scientific method was developed in England and France, and he is certainly right about the differences in method. But it is surely too much to attribute those differences in scientific method (even in part) to different experiences of miracles in each country: the evidence cannot bear that interpretation. Dear is right that the handling of miracles was a more regular and therefore more routinised practice in Roman Catholic France; but he is wrong to assume, as he does, that because there was a *doctrine* of the cessation of miracles in England, then miracles had necessarily ceased there. Because of this assumption, in which he confuses prescription with practice, he maintains that miracles were 'a threat to Anglicans like Boyle or Locke or John Wilkins'; what he does *not* do is take into account the actual miracle claims – events that were regarded as out of the ordinary course of nature – which were investigated by those English experimental philosophers. In short, he presumes theory over practice, in a way that would have been anathema to Boyle and his colleagues.[12]

The intellectual debate about miracles was therefore determined and shaped by actual claims of miraculous healing, and their being witnessed, not by abstract speculation about the miraculous. This engagement with lived religion was true to the experimental method as it was developing in England: it was more important to participate in experimental work than to formulate methodological *a priori*. In that sense, practice was always more important than theory. Thomas Sprat, in his *History of the Royal Society*, published in 1667 just after Greatrakes' visit to England, even went so far as to describe Christ's miracles as experiments 'with which he asserted the Truths that he taught'. Thus Sprat described miracles as 'Divine experiments of his [Christ's] Godhead'.[13] The implication here is that because God conveys the truth of his doctrine by miracles – that is, through events that were contrary to the ordinary course of nature – then experiments should be concerned not only with exhibiting the *ordinary* course of nature, but also with those phenomena which are outside, above or contrary to the ordinary course of nature.

A brief perusal of the *Philosophical Transactions* of the Royal Society indicates the ways in which members were concerned to investigate widely varying, strange phenomena – what the general populace called 'wonders'. Monstrous children; people who fasted and survived; the extraordinarily old;

people cured by unusual means: accounts of all these phenomena filled the pages of the *Philosophical Transactions*. For example, in 1685, Dr Peirce wrote describing the cure of palsy and barrenness by the waters of Bath; in 1695, Dr Henry Sampton, a fellow of the Royal College of Physicians, related the story of one Hannah Taylor who was prodigiously large at an early age; in 1705, Dr William Oliver related 'an extraordinary sleepy person' who slept almost constantly and ate very little; in 1742, an account of one Margaret Cutting, who spoke without a tongue, was published.

In this exploration of the extraordinary, as in so many other ways, the influence of Francis Bacon's method on the early work of the Royal Society can be seen. In his *Novum Organum* (1620), Bacon had called for the compilation of natural histories of monsters, prodigious births and everything that was new, rare or unusual in nature. Such a project was to be undertaken with rigorous selection to ensure that it was worthy of credit. As K. Theodore Hoppen notes, the early Royal Society had a 'thirst for news of "monsters" and "singularities"'. He continues,

> In 1667 Oldenburg was writing excitedly to Boyle about a 'pretty young hermaphordite' which he had seen and about which the Society would shortly receive an account, . . . and Wilkins reported on 'a maid in Holland who voided a seed by urine, which being sown grew'. Dr Timothy Clarke discoursed of a woman pregnant with a child for eighteen years; Kenelm Digby of werewolves; Walter Charleton of a monstrous birth weighing twenty three pounds without any bones or head. Oldenburg relayed news of a woman in France with four breasts.[14]

Sprat was aware of possible criticism of this investigation of oddities and in his defence of it tried to present a balanced approach. Thus, 'it is an unprofitable and unsound way of Natural Philosophy to regard nothing else, but the prodigious and extraordinary causes and effects', and yet 'it is also as true, that there are many Qualities and Figures, and powers of thing, that break the common Laws and transgress the standing Rules of Nature'. A middle way was to be found: 'To make that [Natural History] only to consist of strange and delightful Tales, is to render it nothing else but vain, and ridiculous Knight Errantry. Yet we may avoid that extreme, and still leave room, to consider the singular and irregular effects, and to imitate the unexpected and monstrous excesses, which Nature does sometimes practise in her works.' The task was to 'imitate' nature by the most accurate reporting possible of these singular phenomena. This could be done by following the methods of the Royal Society:

If this was of general receiving all credible accounts of natural, and Artificial productions, shall seem expos'd to overmuch hazard, and uncertainty: that danger is remov'd by the Royal Societies reducing such matters of here-say and information, into real, and impartial trials, perform'd by their own hands.[15]

Greatrakes' cures were regarded both as potential miracles to be investigated for the sake of Christian orthodoxy but also as especially interesting examples of such phenomena, and so it is to the investigation of those cures that we now turn.

It was in 1662 that Greatrakes had his first 'impulse', or knowledge, that he was bestowed with the gift of curing the King's Evil. After the successful healing of a boy with scrofula, news spread of his gift, and many flocked to his estate in Affane, in Ireland, to be healed. Soon thereafter, he received a second 'impulse', which led him to heal other ailments. Greatrakes was a gentleman – of Irish gentry stock – and, being of comfortable means, he did not need to charge a fee for his healings; he could therefore avoid being confused with the many 'quacks' who charged for their cures.[16] But he had been a member of the Cromwellian army in the civil war (though in 1661 he was secured from reprisals for this military past) and it seems that he also had Muggletonian connections, though his acquaintance with Lodowick Muggleton actually appears to have occurred in the 1670s. (His wife's family was, incidentally, soundly royalist.)[17] While Greatrakes may not have intended his healings to be disruptive, they were sometimes interpreted in that way, not least by royalist clergy who knew of his Cromwellian connections, and saw his healings by touch as a political challenge. By this time, of course, the monarchy had been restored and Charles II was touching for the King's Evil. Greatrakes was summoned to the bishop's court at Lismore to discuss his cures, and while there he was commanded to stop what he was doing, but he continued. Even before he arrived in England in 1666, his healings were therefore attracting attention – and some admiration for their success rates – as well as provoking a political interpretation.

Greatrakes' welcome party at Ragley Hall in Warwickshire, the home of Viscount and Viscountess Conway, hinted at the sort of attention he would receive during his time in England. He was greeted by an illustrious crowd: his hosts Anne Conway and her husband, Edward Conway; Henry More and his Cambridge Platonist friends, Ralph Cudworth, Benjamin Whichcote, George Rust and John Worthington; and, finally, Henry Stubbe, who had a medical practice in the Warwick area and was physician to the Conway family. This meant that, from the very beginning of his visit to England, Greatrakes attracted the attention of a number of men and women who were

profoundly interested in the relationship between the natural and the supernatural, and the means and methods by which Greatrakes' cures might be
observed, examined and explained. The Cambridge Platonists in particular
were interested in the relationship between reason and revelation, wishing not
to dismiss the possibility of the supernatural out of hand if the evidence
suggested its plausibility – More was especially concerned not to do this, as
his support of Glanvill's work illustrates – and yet opposed to any form of
'enthusiasm'. Greatrakes went on attracting the attention of the virtuosi, most
notably Robert Boyle, when he moved from Ragley to London.

Once in England, Greatrakes soon began to perform cures; his healings do
indeed seem to have been dramatic *performances* by which he literally stroked
the disease out of the ill person, often praying as he stroked and always giving
thanks to God afterwards. He cured people with eczema, asthma, headaches,
rheumatism and arthritis, tumours, dropsy, deafness and, even, an accident
victim who had internal bleeding. However, as he readily admitted, he was
not always able to cure people – his most notable failure was, of course, Anne
Conway herself – and sometimes his cures were only temporary. At the beginning of his visit to England, Greatrakes spent several weeks at Ragley, healing
people on the Conways' estate and from the surrounding countryside. Henry
Stubbe was present on the estate when Greatrakes was at work, and he
described in some detail what Greatrakes was *physically* doing. Stubbe 'saw
him put his Finger into the Eares of a man who was very thick of Hearing;
and immediately he heard me when I asked him very softly severall questions'. Other cases of deafness were cured, swollen limbs were brought back
to normal size, boils, tumours and wens (or wennes – sebaceous cystic
tumours under the skin, often found on the head) were dissipated, as Stubbe
recorded: 'I saw him launce a Wenne that covered the Eye of an old man;
there issued out an abundance of matter in smell, and consistence, and colour,
resembling a rotten-Egge; after which he crushed out the less digested matter,
which resembled the braines of any Creature: which being done, he stroked
the place gently, and the flux of blood and pain (which was great by reason of
his crushing it hard) presently ceased.'[18]

In February Greatrakes moved on to Worcester where, again, crowds gathered to be healed by him. While he was there, he was summoned to London
by the king, to perform his cures at Court, at Whitehall. Jostling crowds –
both friendly and hostile – surrounded him in London, and he became the
talk of the town. George Rust wrote to Joseph Glanvill, 'The great discourse
now at the Coffee Houses, and everywhere, is about M[r] G, the famous Irish
Stroker ... He undergoes various censures here, some take him to be a
conjuror, and some an impostor, but others again adore him as an Apostle.'[19]
It was now, while Greatrakes was in London, that the debate about what he

was actually doing, and how it could be explained, really took off. There was general agreement that he was healing people, but beyond that, there was disagreement as to what was actually happening when that healing occurred. Some thought his cures miraculous while others wished to root Greatrakes' ability to heal in a variety of naturalistic explanations. Yet others were upset by his audacity in healing scrofula by touch, and the political implications of that.

The doctrinal question that had been asked of the Baptists and Quakers was also asked of Greatrakes. Could miracles occur in the present age? Theological issues remained significant in the debate about Greatrakes, though they were not the only live issues. The anonymous author of the pamphlet *The Great Cures and Strange Miracles* immediately thought Greatrakes' cures were miraculous. After describing some of Greatrakes' healings that he and so many others had witnessed in Ireland and in London, he concluded,

> It is now clear this Gentleman hath no universal Charm against all Diseases, as some out of prejudice at first conceived, but that the Things are absolutely wrought by the power of a Divine Hand, in which there can be no Juggle or Delusion as to the verity thereof; the Truth being evinced by hundreds of Eye-witnesses; for he onely calleth upon the Name of God whilst he is doing of it, and though briefly, yet divinely.[20]

Greatrakes himself thought his capacity to heal came from God; he described his actions as 'what has been done by the Instrument, to the commemoration and admiration of the first and principal Agent, Jehovah'.[21] Asking the question as to whether the operation of his hand came from the temperature of his body or from a divine gift, he answered quite clearly, 'I have reason to believe that there is something in it of an extraordinary gift of God', noting that there had once been a time in his life when he had not been able to heal with his hands (though he had tried on his own headaches and on sick friends – and failed) and then there was a time when he *could* heal by touch, following his 'Impulse'.[22]

Greatrakes provided an extensive theological discussion of why his cures might, at the very least, be of God. He explicitly addressed the question as to why 'God should now cure diseases in an extraordinary manner' and gave three reasons. First, he presented an oft-made argument by those who believed that miracles could occur in their own age and that was: 'to convince this Age of Atheism, which (I am sorry to say it) many of our pretended wits I fear are falling into, who make it their pastime to deride Jesus and Christianity, who cannot yet but believe Jesus to Be God.' Secondly, he suggested, 'the goodness of God, out of compassion to poor distressed man, may make use of never so worthless an Instrument to magnifie his own mercy and power.' And thirdly, he posited these true Protestant miracles over and against Roman Catholic shams: 'God may, to abate the pride of the Papists (that make miracles the undeniable Manifesto of the truth of their Church) make use of a Protestant to do such strange things.' Greatrakes recognised that this all begged the question as to 'why some are cured and not all, and if this work were of God all would be cured?' – a question that sceptical witnesses of his work also asked. Greatrakes' answer is reminiscent of the Baptists who believed that a person's faith was an important ingredient in the possibility of their being healed: 'That God may please to make use of such means by me as shall operate according to the disposition of the Patient; and therefore cannot be expected to be like effectual in all.'[23]

The political repercussions of such miracle claims in the present age were also discussed: politics and religion were constant, intertwined themes in Restoration England. One high church cleric, David Lloyd, who wrote a pamphlet on the subject called *Wonders No Miracles*, described Greatrakes as a man 'bred up in loose times' who had 'prostituted his understanding to a variety of opinions and errors, for he hath been in his time of most of the Factions that were lately extant'. What Greatrakes called his 'Impulses', Lloyd labelled 'Fancies and Imaginations':[24] Lloyd was attacking the notion of indi-vidual claims to divine authority that had been such a hallmark of – and had led to the proliferation of – the sectarian groups of the civil war and Interregnum period, and he immediately made the link between the Quakers and Greatrakes' own sectarian religious connections and miracle claims:

> How dangerous it is to admit of Impulses & Visions, and how common it was with men of Mr Greatrates former way to obtrude; need no further proof than . . . James Naylor, and other Quakers visions and light within, which would have superseded, if allowed, all religion, Law, Duty, Right, and wrong, and common honesty, there being hardly any villany Imaginable, against any of these that hath not been, and may be, perpe-trated upon the account of this Impulse and Inspiration; and if people will but allow any thing to to be true, upon these Enthusiastick grounds, they must allow all things that a deceivers fancy, or interest shall suggest to them.[25]

Greatrakes, who responded to Lloyd in his *Brief Account*, was particularly affronted by this charge, writing 'I never was a member of an *Independent* Church in my life, and so could not be excommunicated by them, neither do I acknowledge any such power in such a Church'.[26] But for Lloyd, a keen royalist, the matter was clear: Greatrakes was a republican, provoking disorder; he represented a challenge to the king's authority, especially for his presumption in curing those who had scrofula including some, it was rumoured, whom the king had failed to cure. Ralph Thoresby, a Fellow of the Royal Society, writing to John Evelyn some thirty years later about Greatrakes, gave an example of such a case: 'Mr H—'s Daughter in law Mrs S—n told me her self, that she was, when a Child, extremely troubled with the Kings Evil, her Mother sent her to be strok'd in King Charles the 2ds Time to London, but she was nothing the better, but Mr Greatrix perfectly cured her.'[27]

In Lloyd's eyes, men like Greatrakes and the Quakers who had claimed the performance of miracles had 'set up an healing Power, as well as the King; levelling his Gift, as well as they would his Office'.[28] Furthermore, Lloyd even saw a conspiracy theory behind Greatrakes' cures to discredit the Restoration:

Since the true Wonder of his Majesties Restauration, evidencing the pres-ence of God with his Person and Government; the men of Mr Greatrates party have spent their time in venting and dispersing false Prodigies, to delude men into an Opinion of the displeasure of God against both: and those that look narrowly into things, are apt to suspect, that Mr Greatrates being concerned, that the reports of Miracles and Prodigies did not work upon us, imagined he might promote the cause further, and perform Miracles himself. It is a dull thing to sell strange things only to amuse people, when men can doe strange things to convince them.[29]

For Lloyd, the gift of healing belonged to one person alone, and that was the monarch, in the exercise of his divinely bestowed authority. The monarch's gift of curing the King's Evil was 'a gracious gift of God, that Gods Viceregents hand should cure that malady which Gods hand hath inflicted'.[30] Nevertheless, it may be argued that Lloyd's anxiety about Greatrakes and reit-eration of the divine right of kings reveals how tenuous high churchmen thought the Restoration was, in the mid-1660s; this was at a time when the fear of another civil war was frequently invoked.[31] Lloyd's anxiety also echoes the fears of the royalists who wrote so loyally of Charles II's touching for the King's Evil in the 1660s, as discussed in the previous chapter.

In the same month that Lloyd published his work, March 1666, the radical physician Henry Stubbe, who had seen Greatrakes at work on the Ragley estate, published a pamphlet defending Greatrakes' miraculous gifts. The title of the pamphlet, *The Miraculous Conformist*, reveals one of Stubbe's purposes: he wanted to reassure readers, especially the prominent Anglican clerics and scientists who were taking an interest in Greatrakes, such as Boyle to whom he dedicated the work, (though Boyle did not want either the dedication or the reassurance from Stubbe!), that Greatrakes was free of the taint of enthusiasm, that he was 'reclaimed from all that is fanatique'.[32] His analysis of Greatrakes' gifts mixes a natural explanation with rather grand claims for Greatrakes' status as a miracle-worker. He postulated that Greatrakes may have been given by God 'a peculiar Temperament' or some 'particular Ferments' in his body, the 'Effluvia' of which 'being introduced sometimes by a light, sometimes by a violent friction, should restore the temperament of the Debilitated parts, reinvigorate the Blood, and dissipate all heterogeneous Ferments out of the Bodies of the Diseased'. Stubbe wrote that Greatrakes placed 'the gift of healing in the temperament or composure of his body; because I see it necessary that he Touch them, or otherwise rubbe their Eyes with his Spittle'.[33] In explaining what was happening in the bodies of those whom Greatrakes healed, Stubbe drew on the theory of fermentation, recently formulated by the Oxford physician and natural philosopher Thomas Willis, who had been Stubbe's tutor at Oxford, and to whom, in *The Miraculous Conformist*, Stubbe wrote a special dedicatory preface.[34] (This theory of fermentation continued to prove attractive in explaining in naturalistic terms other extraordinary events and wonders that altered people's bodies, as we shall see in the next chapter, in the case of Martha Taylor.) Willis had proposed that fermentation was the primary life process, enabling and promoting life and growth in any organism; essential to curing any diseases was the control of fermentation in the body. Stubbe related this theory to what he had seen Greatrakes doing:

> Considering that our life is but a Fermentation of the Blood, nervous Liquor, and innate constitution of the parts of our Body, I conceive I have represented those hints and proofs which may render it imaginable that Mr Greataricks by his stroking may introduce an oppressed Fermentation into the Blood and Nerves, and resuscitate the oppressed nature of the parts.[35]

As proof for his theory, Stubbe evoked the ways in which, by Greatrakes' stroking, pain travelled around the body:

> I saw him Stroke a man for a great and settled paine in his left Shoulder, which rendered his Arme useless; upon his stroking it the paine moved instantly into the end of the musculus Detodes: being stroked there, it returned to the shoulder again: thence (upon a second Stroking) it flew to the Elbow, thence to his Wrist, thence to his Shoulder again; and thence to his Fingers; Whence it went out upon his last stroking, so that he moved his Arme vigorously every way.[36]

This movement of pain was something that several people commented on. Daniel Coxe, a physician and natural philosopher, gave a similar description of *seeing* the pain moving about a person whom Greatrakes was healing, when he wrote to Boyle with his own eyewitness account of Greatrakes at work.[37]

For Stubbe, this naturalistic explanation of what was going on sat comfortably alongside his firm belief that Greatrakes' gift (that which enabled him to do this in the first place) was a 'miraculous gift of healing'. He wrote that in Greatrakes' faith, his charitableness and his soul, he saw 'some graines of the Golden Age, and . . . a relique of those times when Piety and Miracles were sincere'.[38] Indeed, he went so far as to suggest that Greatrakes 'doth the things that never man did, except Christ and the Apostles', and therefore concluded: 'to say that Miracles are ceased is a groundlesse folly'.[39] As we shall see in a moment, these sentences, set alongside Stubbe's naturalistic explanation, caused suspicion amongst some of his readers, such as Daniel Coxe.

Stubbe's pamphlet is interesting for its attempts to fuse religious and natural explanations. He offered it to members of the Royal Society for consideration, writing to Robert Boyle directly in his text, that he would 'leave you and those other worthy members of the Royal Society to determine concerning these Effects, which I apprehend miraculous'.[40] Barbara Beigun Kaplan has pointed to the ways in which the different interpretations of the Greatrakes case 'reveal the main lines of seventeenth-century debate concerning the general operations of nature and the explanation of disease by ascribing Greatrakes' ability to ferments, effluvia, and friction in addition to the more commonplace explanation – the operation of faith'.[41] We can go a step further than this and say that the Greatrakes case – like other cases that we shall examine in later chapters – provided the body of evidence through which emerging ideas about nature, reason and revelation could be discussed and debated by members of the Royal Society and other clergymen, philosophers and keen amateurs. It is not just that natural philosophy changed the shape and direction of the discourse on miracles but also that claims of miracles enabled that very discourse – which encompassed broader questions about the natural and supernatural – to develop.[42]

Certainly, Stubbe's pamphlet provoked a reaction amongst Boyle and others, many of whom had been keeping each other informed of Greatrakes' activities for some months, as we have seen. Boyle and Stubbe knew each other, and were on friendly, or at least collegial, terms but Stubbe was an awkward character, described even by Anthony Wood, who was his friend, as 'extream rash and imprudent, and wanted common discretion to manage his parts' even though he was 'admirably well qualified with several sorts of learning and generous spirit'.[43] Boyle was displeased that Stubbe had addressed the work to him, without permission, as Henry More reported to

Anne Conway: 'Mr Boyle resented Dr Stubs his letter very ill, I perceiv'd by what he sayd to me.'[44] Boyle had been prepared for Stubbe's pamphlet by his friend Daniel Coxe, who wrote to him on 5 March 1666 saying that Stubbe was 'making a collection of G. cures' and 'this book hee intends to addresse to your Honour'.[45] Forewarned, Boyle wasted no time in responding to Stubbe, and he wrote a long reply to Stubbe's pamphlet on 9 March.

What is striking about Boyle's response to Stubbe is the long refutation of Stubbe's *theological* argument. Boyle refuted this just as strongly – perhaps even more strongly – than he did Stubbe's natural explanation of Greatrakes' cures, even though he thought that Willis' theory of fermentation was not yet thoroughly developed and was too speculative to explain a case such as this. Boyle may have been alarmed by Coxe's letter, for Coxe – taking Stubbe's naturalistic explanation of Greatrakes' cures alongside his statements that the cures were like that those performed by Christ and the apostles – had represented Stubbe's views as atheistic: 'I am informed that Dr S. intends to Demonstrate from what Greaterex hath performed that the miracles of our blessed Saviour were not derived from any extraordinary assistance of a Divinity, much less from the Union of the divine nature with Humanity; But that as G. they might be merely the result of his Constitution.' This was not quite Stubbe's argument, but it was what was circulating in Coxe's circle, and Coxe put the matter in such a way that Boyle may have felt he had to distance himself from Stubbe in order to preserve his own reputation as a person of proper Christian belief. Coxe wrote:

> But wee here have all such a Strong persuasion of Mr Boyles good will and unfained Love of Christianity that wee Cannot imagine hee should Patronize any such thing which hath such a direct tendency to Atheisme and doth most positively enervate the very Basis of Christianity; & invalidate (att least seemingly) the strongest motive to beleive the veracity of those Excellent Dictates which all that rightly improve their Reason make the rule of their present life & the foundations of their hopes of a future felicity exceeding imagination.[46]

Here was the dilemma of the natural philosophers in a nutshell: they could not allow their investigations of miracle claims and other cases of the supernatural to be seen to undermine their faith. As Larry Stewart has put it, 'Heterodoxy haunted the new Philosophy'.[47] As men of orthodox Christian faith, their appeal to reason in understanding the natural world – as Coxe points out – was not divorced from traditional Christian beliefs about that world and the next. Boyle's own writings repeatedly reinforced this, as did his endowment of a set of lectures. In refuting Stubbe, Boyle immediately stated,

'I remember not, that I have hitherto met with (no more than you have done) any, at least any cogent, Proofe that Miracles were to cease with the Age of the Apostles'. If Greatrakes' cures were miracles, then they should not be regarded as on the same level as those of Christ and the apostles, for there were many diseases Greatrakes could not cure, and some of the cures he had affected were temporary. Furthermore, 'our saviour could communicate the power of working Miracles to others at his pleasure (which I think you doe not believe Mr Greaterick can doe to you) as in the case of the 70 Disciples.' Boyle's statement on the plausibility of miracles is important for indicating his general position on miracles; this was, of course, before he had observed Greatrakes at work. He declared himself 'backward to believe any strange thing in particular', and thought them 'purely Naturall, unlesse the Testimonyes that recommend it be proportionable to the Extrardinarinesse of the thing propos'd'. Nevertheless, should such testimonies be convincing, Boyle declared, 'I shall not scruple, since his Belief and Life give me no suspicions, to acknowledge my Conviction, and to rejoyce in the appearing of a Protestant that is Enabled, and forward to doe good in such a way; especially in an Age, where so many doe take upon them to deride all that is supernaturall; & while they loudly cry up Reason, make no better use of it, then to imply it, first to Depose Faith, and then to serve their Passions and Interests.'[48]

Boyle therefore decided to investigate the matter, using the method of observation that was a hallmark of the early Royal Society generally, and of his own experimental work in particular. He observed Greatrakes going about his healings; Henry More reported that Boyle 'had been a spectatour of at least 60 performances of his'.[49] In fact, Boyle was more than a spectator; at one point, he even took over the (successful) stroking of a patient. On 6 April 1666, Greatrakes was stroking a tinker, whom Boyle and Dr Fairecloth had previously examined, who had been lame and used crutches, and for whom hospital treatment had been unsuccessful. The tinker had already had some relief from pain, from Greatrakes' stroking a few days before. On this occasion,

Mr G. began to stroak his shoulder, where the patient complained of a paine, which by his stroaking being as the Tincker sayd presently removd unto his Elbow & thence towards his hand, I tooke Mr G's Glove, which was thick and sought, & turning the inside outward stroakd therewith the affected Arme, as (I ghesse) within a minute of an hower drove the paine as the Tincker told me into his wrest where he sayd it much afflicted him, Then stroaking that part also with the Glove, he told me felt a sharp Paine in the middle jooynts of his fingers, & stroaking those parts also he sayd he felt it exceding uneasy under his Nailes, which being likewise stroakd he sayd his paine was quite gone from his shoulder, arme & hand.[50]

Boyle noted all this, along with his other observations of Greatrakes between 6 and 16 April 1666, in his work diary; these were factual descriptions of what he had observed, and the answers Greatrakes gave to his questions. Boyle did not offer here any explanation of what he thought was happening, not even when he put on Greatrakes' glove and took over the healing.[51] Boyle also urged Greatrakes to collect accounts of his healings and sworn certifications of his cures from a range of illustrious witnesses. Greatrakes wrote of his meeting with Boyle when he arrived in London and its influence upon him:

> I met with your Honour, whose Judgment and Wisdom was so great that you would not credit or distrust matters of fact or bare report, and were therefore pleased several times at the place where I used to be in Lincolns-Inn-Fields (and elsewhere) to be an eye-witness of what was done, and to bring several other learned and worthy persons with you, that they might also bear testimony to the truth of what appeared, and to encourage me to give this account to the world, and to take Testimonials of some remarkable Cures as I could remember were done since I came to London, and in the presence of the men of Note.[52]

The sworn certifications of cures were attached to Greatrakes' *Brief Account* and included several for which Boyle served as a witness. Other witnesses included Daniel Coxe, Nathaniel Hobart, Master of the Chancery, and various medical doctors. Ralph Cudworth, the Cambridge Platonist, wrote of the cure of his son: 'I can certifie you that the tumours in my little son Charles his breast are happily cured by Mr Greatrak's, who opened the same, and let out the corrupt matter, and since the sores are healed, and the wounds dryed up.'[53]

Boyle, in his investigation, used his developing experimental method so that Greatrakes' cures could be established as 'matters of fact'. In those early days of the Royal Society, it was realised that certain standard criteria had to be established for conducting experiments. Members of the Royal Society asked how claims – especially competing claims – were to be established as knowledge. They asked: what was to count as knowledge? How was this to be distinguished from other epistemological categories such as 'belief' or 'opinion'? Boyle was prominent in constructing what Steven Shapin calls the 'material, social and literary technologies' for the conduct of experiments and the production of knowledge. Prominent amongst these technologies were the performance of experiments in a public space (the scientist's laboratory rather than the alchemist's closet); the testimony of witnesses present at those public events and the means of ensuring that these witnesses were reliable; and the development of clear 'scientific' prose for describing those events for people not present (described by Shapin as 'virtual witnessing').[54]

Greatrakes' healings occurred at just the moment that these 'technologies' were being developed. It is not surprising, then, that Boyle and his colleagues from the Royal Society used these techniques and methods to try and establish the truth about Greatrakes. Such methods accrued the evidence by which the virtuosi made their judgements on the probability of a particular phenomenon. We can see the ways in which Greatrakes' healings were treated as experiments and therefore subject to the same criteria. First, they were performed in public spaces, out in the open, for all to see: this was for both religious and 'scientific' reasons. Greatrakes himself commented on this, and contrasted his open approach – which he understood as part of his Protestantism – with the closeted performance of supposed miracles by the Roman Catholics: 'God may, to abate the pride of the Papists (that make miracles the undeniable manifesto of the truth of their church) make use of a Protestant to do such strange things in the face of the Sun, which they pretend to do in cells.'[55] The Protestant attack on miracles had been, in part, rooted in their scepticism about the apparatus of Roman Catholic miracles, and therefore if they were to claim miracle working, their methods had to be transparent. This suited men such as Boyle on both religious and scientific grounds.

Secondly, the testimony of reliable witnesses was a central part of the observation of Greatrakes' healings: members of the Royal Society, medical doctors and other gentlemen whose word could be believed witnessed to the truth of these cures. As Greatrakes put it to Lord Conway:

The virtuosi have been daily with me since I write to your honour last, and have given me large and full testimonials, and God has been please to do wonderful things in their sight, so that they are my hearty and good friends, and have stopt the mouths of the Court, where the sober party are now most of them believers and my champions.[56]

This was significant because if testimony was to receive its due respect, the reliability of the witnesses was vital. As Shapin puts it: 'Oxford professors were accounted more reliable witnesses than Oxfordshire peasants. The natural philosopher had no option but to rely for a substantial part of his knowledge on the testimony of witnesses; and in assessing that testimony he (no less judge or jury) had to determine their credibility. This necessarily involved their moral constitution as well as their knowledgeableness.'[57]

There were differing opinions about Greatrakes: as George Rust had put it, 'some take him to be a Conjuror, and some an Impostor, but others again adore him as a apostle'.[58] The testimony of the 'worthy' therefore stood for a great deal: Henry More wrote, of Boyle's interest in the case, 'I believe that gentleman [Boyle] is likely to doe him [Greatrakes] more credit than any body.'[59] It was thought that a gentleman, who was his own master and had economic, social and political independence, was more capable of being impartial, and therefore more truthful, than an ordinary man or any women who owed their allegiance to others because of their subservient positions. A gentleman's supposed disinterestedness made him a good witness, whereas those who were dependent on others were, for that very reason, less reliable. As Boyle himself put it, 'vulgar men may be influenced by predispositions, and so many other circumstances, that they may easily give occasion to mistakes'.[60] Such attitudes were in part rooted in old chivalric codes, whereby honesty and honour were equated, but they were also found in prevalent ideas about human nature, which saw 'vulgar' men and just about all women as inherently irrational. In making his case, Shapin quotes Sir Thomas Browne, who wrote in his *Pseudodoxica Epidemica* of 1646, of the 'erroneous disposition of the people' who were 'bad discerners of verity'.[61] (This, of course, is one reason why elite writers of the period thought that ordinary people were more prone to the superstitions of Roman Catholics and the enthusiasm of the civil war sects and their successors.) Both Shapin and Schaffer therefore emphasise the social location of the witness. As Shapin writes:

> All 'normal' gentlemen were deemed to be perceptually competent –
> indeed, the reports of such people largely defined what perceptual compe-
> tence was – but not all 'normal' members of other social categories were
> assumed to be so. Assessments of the reliability of empirical narrative, in
> early modern society, were therefore founded upon largely informal, but
> hugely consequential, theories about the 'natures', 'temperaments' and
> 'dispositions' of different types of people.[62]

A tinker might have been cured by Greatrakes but for that to be believed (at least by those in the Royal Society and their like-minded colleagues), people needed more than the tinker's word for it. Stubbe also knew the importance of good witnesses and wrote of the cures he had witnessed in the countryside around Ragley, before Greatrakes came to London:

> I do not relate unto you the reports of interested Monks and fryers
> concerning things done in Monasteries and private Cells; An infinite
> number of the Nobility, gentry and Clergy of Warwickshire and

Worcestershire, persons too understanding to be deceived, and too Honourable and Worthy to deceive, will avow, that they have seen him publickly cure the lame, the blind, the deaf, the perhaps not unjustly supposed Daemonicks, and lepers; besides the Asthmas, Falling-sicknesse, Convulsion-fits, Fits of the Mother, Old aches and pains.[63]

Of course, witnessing had always been important in English culture; many of the features of witnessing that became so important to the world of Restoration natural philosophers already existed in legal culture, as Barbara Shapiro has pointed out. For example, the social status of witnesses was already deeply embedded in both common law and civil law traditions. Shapiro argues that Boyle adopted aspects of this legal culture as he developed his technologies for the witnessing of experiments and the formation of matters of fact. Shapiro notes: '"Matter of fact" was indeed a social as well as an epistemological category as Shapin and Schaffer insist, but that social category was being transferred from one kind of institutional setting to another – from the courts to scientific inquiry'.[64] This is, of course, true, and Boyle himself made analogies with the use of evidence in legal cases when formulating his methods:

> The practice of our courts of justice here in England, affords us a manifest instance in the case of murder, and some other criminal cases. For though the testimony of a single witness shall not suffice to prove the accused party guilty of murder; yet the testimony of two witnesses, though but of equal credit, that is, a second testimony added to the first, though of itself never a whit more credible than the former, shall ordinarily suffice to prove a man guilty; because it is thought reasonable to suppose, that though each testimony single be but probable, yet a concurrence of such probabilities . . . may well amount to a moral certainty, i.e. such a certainty as may warrant the judge to proceed to the sentence of death against the indicted party.[65]

We do not have to reject the work of Shapin and Schaffer to accept Shapiro's refinement of it.

All sorts of people, from different stations in life, were familiar with the legal technologies of establishing 'matters of fact' in common law; they knew that in a way that they could not know or enter the rarefied and elite world of Restoration science.[66] I would therefore suggest that many different sorts of people were consequently all the more readily able to absorb and appropriate for their own uses the developing scientific methods of observation and witnessing. The case of Greatrakes represents a moment when the virtuosi who developed this scientific method turned it upon a set of incidents that were being claimed – by some – as miracles. We will see in chapter 6 how ordinary women such as Marie Maillard and Elizabeth Savage, who wanted to prove that their healings were miraculous, knew that the first-hand testimony of credible witnesses was important, as was the number of witnesses, aware that their claims would attract the attention of medical men, natural philosophers and churchmen who were still not certain whether miracles had indeed ceased in their own age. When Charles Doe published an account of the healing of the lame Anne Munnings of Colchester with healing oils in 1705 by William Rawlings, a Baptist minister (the case discussed at the end of chapter 2), he attached to it the names of sixteen men and eight women from his church who did 'attest the truth thereof, and know of no other means that hath been used, but that God hath shewed his great power therein'.[67] Interestingly, two of these witnesses – Hicks and Todd – became French Prophets, the group discussed in chapter 7.[68]

Context was also important; the validity of miracles depended too on the overall situation in which they occurred. For example, Glanvill considered that the evidence for Jesus' miracles being of divine origin was good because of 'the conjunction of other circumstances, the holiness of his life, the resonableness of his religion, and the excellency of his designs'.[69] Greatrakes' own character was a significant consideration in the overall assessment of the evidence of his case. Many of the illustrious witnesses therefore also attested to Greatrakes' own reputation. Benjamin Whichcote, the Cambridge Platonist, gave a certificate of Greatrakes' good character and of his solid, Church of England Protestantism.[70] Others anticipated that Greatrakes' character would be discussed: Stubbe wrote of Greatrakes' faith and charitableness and emphasised his good character 'because some will be very inquisitive herein'.[71] Both context and witnesses were therefore vital in the overall 'believability' of the investigation. William Beckett, the Whig surgeon and fellow of the Royal Society writing in 1722 about the royal touch, looked back to the success of cures effected by those who were not of 'Royal Dignity', such as 'the Touching of Valentine Greatrakes, Esq.' in the 1660s. Illustrious witnesses and Greatrakes' own character were regarded by Beckett as primary features of the story:

> This Gentleman, a member of the Church of England, of great Honesty and exemplary sobriety, and who always refus'd any Gratuity for his Performances, cured a Prodigious Number of Persons of the King's Evil, and other Distempers in London, and elsewhere, by the stroaking of his Hands, as is beyond Contradiction testified by the Hon. Mr. Boyle, and other Eye-Witnesses of High Distinction in Church and State, as may be

seen at large in Mr. Greatrack's Letter addressed to Mr. Boyle, and every-
where King Charles the 2d himself had failed, as appears by the
Philosophical Transactions, No. 256.[72]

Beckett's description of Greatrakes, some sixty years after Greatrakes' healings had taken place, is interesting for it suggests that Greatrakes' activities,
many decades later, were remembered as uncontested. Indeed, Beckett
assumes this to be the case precisely because of the reliable evidence of Boyle
'and other Eye-Witnesses of High Distinction in Church and State'; and,
perhaps, because Greatrakes was remembered as a gentleman and member of
the Church of England.

But what of Boyle, the Royal Society and Greatrakes? Boyle scrupulously
observed Greatrakes, made careful notes of the 'matters of fact' in his work
diary, and ensured that Greatrakes gathered the ample testimony of credible
witnesses, often providing the witnesses himself. He seems to have come to
no certain conclusion as to what was happening when Greatrakes stroked and
cured people who were suffering from a whole range of illnesses.[73] Some of
his colleagues were less hesitant to offer explanations. Henry More recycled
his earlier explanation of how Matthew Coker had healed people, which he
had published in *Enthusiasmus Triumphatus* in 1662; namely, that there was a
'sanative and healing contagion' that could be passed from one person to
another.[74] The very nature or temperament of Greatrakes' own body was the
source of his healing power, and this could be conveyed, by stroking, to
another person. Lord Conway repeated this theory in a letter about Greatrakes
to Sir George Rawdon. Conway, at first sceptical about Greatrakes, believed
that he was performing cures once he had seen him at work (even though he
had failed to heal his wife) but noted, 'I am far from thinking them miracles
or that his cures are at all miraculous; but I believe it is by a sanative virtue
and a natural efficiency'.[75] This explanation was echoed in a number of the
letters and testimonies attached to Greatrakes' *Brief Account*. Henry
Oldenburg, who was also largely convinced of Greatrakes' healing ability,
believed that the healing occurred by friction. He wrote to Boyle, 'Greatrix
does certainly some cures by his frictions, insinuating (perhaps) some salu-
brious steams or spirits of his owne into sickly people's bodies.'[76] An article
on the effects of touch and friction was published in the Royal Society's
Philosophical Transactions in May 1666, and this was quite possibly written by
Oldenburg, who described this theory as 'confessedly Mechanical'; the article,
interestingly, does not mention Greatrakes.[77] Some hedged their bets but, in
the end, expressed a belief that Greatrakes was curing people. George Rust
gave a testimonial: 'I must profess myself convinc'd (however it be, whether
from an immediate gift, or a peculiarity of complexion) that he has a vertue

more than ordinary.'[78] Similarly, in a letter to Glanvill, Rust declared that 'really there is something in it more than ordinary; but I am convinc'd it is not miraculous'.[79] Yet others were willing to declare Greatrakes' healings as miraculous or, at the very least, of God. For example, Benjamin Whichcote, the Cambridge Platonist, gave a careful account of his own healing at Greatrakes' hands:

> And for my own particular, he hath been to me an happy instrument of God, to relieve and ease me of a dangerous and painful malady, which for many years had greatly disabled and sorely afflicted me, for which before my coming to him I could have no remedy; but not withstanding the use of all means I could hear of, which all proved unsuccessful, I was wholly left in despair of ever obtaining a Cure, yet I neglected not the advice of persons of art and skill. But now by his means, and his often application of his hand and spittle, I am rid of all the pain and inflammation of the part disaffected, and the tumour, fungus and superfluous flesh, formerly very grievous to me is greatly abated, and decrease the more and more daily; so that I am in very great hope that in a little more time by his means it will wholly wast away and consume, as the greater part since his touching already is, through God's mercy, for which I give hearty thanks to the Divine goodness. This I account myself bound, in acknowledgement of God as principal, of doing right to Mr Greatrakes as his instrument, to testife and declare, and in witness whereof I subscribe my name, April 3, 1666.[80]

This range of responses to Greatrakes was typical of future debates about miracle claims in the succeeding decades: some fused religious and natural explanations, others relied solely on supernatural interpretations while yet others offered only naturalistic or mechanistic explanations. The point was that this was no longer just a doctrinal debate about whether miracles had ceased in apostolic times: the Protestant Reformation thinkers who argued for a limited age of miracles did not challenge whether God could or might yet do these things; rather they argued that God had no need to do them any longer. The shift that occurred in the latter part of the seventeenth century in England – the early Enlightenment – was that this was now a debate about the very nature of revelation itself. Did God do such things at all? Could such events be satisfactorily accounted for purely in terms of the natural laws that governed the universe and explained the workings of the human body? Many feared that to go down this path would lead to atheism, and so very few rejected the *possibility* that God might yet still intervene in human affairs by effecting miracles; rather, many suggested or implied that natural or mechanistic explanations would be offered in the majority of cases that people claimed as miracles, but that divine intervention remained a plausible explanation, at least upon very great evidence. As we will see in the following chapters, people at all levels of society debated these explanations.

Conclusion

The number of people claiming to be miracle-workers increased rather than declined in the second half of the seventeenth century and early eighteenth century. This in itself serves as a check against a too ready acceptance of the secularisation thesis, which is sometimes applied to this period. Theological and political factors combined to bring about this increase, and both theological and political factors remained a force amongst all those who claimed to heal by touch, from the Quakers to the Jacobites. Such miracle-workers also had an increasingly public profile. They were controversial and thus their claims were debated and, increasingly, not just in theological terms. No longer was the question, as to whether miracles has ceased or not, asked and discussed on purely doctrinal grounds. The ideas and technologies of the new philosophy were the impetus for new questions, investigations and explanations. The case of Valentine Greatrakes marked a particular turning point, coming as it did just a few years after the foundation of the Royal Society. Such miracle-workers and their means of curing became the evidence for 'scientific' investigation as people tried to discern the relationship between the natural and supernatural worlds, between reason and revelation. Furthermore, the sheer number of people who claimed to be able to heal by touch – challenging the king's role as sole healer in the land, either implicitly or explicitly – raised questions about who could heal by touch and on what grounds. In some circumstances, in the late seventeenth and eighteenth centuries, this ultimately paved the way to scepticism about any miracle claims at all. Contemporaries who tried to steer a middle course were aware of this danger, as we shall see in chapter 6.

In the next two chapters, our focus will shift from investigations of the miracle-worker to investigations of miraculous and extraordinary phenomena as they were experienced and embodied, and thus to the development of the debate about miracles as it happened 'on the ground'.

CHAPTER 5

Fasting Women

Just as the civil war and Interregnum period provided the impetus for a revival of miraculous healing, so it also witnessed claims of miraculous fasting and survival. George Fox, James Nayler and other Friends fasted for several days or weeks at a time and then described their survival as miraculous. Their capacity for such fasting, and their survival during and after it, were interpreted as signs – just like the healing miracles they claimed to perform – of the special truth of their religious and political claims in the midst of a great proliferation of such claims in that period. From the earliest days of Christianity, in the ascetic movement, fasting was given a special place and particular meaning in the practice of the religion, and fasting remained an important devotional practice in the middle ages.[1] As with healing miracles, so with fasting: Protestants adapted a practice regarded as predominantly Catholic for their own use; this happened both informally and at an official level, and even before the chaotic civil war period called forth such a response. From Elizabeth's reign onwards, the Church of England set fast days in times of difficulty, and the Puritans used this ritual to such an extent and so rigorously that in 1604, the Anglican canons forbade special meetings for fasting and prayer unless authorised by the diocesan bishop. Fast days acquired new significance in the Interregnum at times of political crisis, and public days of fasting remained in use in the Church of England until the late eighteenth century, as a way of atoning for or turning around God's judgement on the nation.[2]

There were, however, still those who attached a special significance to fasting and survival without food for periods of longer than a day or so. This chapter looks first at two examples of female prophets in the civil war and Interregnum period, for whom fasting was integral to their prophesying. These women were examined and investigated not primarily in terms of the 'truth' of their fast, but rather for the origins of their spiritual authority. Martha Taylor, just a decade or so later, however, who claimed that she survived without food for at least eighteen months, was subjected to a series of interpretations and investigations of her fasting body primarily in terms of her capacity to survive without food or drink. Indeed, Taylor's case may be seen as a turning point in attitudes to fasting women just as Greatrakes' case was a turning point in attitudes towards healing work. But, as with Greatrakes, so a variety of explanations of Taylor's survival co-existed, causing debate and discussion about the natural and the supernatural at the local level. Nor does a case such as Taylor's represent an irreversible turn towards a purely medical interpretation of fasting women; religious interpretations remained important, but the agenda of the men who came to investigate her and wrote pamphlets about her was such that she was interpreted in terms of providence, rather than the miraculous, giving us an insight into the religious divisions over these terms, especially amongst the dissenters, in Restoration England.

I. Female Prophets and Fasting

Those who gave fasting particular political and religious meaning in the civil war and Interregnum periods were the female prophets, of whom there were many in this period. At the root of the proliferation of religious sects was the idea that anyone could be directly inspired by God and did not need the institution of the church to mediate their relationship with God. Political turmoil quickly led to a charged atmosphere in which prophecies were spoken, heard and printed daily. Women were thought to be particularly good prophets, empty vessels who could more easily receive God's word and speak it. This, paradoxically, gave them a voice in the public sphere, and they frequently published their prophecies: over half of the texts published by women from 1549 to 1688 were prophetical writings.[3] Phyllis Mack has shown, in her study of female prophets in this period, that at the heart of women's religious agency in this period was self-abnegation. In the broader culture, women and suffering were linked. Within this context, suffering was a way of establishing religious authority.[4] The 'art of suffering' was an important strand within sixteenth- and seventeenth-century godly Protestantism,[5] and female prophets developed this, gaining a particular authority from the bodily suffering they endured when they fasted, an authority with which their prophetical utterances became imbued. As Diane Purkiss puts it, 'Illness and physical incapacity stage the body as the passive prey of external forces, hence an authentic site of divine intervention.'[6]

Anna Trapnel and Sarah Wight were two prophets from this period who claimed political and spiritual authority through their fasting. Trapnel came to public prominence in January 1654 when she went to Whitehall and for twelve days poured forth her religious visions near the room where Vavasour Powell – whom we encountered in chapter 2 – was being examined for treason by the Council of State for his Fifth Monarchist connections. Trapnel was, like Powell, a Baptist who had Fifth Monarchist beliefs: millenarian ideas about Jesus' second coming; the centrality of prophecy and the interpretation of scripture in terms of present and future events; and the radical egalitarianism of God's saints (the elect). Believing in the imminent arrival of King Jesus, Fifth Monarchists felt called to prepare the way for his arrival, by force if necessary, and the Cromwellian regime therefore perceived them as a threat. Trapnel's prophesying was in this Fifth Monarchist paradigm. Trapnel had had visions since 1642, and she had been prophesying since the late 1640s about the political situation, often making accurate predictions about the course of the civil war; in particular she prophesied against Oliver Cromwell.[7] This prophesying began after she had experienced her 'call', a religious experience in which the Lord had told her, 'I will make thee an instrument of much more; for particular souls shall not only have benefit of thee, but the universality of Saints shall have discoveries of God through thee.'[8] For Trapnel, fasting was always intimately connected with this personal authority received from God, and the prophecies came thick and fast when she had endured a period of fasting. The opening of her book *The cry of a stone*, which described her experience of prophesying at Whitehall in January 1654, makes this connection clear:

> The first five days neither eating nor drinking anything more or less, and the rest of the time once in twenty-four hours, sometimes eat a very little toast in small Bear, sometimes only chewed it, and took down the Moysture only, sometimes drank of the small Bear and sometimes only washt her mouth therewith, and cast it out, lying in bed with her eyes shut, her hands fixed, seldom seen to move, she delivered in that time, many and various things, speaking every day, sometimes two, three, four, and five hours together . . . she uttered all in Prayer and Spiritual Songs for most part.[9]

Some of Trapnel's companions questioned her fasting, for she reported, 'I was judged by divers friends to be under a temptation . . . for not eating' so she tested the practice of fasting by scripture and by asking God directly. The answer she received was that fasting was in fact a sign of purity, and in February 1653, she reported, 'I durst not eat nor drink for four days together, because it was said to me, If thou doest, thou worshippest the Devil.'[10]

Trapnel was inspired, at least in part, by the activities of Sarah Wight, an Independent/Baptist who worshipped at Henry Jessey's church. Wight, aged sixteen when she was in her period of most intense prophesying, also made fasting central to her practice, understanding it as a sign of purity in her battle between good and evil. Enduring a seventy-five-day fast in 1647, at a time of intense spiritual despair and agitation, she gave up eating and drinking on 27 March 1647 and declared that she needed nothing but Christ to survive: 'Now I have my desire; I desired nothing but a crucified Christ and I have him; a crucified Christ, a naked Christ; I have him and nothing else.' This meant that she was 'so full of the Creator that I can take in none of the creature'. So, she reported, 'I do eat, but it's meat to eat that the world knows not of. His words were found, and I did eat them.' Thus Wight even refused the bread and wine of the Lord's Supper because she was already so full of Christ.[11] By contrast, Trapnel relied on the Lord's Supper for sustenance. On the day before she set out from London for her ill-fated prophesying tour of Cornwall in 1654, she went to the All Hallows congregation, of which she was a member:

And I that day saw great shinings and tasted much of my saviour that day, who was presenting his loveliness in the ministery, and his sweetness in the supper of breaking bread, which filled my heart with joy unspeakable and glorious in the believing, . . . And having thus spent the night in sweet communion with God I was prepared for my journey; I wanted not sleep nor food-preparation, having had the cordial revivement liquors from my Lord Jesus which strengthened me for my travelling to Cornwall.[12]

Here, despite the Protestant language for the eucharist – 'the supper of breaking bread' – Trapnel sounds very like the medieval and early modern mystics who survived on the host.[13] She and Wight, like those Catholic predecessors, used what was close at hand to exercise religious authority: their bodies and food. In Trapnel's case, fasting was intimately entwined with her power to prophesy, and involved explicitly political prophecies against Cromwell. Sarah Wight's seventy-five days of fasting and related illnesses were, rather, an essential part of her wrestle with the forces of evil, so that her fasting body became an authoritative sign of the triumph of good, of the healthy state of her soul and of the ultimate victory of the Independent church of which she was a member. This in turn gave Wight the authority not only to pour out her scripturally-based prophecies (which visiting ministers recorded), but also to offer spiritual advice to the many people who visited her, including Dinah the Black, a young woman to whom Wight offered counsel about her suicidal tendencies and pain at being and looking different.

Both Trapnel and Wight were read as 'signs' by the many people who visited them and by other commentators and observers. By virtue of both their prophesying and their fasting, their bodies were on public display. Like the fasting women who came before and after them, they attracted attention and investigations. But in this political context they were investigated not so much for the 'truth' of their miraculous fasts, but rather for the veracity of their words and the origins of their prophetical authority. In the chaos of the civil war and Interregnum years, questions of epistemology were thrown into question. As Phyllis Mack puts it, 'The crisis of knowledge and moral authority that dominated the Civil War period was every bit as confusing to ordinary people as it was to the magistrates and intellectuals who interviewed the visionary in Parliament or debated the nature of prophecy in university common rooms.' Mack gives the example of Margaret Muschamp, an eleven-year old who 'lived for sixteen weeks without solid food, suffering fits and announcing visions of both angels and the devil, while her mother summoned all the representatives of secular and spiritual authority: the minister, in case she turned out to be a true prophet; the physician, in case her trouble was "only" convulsions; the judge, in case she was the victim of the crime of witchcraft'. [14]

Both Trapnel and Wight attracted visitors and investigators. While at Whitehall, Trapnel 'Uttered all in Prayer and Spiritual Songs for most part, in the ears of very many persons of all sorts and degrees, who hearing the Report, came where she lay.' Amongst those who came to visit her were members of the Barebones Parliament, Independent ministers, military men, Lady Darcy and Lady Vermuden. [15] While she was in London she was treated with respect, but on her tour of Cornwall she met with hostility, for 'the clergie gave information in many places of the country, what an impostor, and a dangerous deceiver was come into Cornwall'. Ministers came to speak to her, though she regarded their words as mere 'clergie-puff', and they were followed by justices and constables who came up the stairs crying witch, and pulled her eyelids up and pinched her nose. Trapnel went into a trance to avoid them, but she greatly feared the 'witch tryer-woman of that town' who had a 'great pin which she used to thrust into witches, to try them'. [16] The tests for prophets were no more sophisticated than the tests for witches, and both were similarly tested to see if their words were of demonic origin. As Mack puts it, 'the kinds of evidence one looked for in trying to determine the sanctity of a given prophet was as slippery as that admitted in witchcraft trials'. [17] Trapnel was accused of witchcraft, madness, whoredom, vagrancy and seditious intent, accusations against which she had to defend herself; she then spent three months in prison, but after her release she was able to continue her prophesying.

When prophets were tested, it was their spiritual authority that was being tested and so they needed to offer evidence of their piety. Trapnel did this in her published writings. In *The cry of a stone* she related the details of her conversion, her regular attendance at All-Hallows-the-Great (John Simpson's millenarian Baptist congregation) to which she was attached and her many personal conversations with God. Fasting was central to this piety, and while waiting for God to speak to her, she would remain 'silent, waiting with prayer and fasting, with many tears before the Lord'. Her reward came in God's reply: 'I let thee see that thou art in thyself to keep thee humble, I am about to show thee great things and visions which thou has been ignorant of.'[18]

Wight's fasting was inextricably bound up with the testing of her spiritual authority. Henry Jessey assembled a group of witnesses who were 'reliable' in terms of his, and Wight's, religious sensibilities. They were the prophet's father, Mr Thomas Wight, a preacher in Tewkesbury; her mother, Mrs Mary Wight, who 'above seven years ago was also deep in terror and distraction of the Spirit . . . till the Lords good time of refreshing came'; and the maid who tended her, Hannah Guy, whose father went to Ireland 'to avoid the ceremonies here urged'. Jessey reported that, 'the testimony of these two, the Mother and this Maid, of her drinking so little, and not eating at all, for so long (from 27 March till 11 June), *both those being of approved faithfulness* may be sufficient' [my italics]. In this case, then, credible witnesses were not gentlemen who were thought to have no stake in the matter – as we saw in the case of Greatrakes – but rather those of the same religious sensibility as Wight who would not wish to catch her out. Similarly, Jessey listed those who 'have been with this handmaiden' in her days of fasting and illness, and these witnesses were credible, Jessey maintained, because of 'esteeme amongst many that fear the Lord in London'. Nevertheless, he understood the need to name as many witnesses as possible so 'that some more incredulous, might the sooner believe, and reap benefit, and not reject the mysteries of God, against themselves, to their hurt (Luke 7:30)'.[19] Doctors examined Wight during her long fast, and their diagnosis covered both the physical and spiritual dimensions of her fast and illness. As Barbara Ritter Dailey has pointed out, these doctors (Thomas Coxe, Benjamin Worsley, Nathan Paget and one Dr Debote – probably either Gerald or Arnold Debote) had connections to the radical religious and political circles with which Wight and Jessey were associated, so they would not dismiss the religious significance she attached to her illness and fasting, nor the prophetic utterances she made in her weakened state.[20] At the end of seventy-five days of partial fasting, Wight exhibited her body because it was for her 'the site of triumphant combat between the forces of good and evil'.[21] That was why she had no need of food, 'the creature'; she was full of Christ crucified, by and with whom she had done battle against the forces of evil – and won.

II. The Case of Martha Taylor

With the Restoration came persecution of the radical sects and an end to female prophecy. The practice of fasting did not, however, come to an end, and the case of Martha Taylor, who fasted for over a year – and survived – between December 1667 and mid-1669, illustrates a shift in the ways in which fasting women were seen and interpreted in the Restoration period and beyond.[22] Although Taylor was, variously, understood in religious, political and medical terms by those who visited and heard about her, she herself laid no claims to spiritual authority in the ways that Trapnel and Wight had done. However, like them, she (or her fasting body) was interpreted as a sign by those who offered a religious explanation of her extraordinary survival and, again like Trapnel and Wight, her piety was considered important by some of those who wrote about her. Furthermore, her piety was linked to her suffering as a woman. Survival without food was the central issue in her case – fasting was her claim to fame – and the debate generated by her case revolved around the question of whether her survival was of God or could be explained in entirely natural, medical terms. Taylor was, moreover, entirely an object of investigation: her fasting did not lead her to claim agency on behalf of any particular cause. Rather, she was whatever those who interpreted her made her out to be: a wonder, a providential sign to a sinful nation, an impostor, a purely medical phenomenon. Interestingly, neither she nor her survival while fasting were interpreted by anyone – at least in print – as a miracle, though a Presbyterian minister practising physic offered his medical explanation to refute the idea that her survival was a miracle, an idea that no one had in fact mooted. Her case therefore gives evidence of the theological stakes that still existed for some religious groups – notably the Presbyterians – in using the language of providence rather than the language of the miraculous.

Martha Taylor came from Over-Haddon, then a hamlet of about one hundred and thirty-five people and thirty houses, near Bakewell in Derbyshire; she was the daughter of a lead miner, William Taylor, 'a man of good Credit amongst the better sort of neighbours', whose wife, Martha's mother, was described as 'of something an higher Rank than himself, both as to Birth and Education; A person in her common carriage very careful, and cautious about her words and actions'.[23] Martha was one of several children that William and his wife had and she was baptised at the parish church in Bakewell. Her fast began as a result of illness. One interpreter of her case wrote that 'the Fountainhead of all her Afflictions was her Lameness', which occurred in 1661, 'by the unhappy stroke of a Miller her next neighbour, over the Hips and small of the back'. The lameness soon turned into a general debilitation that left her 'whole Body as an useless Lump' so that by May

1662, 'she bid farewell to the open, Refreshing Air, and then entred close Prisoner to her tedious Bed. From which place, since that time, she hath never moved, without the help of other hands and feet beside her own.' By 1667, she was suffering from a variety of afflictions. In November of that year, she 'did begin her strange and wonderful Bleedings at several external Parts, as at the Mouth, the Nose, the Ear, the Eye', caused perhaps by her 'violent continued vomiting, which broke open convenient passages, through which the Blood might vent itself'. This vomiting was accompanied by 'violent hiccups, cramps in her joints, convulsions and strange sightings.'[24] By December 1667, she had stopped eating and had little speech and few senses, though these were gradually recovered, so that many visitors commented on her liveliness of speech when they visited. Her fast lasted, so far as we know, until the middle of 1669.

Her extraordinary survival was given a religious interpretation by several observers and interpreters, but they all framed it as a providential wonder. H. A., the author of a pamphlet entitled *Mirabile Pecci*, saw Taylor as a sign of the providential care of God:

Martha Taylor's case, which was beyond controversie a more than ordinary discoverie of the care and Providence of God, whence You may read the ground of my first thoughts, that the care and providence of God hath not done with the world. All that have seen her, or heard her story, have presently set the crown upon the Head of Providence.[25]

This pamphlet was published by the Presbyterian, Thomas Parkhurst and, it is therefore perhaps not surprising that H. A. interprets Taylor in terms of the providential rather than the miraculous. H. A. also interpreted Taylor as a suffering and pious woman, setting her − at least implicitly − in a long Christian tradition of suffering and fasting female saints. It was important, then, for her piety to be remarked upon. In prayer, H. A. observed her to be 'constant . . . either in Confessing Sin, Begging Mercy, or Praising God. She seemed to be made up of prayer when most afflicted.' He even suggested that her pious utterances in prayer led to mystical experiences:

Her voice, when at the weakest, would be spending itself upon her God, by fervent, pious Ejaculations, to hold up an heart-chearing Intercourse between Heaven and her hungering soul . . . She seemed by a sensible struggling, melting frame of Spirit, to go as it were out of her Self into an Upper region; so that when a rousing Prayer hath been ended, she would be puzzled to reduce her self, and compose the humane frame.[26]

He listed a variety of her 'ordinary sayings', responses she gave to certain questions about the role of Christ in her life, 'taken from her mouth by the Hand of a Friend'. The place of suffering is central in these sayings; in particular, the suffering caused by those who were sceptical about her survival without food and therefore did not believe that her illness was real: 'The Reproaches of the World, which are many, and Crowd in upon me, do not, cannot rob me of my joy which I have in Christ Jesus, my Lord, my portion, my righteousness, my Life, my All.' For H. A., 'our Derbyshire Damsel' showed 'that spiritual comforts may be enjoyed, and Serious Holiness exercised, under great and continuous Bodily Afflictions'.[27] Her illness and suffering were closely related to her piety. For women – associated with suffering in the wider culture – suffering could be a source of authority, as illustrated by the sayings that H. A. attributed to Taylor. H. A. therefore emphasised the godly nature of her survival, but he did not interpret her case as a miracle. His conclusion was that cases such as Taylor's (and many other examples of extraordinary abstinence that he cited from history) 'may deservedly be called wonders, though they have not been advanced so high as to be undoubted miracles'.[28]

One Thomas Robins, described as a 'B. of D, a wellwisher to the gospel of Jesus Christ' (with B. of D variously interpreted as Bachelor of Divinity, Balladmaker of Derbyshire, and Bellman of Derby),[29] also interpreted Taylor in terms of providence, in his two pamphlets. In the second pamphlet, *The Wonder of the World*, written after he had visited her in October 1668, he described Taylor's survival without food as a public, interpretable, sign of a mysterious work of God. He suggested that God 'hath made his chosen vessel of this Damsel, for to work this marvellous work upon her as a comfortable sign to a sinful and hypocritical nation'.[30] Robins was writing within a culture of reading signs and prodigies in relation to the nation's political and religious fate, a culture which had flourished in the civil war and Interregnum period, and which continued after the Restoration in both the (re)-established church and dissenting congregations. In Robin's other pamphlet, the first that he wrote about Taylor, in 1668, *Newes from Darby-shire; or the Wonder of all Wonders*, he described her as 'one of the strangest wondrous works ... wrought by the handy work of God in love to sinners upon earth'. He pointed out that while Moses and Jesus fasted forty days and forty nights, this maid 'has fasted for every day for a year or more'. He claimed that 'it is for love that the Lord bears to that poor creature, which makes him to work this wonderful work upon her, for indeed I could wish with all my heart, that I and every poor soul living were but in as good a condition as the soul of that poor Christian is in, for ... she is fed with Angels food and the power of heaven is with her'. He compared Taylor, as a wondrous work, with those miracles worked by Jesus, such as the raising of Lazarus from the dead, but he stops short of describing her survival as a miracle and, rather, exhorts his readers 'to consider the Lord hath not shown his handy work upon her only for her own sin'.[31]

If Taylor was, for some of those who came to see her, like Robins, a public and interpretable sign, then what was she a sign of, or for? Simon Schaffer, in his article discussing Taylor's case, writes, 'the Restoration crisis of enthusiasm and dissent gave the events at Over Haddon their peculiar significance'.[32] In the aftermath of the Restoration, all dissenters were expelled from the Church of England, even moderate Presbyterians who tried to avoid expulsion; in March 1668, persecution of dissenters increased as the government issued a proclamation against conventicles, quickly followed by a bill in the House of Commons to ban dissenters' meetings. If Martha Taylor was, then, a public sign 'to a sinful and hypocritical nation' for Robins, quite possibly a Calvinist,[33] and for H. A., with his Presbyterian connections, the nation's hypocrisy was bound up with its persecution of all those who were not Anglican. But, further, if Taylor was interpreted as a providential sign rather than a miracle, she also became a sign to others that the age of miracles was past, and by interpreting her thus, H. A. and Robins reinforced the Presbyterian and Calvinist rejection of miracles in their own age.

Schaffer makes much of the fact that the Peaks region in Derbyshire was an area of various strands of dissent, but he seems to overemphasise this, at least in the case of Martha Taylor, for we receive only a glimpse of any dissenting activity other than that of the Presbyterians. For example, John Gratton, 'an ancient servant of Christ', who lived in Monyash, two miles from Over Haddon, was a man on the search for authentic Christianity when he visited Martha Taylor in 1668 – he described himself as 'one alone, like a speckled bird, none like me' – and he went through several different groups and churches (including a period with the Baptists and a time of reading Muggletonian writings) before becoming a Quaker in 1671. He wrote in his journal of a visit he made to Martha Taylor; his comments about her are brief and rather dismissive but because he was always on the lookout for new preachers and someone to follow, his account gives a sense of the religious activity in Over Haddon, some of it provoked perhaps by the wonder of Martha Taylor:

Sometimes I went two miles to see a woman at Over-Haddon, who *pretended* to live without meat; where I met with professors (I think I may say) of all sorts. And one day a man of London came, called an Independent, and there was a meeting: and he having heard of me, desired me to pray before he began to preach: but I felt a zeal to rise in me against putting men upon that service, which only belonged to God to require and move men to; so I refused, and he went on, who could do what he had a mind to do, as far as I saw, in his own will. [my italics][34]

Perhaps if Gratton had, by that time, already become a Quaker, he might have been more willing to see her survival without food as a miracle but, as it was, he seems to have thought her an impostor, and the Presbyterian/Calvinist interpretation of her feat of survival as a sign of God's providence won out. Schaffer claims, 'The Quaker John Gratton may not have been the only pilgrim at Over Haddon during 1668–69 who saw there another sign of remarkable workings of the inner light, and thus of confirmation of the faith delivered to the saints.' In fact, Gratton described Taylor's fast as 'pretended' and he did not become a Quaker until 1671, *after* he had visited Martha Taylor.[35]

If the case was indicative of 'the Restoration crisis of enthusiasm and dissent', as Schaffer suggests, then that crisis was evidenced here by the intra-Protestant differences about miracles, differences which took on new meanings in the Restoration period when, in seeking respectability, certain groups (in particular the Presbyterians) had no wish to be associated with those whom *they* considered enthusiasts. Men such as H. A. and Robins may therefore have felt the need to refute an *imagined* Quaker argument that Taylor's abstinence and survival was a miracle, and to distance themselves from it at a time when they wished to present themselves as respectable dissenters; in reality, they faced no real challenge to their interpretation from Quaker opponents, at least none that has made it into print. It is perhaps relevant to these prevalent interpretations of Taylor's case that Presbyterianism was particularly successful in the area of the Peaks, not least because of the itinerant preaching and teaching of William Bagshawe, a minister who was ejected from his Church of England living of Glossop in 1662, became known as the 'Apostle of the Peaks' and was successful in collecting Presbyterian congregations in several places in that area.[36] Others visited Taylor, with religious interests, but did not offer any particular theological interpretation or explanation of the case, even if they thought the visit worth noting in their spiritual journal, as did one Leonard Wheatcroft, a tailor, poet and the parish clerk from Ashover, who went to visit Martha Taylor on 6 January 1669. He reckoned, she 'had received no food for the space of 40 weeks' and 'had much discourse of God, and Jesus Christ, of her selfe and of her distemper. But no food she tooke meate or drinke for the space of many years after'.[37]

No one was calling Martha Taylor's survival without food a miracle – not in print at least; we do not know what was being said on the ground. Nevertheless, John Reynolds, another Presbyterian minister, wrote explicitly against any suggestion that she was a miraculous maid. In 1669, he published his medical explanation of her survival, *A discourse upon prodigious abstinence occasioned by the twelve moneths fasting of Martha Taylor, the famed Derbyshire damosell*. The subtitle was 'proving that without any miracle, the texture of humane bodies may be so altered, that life may be long continued without the supplies of meat & drink.' Early on his treatise he wrote, 'Some persons as scant in their reading, as they are in their travels, are ready to deem everything strange to be a monster, and every monster a miracle: true it is, the fast of Moses, Elijah and the Incarnate Word was miraculous, and possibly of some others; yet why we should make all miracles, I understand not; for what need have we now of miracles.'[38] Reynolds used Willis's 1659 theory of fermentation (used by Stubbe to explain Greatrakes' healing methods) and his mentor Walter Needham's anatomy of the foetus from 1667, to suggest that the body could 'store up' nourishment. For Willis, the seminal vessels and genital parts were filled, as were other major organs of the body, with fermentative particles made up of salt, sulphur, earth and water. These bodily elements could ferment within the organs and move in the blood, making it hot. Commenting on the ways in which fermentation could be continued in the blood without new additions of 'chyle', produced by eating and digestion, and pointing out that the natural evacuations of the bowels and saliva and sweat glands stopped when eating and drinking ceased, Reynolds concluded that the body actually conserved elements in Taylor's blood, and therefore nourished her and allowed her to survive.

Why might Reynolds wish to refute the possibility that Taylor's survival without food for so many months was a miracle? If we imagine his imagined audience, we will begin to understand what was at play for Reynolds. First of all, Reynolds was a Presbyterian. He had been a minister in Wolverhampton from 1657 to 1660, but was ejected from his living at the Restoration and, after preaching in various local churches, he retired to live in King's Norton where he practised physic or medicine.[39] It is no surprise, then, that in the Preface to his *Discourse*, he wrote 'A Just Reverence to Reformed Theologues, asserting a total cessation of miracles, forbad me to immure myself in any such supernatural asylum.'[40] His *Discourse* was distributed by Nevill Simmons, a bookseller in Kidderminster, who was also Richard Baxter's publisher; indeed, Baxter and Reynolds were friends. Reynolds was holding firm to the Presbyterian line against miracles in the present day, and he needed to indicate this to his readers from the opening page. He did not refute the possibility that Taylor had survived for over a year without food – he did not think she was an impostor – but he wanted to provide an entirely natural explanation for her survival over and against any *possible* suggestion that it was miraculous. Reynolds was a great opponent of the Quakers, engaging in controversy with the Friend Thomas Taylor in 1662:[41] Reynolds disliked the notion of inspiration and the Quakers' associated belief in miracles. When he wrote 'Some persons as scant in their reading as they are in their travels, are ready to deem everything strange to be a monster, and every monster a miracle', he was perhaps thinking of the Quakers, whom he disliked intensely, but he was also sending out a signal to his Presbyterian readers that he was presenting a tract which was 'sound' in terms of Reformed theology's attitude to miracles.

Reynolds had other imagined readers too. As one who read the work of the leading lights of the Royal Society, Reynolds perhaps wished to make an impression in that world with his own treatise. His whole text is peppered with references to important figures in the world of Restoration science, most notably Robert Boyle, and he included an obsequious dedication to 'the deservedly famous and my Honoured Friend, Walter Needham, Doctor of Physick as also a member of, and Curator Elect to, the Royal Society'. (Walter Needham was an anatomist in Shropshire.) He sent the published work to the Royal Society; it was quite common for scholars and other gentlemen in the provinces, interested in the Society's work and the new philosophy, to send in such reports in the hope that they would be discussed at the Society's meetings. The Society had already heard about Martha Taylor, having received a report from Thomas Hobbes in his letter to John Brooke of October 1668, and, in January 1669, received information via a Fellow of the Society, Joseph Williamson, who had had the following report from Ralph Hope in January of that year:

> I suppose you have heard of the woman at Hatton in Derbyshire, who has not taken any manner of sustenance since St Thomas's Day was a twelvemonth; she lies in bed talking much, although worn to a mere skeleton; all her refreshment is having her lips anointed now and then with a little oil, &c.[42]

The Royal Society Fellows were also interested in cases of 'prodigious abstinence', publishing reports in the *Philosophical Transactions* from time to time.[43] Despite all that, they did not discuss Reynolds' tract or publish it in the *Philosophical Transactions*. But in shaping his *Discourse* as a report to the Royal Society, Reynolds would have wished to show not only his medical credentials and range of reading, but also his clear position that while he did not think Taylor an impostor, his readiness to believe in her survival without food did not indicate that he believed in a miraculous explanation for wonders or prodigies, as other dissenters might. Finally, we should remember that Reynolds never visited Taylor; he had no idea – just as we do not – whether the visitors who crowded into the parlour of her parents' tiny cottage described her survival without food as a miracle or not. He did not hear their discussions and musings about Taylor in the pub or the church porch; he therefore followed his own agenda and a good part of that agenda was to show that miracles had ceased in his day.

The fact that John Reynolds, who lived in King's Norton and had never visited Martha Taylor, wrote such a detailed and careful medical tract to explain her survival indicates how widely news of Martha Taylor's spread and what interest her case attracted. The diary accounts of Gratton and Wheatcroft also illustrate this, and suggest that all kinds of people came to visit her. People flocked to the little cottage by the mill where she lived with her parents and siblings, and, walking up the path to the front door, they heard her loud hiccups. Local ministers, local gentry, neighbours from Over Haddon and outlying villages all came to see her. When they arrived inside, they found her in bed, in the parlour downstairs, often surrounded by visitors. The emaciated body that greeted them was, to some, shocking. The philosopher Thomas Hobbes, who was the tutor at Chatsworth, reported on the Earl of Devonshire's visit: 'My Lord himself hunting the Hare one day, at the Towns-end, with other Gentlemen and some of his servants, went to see her on purpose'. They found a woman with part of her belly touching her backbone, and were given a report that 'her Gutts . . . lye out at her Fundament, shrunken'. Hobbes also reported that 'the neighbouring ministers visit her often' and 'others that see her for Curiousity give her money, sixpence or a shilling, which she refuseth, and her Mother taketh. But it does not appear they gain by it so much, as to breed a Suspition of a Cheat.'[44] There were those who were sceptical, however; H. A. remarked that 'Divers sort of Persons there were who employed themselves to vilifie her, and cry her up for a cheat, about the Country', and Robins reported there were 'some so hard of belief, that they will not stick to say; I mean concerning this maid; that there is some desembleation in it'.[45]

It was most probably because of this scepticism, and the possibility of a 'cheat', that a watch was set up, with twenty maidens from Over Haddon and other villages nearby, each taking their turn to check that Martha Taylor did not eat or drink anything. Local gentry who had a 'great desire to be more fully satisfied in the truth' set up the watch. Accordingly, 'they thought good to make choice of twenty maids to watch and wait for her, that they might be satisfied in the truth'.[46] When the Earl of Devonshire visited Martha Taylor, he set up another watch, perhaps because he was still unsure about the truth of the matter; perhaps because he thought he felt that the first watch was not credible; or perhaps because there was some rivalry between him and the other gentry and he wished to be in control of the watch and the choice of maidens. He therefore sent fourteen maids to wake and watch with her, that he might be the more satisfied in the truth; these Maids wake with her by two at a time, for four and twenty hours, and so every two did so, till they had waked seven nights and seven days, and when they had so done, they certified that she did receive no mortal Food, but onely the wetting of her lips with Spring water in a spoon; and as it is very credibly reported, this hath given him very good satisfaction, and he doth believe it to be true.[47]

Schaffer likens this watch to a lying-in scene at childbirth, which was 'a place of female collectivity, . . . a profoundly consecrated space, the gossips present there as witnesses and members of a wider community'.[48] Of course, the scene of Martha Taylor in her bed, surrounded by local women, in the parlour is immediately reminiscent of that, but we can push Schaffer's point much further if we look at the broader picture. The 'lying-in' situation was one in which women were called to serve as witnesses, as Laura Gowing points out, 'With such concern about the presence of witnesses at labours, women were also there to function as honest observers, proof that the midwife had done her work well, that the mother was the true mother, that a stillbirth or infanticide had not been abetted or concealed.'[49] The 'watch' was, in fact, not a lying-in scene – though it was reminiscent of one – but it was a kind of experiment, a similar attempt to get at the truth of the situation by controlling and observing Martha Taylor at all times, and the maidens were the witnesses. Female witnesses – generally thought less reliable than men – were less desirable in the public sphere, but this situation and its intimacies called for women to take up the role, just as childbirth did. Male commentators were keenly aware of this problem, as Hobbes wrote:

> To know the certainty there bee many things necessary, which cannot honestly be pryed into by a Man. First, whether the Gutts has (as 'tis said) lye out. Secondly, whether any excrement pass that way or none at all. For if it pass, though in small quantity, yet it argues food proportionally which may being little, bee given her secretly. And pass through the shrunken Intestine, which may easily be kept clear. Thirdly, whether no Urine at all pass; for Liquors also nourish as they go.[50]

Nevertheless, the fact that the male gentry and other fully reliable witnesses had visited and observed her was also important, as H. A. noted, in establishing his own credibility as one whose account of Taylor could be believed:

> I writ the ensuing sheets upon the irresistible Importunity of some Friends, who know that I had seen and conversed with her several times; and with

her Visiters, Gentlemen, Divines, Physicians, some of both the watch set upon her, and with some of her most sober knowing Neighbours on purpose to get the Truth concerning her; but upon further Trial, I became convinced of the reality of what I had been given an account of.[51]

We have, then, in Taylor's case, a fusion of all the apparatus of the traditional birthing scene (without a birth) with a more modern scenario, an early scientific experiment – for what is also striking about the whole of Martha Taylor's story is that her female body was constantly being examined and commented upon by men. In this sense the Martha Taylor case represents a 'crossroads' moment in the history of medicine and science. For, while her parlour scene may indeed be likened to a late seventeenth-century lying-in scenario, very soon that scenario was to be challenged by the professionalisation of medicine as the traditional role of the midwife was challenged and went into decline, and male midwives became increasingly assertive in establishing their authority, though they were often resisted for exactly the reason Hobbes gave – that 'there bee many things necessary, which cannot honestly be pryed into by a Man'.[52] Similarly, the newly emerging culture of natural philosophy was – with a few rare exceptions – the domain of men. The philosopher Lady Margaret Cavendish, who engaged with the ideas of Boyle and others on the nature and methods of experimental philosophy, may have visited the Royal Society in 1667 but she certainly was not allowed (or indeed invited) to become a member. In the new world of experimental philosophy, women were more likely to be the observed than the observers.

Hobbes may have felt that 'there bee many things necessary, which cannot honestly be pryed into by a Man', but that did not stop other male doctors trying to examine Martha Taylor as thoroughly as possible. The final report on Martha Taylor – also sent to the Royal Society – was from a sceptical doctor who had neither embarrassment nor compunction about examining Taylor as closely as possible. This was Nathaniel Johnston, a Cambridge MD (King's College 1656) and an Anglican,[53] who practised medicine in Pontefract, South Yorkshire and visited Taylor in 1669. That June, he wrote a letter about her in Latin to Dr Timothy Clarke.[54] He began by tracking the very small amounts of moisture that she had received since eating her last meal of apple with meat pie on 21 December 1667: at Easter and in November 1668, she received a little sugar water; at Christmas, the juice of a Damascus plum; in February 1669, more sugar water, and on the 14 April 1669, some claret mixed with sugar. Johnston then began his examination of her body. He reported (as others had done) that her face was lively; that she hiccupped a lot; and that her pulse was that of a healthy person. She said that her intestines had fallen out and that her bladder was in the wrong place; this aroused Johnston's suspicions and he replied that her bladder could not fall out unless she had an ulcer of the womb and he asked her the size of the tumour around her anus. When Johnston told Taylor that her intestines were not coming out of her anus, she replied that they were coming out of another place – that is, her genitals. Johnston therefore asked if he could examine her there; Taylor duly prepared her groin for the examination. As Johnston relates the episode, the reader has an image of the male doctor's hand groping around, attempting to inspect the tumour under cover of the blankets, the young woman resisting and possibly frightened; in any case, the examination failed: 'the light was so dim and the opening so narrow that I could not make out the colour or shape, nor could I feel it, because although I barely touched it, she experienced a sharp pain, even though I had only gently touched the lips of her vulva, as far as I could judge'.[55] Johnston asked if he could remove the blanket but Taylor replied that he had seen enough, after which there was something of a tussle between them – she covered herself with her hands, he tried to move her hands away – until they were interrupted by Taylor's mother who had come in from the garden (Taylor's younger sister had been the other female presence with Taylor and the doctor until then) who said that her daughter was not a hypocrite, that that she had satisfied the whole region, indeed the whole of England, about the truth of her fast. After that, Johnston was allowed to examine Taylor's mouth, which he thought normal if a little dry, as well as her ears, neck (a bit scabby) and hair (of normal thickness).

As Johnston left the cottage, he tried again, this time offering money to Taylor's mother, so that he might be allowed to examine properly the prolapsed uterus. Taylor's mother put him off, replying that she did not know what sort of tumour it was for she was so affected by her daughter's suffering that she had not tried to see it, and when Dr Willoughby of Derby had felt the tumour, he had commiserated with Martha. The implication was that, in comparison with Willoughby, Johnston was a very harsh man, but Johnston's response was that Willoughby had only examined Taylor perfunctorily. In the exchange between Johnston and Martha Taylor's mother, almost by chance we get an interesting insight into how Taylor was discussed and understood in her family (though we are, of course, relying on Johnston's account for it): Taylor's mother described her daughter's survival as a miracle. She felt that 'her afflicted girl, by talking so much about her miracle in God's honour, was wasting her strength'.[56] This is, perhaps, where Johnston himself picks up the language of miracle in his letter to Clarke, for he wrote that, 'when not only the vulgar but also the wise fluctuate in their opinion, and others, who give themselves over to religion, persist in thinking it a miracle, then the certainty of the case should be known, so that the opportunity for doubt can be ended'.[57] Frustrated in his attempts to make a proper examination of the evidence, Johnston turned to second best: a witness. He went to visit a local woman who had been helping to look after Taylor, and she confirmed that there was a tumour; it was not as big as Martha Taylor described it; and it was kept clean – or fomented – with water and milk, just as Taylor had herself told Johnston.

Why was Johnston so suspicious? His theory was that Taylor was secretly consuming food and drink and then relieving herself into an attached bladder. He must also have felt thwarted in his attempts to examine her; despite his qualifications as an expert, the young woman had eluded him. This may explain his rather sharp request to the Royal Society 'that by the authority of his Majesty she might be searched by some intelligent physician, assisted by a justice of the peace'.[58] Johnston's letter to Clarke was read out at a meeting of the Royal Society, and it was copied into the Society's Letter-book, but Johnston's request was not followed up. For all their interest in cases of prodigious abstinence, the members of the Royal Society were not willing to go that far. Hobbes, who had pointed out the improprieties of examining a woman such as Taylor, had already concluded, several months before Johnston went to see her:

I think it were somewhat inhumane to examine these things too nearly, when it so little concerneth the Commonwealth; nor do I know of any Law that authoriseth a Justice of Peace, or other Subject to restrain the Liberty of a sick person, so far as were needful for a discovery of this Nature. I cannot therefore deliver any Judgement in the case.[59]

Johnston's letter is the last extant report of Martha Taylor. It is not known how long her fast lasted after June 1669, or when she died, though Janet Wadsworth has tracked several possible dates for her death.[60] However, her story lived on, told, for example, in the county history compiled by Daniel Lysons and Samuel Lysons, *Magna Britannia*, of 1817.[61] Such stories of 'fasting girls' were retold in numerous wonder books such as Nathaniel Wanley's *The Wonders of the Little World* (1678) and William Turner's *A Compleat History of the Most Remarkable Providences* (1697), and were collected by antiquaries such as Robert Plot. He told the story, in his *Natural History of Oxfordshire* in 1677, of Rebekah Smith, a servant in Minster Lovell, who fasted for ten weeks after communion on Palm Sunday, 1667, and ten years later was still very much alive and well, and he related the narratives of several fasting men and women in his *Natural History of Staffordshire* (1686). Martha Taylor, and numerous other 'fasting girls' have been incorporated into accounts of anorexia nervosa, and sometimes have been retrospectively diagnosed with that disease.[62]

One particular question remains: what did Martha Taylor herself think of what was going on about her? Where is the woman herself in all the interpretations of her? Several of the observers and interpreters commented on 'her talk' as 'most heavenly', as a gentlewoman, who had visited Taylor, reported to Hobbes.[63] H. A. wrote that she 'took great delight to talk and discourse in the Scripture with any Scholar, there very many of the Clergy doth come unto here from far and hear and hath very much discourse, for she is very ripe witted concerning the world of God'.[64] Indeed, she formed something of a contrast with all those around her. H. A. commented that, 'she was not cultivated by education at home or abroad . . . the religion of very many there is but few degrees beyond ignorance'.[65] Hobbes therefore wondered 'how her piety without Instruction should bee so eloquent, as 'tis reported'.[66] It was H. A. who reported her words, and we must rely on those for we have no other source. According to his account, she gave a religious interpretation of her fast, but she spoke neither of providence nor of miracle:

I look upon my Preservation without the use of Creatures to be the Manifestation of Infinite Power, for the benefit and advantage of them that fear God. To let them see how God can preserve life by and of himself, and for the hardening of the obstinate and impenitent; for my own awakening and bringing into a way of holiness.

Her words sometimes echoed the language used by the earlier fasting prophets, Wight and Trapnel:

If I was able to feed upon all the good creatures of God, where as now I cannot, yet they could none of them satsifie or solace my poor, weak, hungry Soul; it is the enjoyment of him, who is the Bread of Life, the Life of my Life, that is my satisfaction to whom be glory.[67]

And yet, she has none of the authority of those prophets, for her words are profoundly second-hand, framed for us by H. A. and his preoccupations. There was nothing in her cultural context to encourage virtuoso fasting behaviour – a holy desire to be ill and a flamboyant performance of it – as there had been for the medieval mystics or even the prophets of the 1640s and 1650s. Indeed, her remarkable case occurred at a time when women's spiritual authority had been suppressed; in Restoration Britain, neither the established church nor the dissenting groups, who desired respectability in the new climate of persecution, wanted women speaking in public. Nor was Taylor a modern girl trying to gain control in a modern world where women feel repressed or oppressed, or both, and therefore become anorexic: there was no such medical diagnosis, nor even the existential conceptualisation of the self that might bring it about. Nevertheless, it was Taylor's *body* which fascinated those who visited her, not her pious words, and all the men who commented upon her case, including H. A. who quoted her words, interpreted her body to their own ends and in terms of their own concerns. Her prodigious abstinence really did occur at a crossroads moment, when the development and professionalisation of medicine was leading to a new focus on the body, and a new emphasis on health (or lack thereof); and yet, when medicine still had few explanations for ill-health (or for phenomena such as bodies which were said to survive without food) so that the supernatural was always a possible explanation – and the bodies themselves might hold signs of that which was beyond the natural. As Laura Gowing, writing about the female body in the seventeenth century, puts it, 'uncertainty was always part of the culture. Stories and claims about the body are, in some way, always attempts to make sense of the mysterious.' Gowing is talking about the pregnant body, but her words are equally applicable to the *extraordinary* female body in this period – the body that was prodigiously abstinent, for example – when she writes, 'The unpredictable body demanded regulation, intervention and surveillance, and those practices, performed by both men and women, officials and neighbours, did much to effect the subordination and vulnerability of female bodies.'[68]

In all the printed sources that have survived about Martha Taylor, there is no evidence that her prodigious abstinence was interpreted as a miracle, except, we learn from a chance remark that happened to be reported by Johnston, by her mother. Hobbes wrote to his friend Brooke, 'The examining whether such a thing as this bee a Miracle, belongs (I think) to the Church.'[69] However, despite the numerous ministers who, it was reported, came to visit her, there was no suggestion from any of them that her fast and survival might be a miracle. The only ministers and laymen who made any public (printed) interpretation of Taylor's case were so bound by the doctrine of the cessation of miracles that they could only interpret her survival in terms of providence. The case is an instructive one, then, for seeing how the language of miracles and providence was shaped by doctrinal differences. All wonders might be interpreted either way: who did the interpreting was the key. In Taylor's case, the Presbyterian and/or Calvinist associations of the key interpreters meant that the wonder of Taylor's survival was necessarily read in terms of the providential and, indeed, over and against an *imagined* argument that it could be a miracle. Another set of interpreters might well have argued that it was at least *plausible* to read it as a miracle. In the next chapter, we turn to a series of cases from the 1690s in which miracles were claimed, and female bodies were examined for their miraculous possibilities. Martha Taylor never explicitly claimed for herself a miracle; the women we will discuss next most certainly did.

CHAPTER 6

Perfectly Protestant Miracles

On the evening of 26 November 1693, a thirteen-year-old lame girl named Marie Maillard was instantly healed while she was reading the Bible. It was a day when she had been especially reminded of her lameness because local boys had teased her and thrown dirt at her as she had been walking home. She had just eaten supper and was reading the second chapter of Mark, 'where is related the cure of the man sick of the Palsy', when her thigh snapped 'just as the words were out of my mouth, and I said, Madam, I am cured.'[1] She ran about and showed her perfectly upright body and now even hips to Madame Renée de Laulan, the French gentlewoman with whom she lived. Maillard was a Huguenot who had escaped with her family to London in 1689 from persecution in France, following Louis XIV's 1685 revocation of the Edict of Nantes, which had formerly protected Protestants. She had been lame since birth because of a tumour that had caused her to tip to one side when she walked. Eminent Huguenot surgeons, including a Mr James De Batt of Leicester Fields, had pronounced her incurable.

The story of her miraculous cure spread widely and quickly, so that the next day, 'Crowds came so thick to see me, that she [Madame Laulan] was desirous that I should be at my father's house, where multitudes of all Ages, and both sexes, came to see me; and the house was so crowded that I hardly had time to eat.'[2] Her story became famous, at least in the environs of London: she was summoned to appear before Lady Sutherland, the Lord Mayor of London (Sir William Ashurst), four surgeons sent by the Queen and at least three bishops (the Bishops of Worcester, Salisbury and London), all of whom wanted to see her and inspect her for themselves. Several publications about her followed swiftly. In 1693, an anonymous ballad, *The Happy Damsel: or, a Miracle of God's Mercy* was written about her;[3] and a narrative of the miraculous events, *A Plain and True Relation of a Very Extraordinary Cure of Marianne Maillard*, was published. In 1694, a sermon on miracles, with particular reference to her case, *Light in Darkness*, and a further account of the cure, *A True*

Relation of the Wonderful Cure of Mary Maillard, were published. Attached to the latter were affidavits, in which people testified to her previous lameness and their observation of her physical cure, and a discourse on miracles by James Welwood, M.D., a Fellow of the Royal College of Physicians in London. This account was translated into French and published in Amsterdam in the same year. It was re-published in 1730, as *An Exact Relation of the Wonderful Cure of Mary Maillard*, this time with Maillard's permission, and with the addition of her own report of the events: by this time, she was married to Henry Briel, a Huguenot minister (they had married in 1700), and living in Rose Alley in Bishopsgate, London. Briel was the pastor of the Huguenot church at Swanfields, Slaughter Street (1721–34). Maillard died the year after that account was published, in 1731.[4] This account was published at least once more, in 1787, indicating the enduring interest of the case – or at least its perceived commercial value to publishers and booksellers – throughout the eighteenth century.

Maillard's case produced a spate of copycat miracles: the mid-1690s witnessed a cluster of cases of women, all living in London or the surrounding area, who claimed they had been miraculously healed. A month after Maillard's cure, on 22 December 1693, Elizabeth Savage, a dissenter, who lived in the parish of St Leonard in Shoreditch, London, was cured of the palsy in her right hand. Like Maillard, Mrs Savage was cured instantly upon reading a miracle story in the gospels, though in her case, her husband was reading the scripture passage out loud. Mr Savage had been inspired by the recollection of Maillard's healing to read a gospel story of Jesus' healing miracles to his wife, at the end of a day that they had set aside for fasting and prayer together. The Savages were unsure as to which biblical passage Maillard had been reading at the time of her healing, but decided that any story of Jesus' miraculous healing could serve the purpose, and so Mr Savage read from the first chapter of the gospel of Mark, Christ's cleansing of the leper. As he read the passage, Mr Savage dared to have 'as much Faith in the Power of Christ as he [the leper] had, as to the curing of her Infirmity' so that at 'about the time when he was reading the third verse, where Christ said, *I will, be thou clean*', Mrs Savage reported, 'I felt the middle joints of my lame fingers greatly ake; and as I remember, immediately or at least before the chapter was read out; my Fingers and Thumbs were stretch'd out with any means used'. That very night, her joints were 'so strengthened that she, without pain, doubled lock'd the fore-door of her House with that Hand, whereas before she could never single-lock it, or as much as lock or unlock her Boxes with it.'[5]

Later in the month, December 1693, Susannah Arch, a dissenter from Battle Bridge in Southwark, testified that she had been cured miraculously from leprosy from which she had suffered for four years, an 'itching and scurf on my head [which] afterwards spread over my body'.[6] She visited many doctors who had pronounced her incurable, each of whom said that they might give her something to curb but not cure her illness; each time this happened, she renewed her hopes that Jesus would heal her. 'This I can truly say', she claimed, 'that all along my Faith was fix'd on the Lord Jesus Christ: it was on him I did and was resolved to rely.'[7] Her miraculous cure had a considerable build-up time: it was punctuated by doubts, recourse to appropriate scriptural verses, a dream (in May) of Christ standing by her and, most significantly, knowledge of Maillard's healing. In November, she learned of Maillard's cure at her church:

> being at Mr Beverly's meeting, and hearing the People talk of a Miraculous Cure of one that was Lame, I asked one that sat by me Concerning it: and she told me, that a maid had been lame 17 years, was miraculously cured on a sudden. Then I told her, I was waiting at the Pool believing that I should be made whole. From that time my heart was drawn out to wrestle more earnestly with God for a Cure, crying out, Lord! Why not I? Why not I, a poor Leper?[8]

When the healing finally happened it was immediate and instant. On 27 December, she was healed while in bed, and putting her hand to her head, she felt skin on both sides of it:

> Then I said, Lord Jesus! Hast thou begun? Thou wilt carry it on. When I arose in the Morning, and had taken off my Head-Clothes, I found the Scurf was gone off my Head, only there remained a little cap on the Crown of my Head, which was easily taken off with a comb, which I made use of for that end: And then appeared firm skin all over my Head. At the same time, my Distemper, which was spread over my whole Body from Head to Foot, even to my very Toes, was likewise taken away.[9]

The final case of this period is that of Lydia Hills, a forty-year-old Baptist spinster of Great Trinity Lane in London, who was cured of lameness nearly a year after Maillard's case, on the morning of 17 November 1694. She had been lame for twenty-two years following an accident in the rain when she had fallen down and had bruised her already defective right hip, after which it steadily became worse, so that she spent periodic spells in the hospital and could no longer walk without two crutches, and was constantly in great pain. She described herself as praying for endurance of that pain, though it finally became so bad that,

I did then beg of God, that he would give me some Token, whereby I might know whether I should live or dye; and (I bless his name) he gave my desire, after I had been earnestly seeking the Lord in Prayer, by bringing those words with power to my mind, John 11.4 *This sickness is not unto Death, but for the glory of God.*[10]

Thus encouraged by the Lord's word, she continued to endure the pain, believing that she would not die in that sickness, 'though it was far from my thoughts of being so restored to my Limbs as to go without Crutches'. Indeed, after some time, she 'had no expectation of being healed, but of being worse; for I thought at the last it would be my Death' – that was, until she heard of Maillard's case:

When I heard of the young Frenchwoman that was miraculously healed, I thought of my self, if the Lord be pleased to work Miracles on others, he is able to do the same for me; and immediately that Word was brought to my Mind, Mark 9.23 *If thou canst believe all things are possible.*[11]

Her faith and hope wavered, as had Susannah Arch's, so that she believed one minute, and not the next. Finally, on Saturday 17 November, she was enabled to cast out all her doubts and throw herself on the feet of Christ, believing that he would heal her:

Whereupon I was in such an exstasie, I scarce knew where I was, and Taking my Bible again, the first words I set eyes upon was, Mat. 25. 28, *O Woman, great is thy Faith; be it unto thee even as thou wilt.* Then I laid down my Bible immediately and stood up, and upon Tryal I found myself able to walk about the Room without any Crutch, and without Pain . . . and from that time to this I have used no Crutch.[12]

These four miracle stories might be described as perfectly Protestant miracles; they involved no intermediary figures, no external trappings, only the reading of the Bible with faith (that quintessential Protestant activity), and they happened in the home. Marie Maillard was cured simply as she had been reading scripture, as she always did every evening, as a devout Huguenot: her faith had led her to identify with a particular passage about Jesus' miraculous healing. The author of *Light in darkness*, the sermon published on Maillard in 1694, called this a miracle '*in pura* . . . done without any second cause'. God performed this miracle immediately and suddenly: 'There was neither the use of ordinary means for the Body, not of Spiritual Means, no prayer . . . God by his immediate Hand of Power joined all in again.'[13] Likewise, Mrs Savage was healed instantly through the reading of scripture.

Significantly, neither Marie Maillard nor Elizabeth Savage *sought* a miraculous healing. Mrs Savage had, with her husband, set aside a day for prayer and fasting, but she wrote, 'my Distemper being no end of it, not so much as having it upon my Thoughts'.[14] They were not, then, engaged in any petitionary prayer (an activity which was thought suspicious by the strictest of Protestants) but rather their faith and reading of scripture were interpreted as enough to affect these 'pure' miracles performed directly by God upon them. For the author of *Light in darkness*, Maillard's faith was but a small part: the emphasis was on God's total power as healer, as is illustrated by his rather dramatic description of the mechanics of the healing:

> God sends her to that particular portion of his Word, that was so suitable to her Case. And sent it into her very Heart, he opened the Heart, he sent in the Word, he raised up her Heart to such expressions as these: O that I lived in that time, I should certainly have been healed . . . he no sooner saw . . . the weak faith of this poor Creature, but he brought health and Cure to her.[15]

There is here a hint of the practice known as 'Bible-dipping', quite often referred to in seventeenth-century England, in which the Bible was opened randomly on a page, at which point, it was believed, God would, by his divine providence, send a message to the faithful reader through the passage thus randomly selected.[16] But it was more than that: both women were engaged in reading the Bible as part of the ordinary course of their devotional practices. This regular reading of the Bible at home was an essential part of household religion, and such domestic piety was a vital component of 'serious' or evangelical Christianity. Indeed, for dissenters, the reading of the Bible and other devotional books at home was a key form of worship in the years after the Restoration and before Toleration, when their public worship was prohibited; the same would have been true for the Huguenots in France.[17] It is no surprise, then, to find Maillard taking up the Bible after supper and reading a chapter to Madame Laulan 'as she used to do every day in the New Testament'.[18] In that sense, the actual passage from scripture did not matter; but there was significance in the fact that Maillard and Savage were both reading stories of Jesus' miraculous cures and – according to the author of *Light in darkness* – their faith allowed them to enter into the text imaginatively, with a longing for healing themselves and, at that point, God's all-powerful miraculous power worked upon them. Furthermore, all of this was happening in the home, the locus of personal piety and devotion; likewise the cures of Susannah Arch and Lydia Hills happened in their homes.

The cases of Susannah Arch and Lydia Hills are, however, different in that they both *hoped* for healing, and they prayed for cures over a period of several months. Scripture was central to both of their cures though neither was reading scripture at the moment of their healing. Lydia Hills was reading scripture just before she was cured of her lameness, and the passage she was reading – Matthew 25:28 'O woman great is thy faith, be it unto thee even as thou wilt' – is revealing of the central struggles not only in Hills' account of her healing, but also in Arch's narrative, and is thus illustrative of the role of scripture in their cures. The tension for these two women was between faith and doubt; between hoping for healing and then thinking they should not and could not ask for a cure; between petitionary prayer and plaintive cries to the Lord in their pain. Scripture acted as guide and sustainer throughout their struggles, so that their texts were peppered with scriptural quotations, and comments that the Lord has shown them a word in their moment of trouble and doubt. For example, Hills wrote in the summer before her November cure:

> But my Faith was ebbing and flowing again; and I thought within myself there was no particular promise from the Word of God, that I could apply for being healed: But when I was thinking of it, that Word was brought to me, 2 Kings 20.5 *I heal thee;* though I did not know it was in the Scriptures, till afterwards, when I was glad to find it there. And the Word was brought to me, when the Lord spake to Lazarus: *This sickness is not unto Death, but for the Glory of God,* which was an argument to me, to go to God by Prayer and plead with him.[19]

The effect is that both Hills' and Arch's accounts read much like classic Protestant spiritual autobiographies of the period. In the spiritual autobiography the author represents himself or herself as wavering between faith and hope, with moments of abjection to the Lord to save their wretched sinner's soul, until they are finally saved. Such accounts are always liberally sprinkled with biblical quotations. Both Hills and Arch, coming from dissenting traditions, would have been familiar with this genre, at least orally in the stories told in their church circles, if not in print. Indeed, Arch made the connection between spiritual and bodily salvation explicit in her account:

> Then was I help'd to look back to former Experience, and remembered that about thirty Years ago, when I was under great Distress about the state of my soul, being under a deep sense of Sin, I was helped to cast my soul on the Lord Jesus Christ. And from that consideration many times since, when I have been in great Distress, with respect to my outward Condition,

I have been able to cast out my Bodily Concerns upon him; and then I cried out, *Lord, I cast my soul upon thee, and my Body upon thee, and now I am resolved to cast all my Diseases upon thee.*[20]

In these two accounts, then, miracles were invested with the tensions of the Protestant belief in faith and scripture alone, and the belief that human beings are inherently sinful but can be saved by faith: that is, the constant struggle between faith and despair; the desire and impulse to ask the Lord for help counterbalanced by a suspicion of petitionary prayer and a feeling of abject unworthiness. In this sense, too, they are perfectly Protestant miracles.

For these women who experienced these miracles and for the faithful Christians who published their comments and opinions on them, there was no question that miracles could and did occur in the post-biblical age, indeed in their own age, and for good reason. The author of *Light in darkness* antici-pated that people would ask, 'is not the Power of working Miracles ceased?', and replied clearly, 'This Power is not ceased . . . if God . . . pleaseth [to] give it again.' Indeed, 'the Instance in hand is a sufficient proof of his powerful Presence to heal this Day as formerly . . . whensoever it may please his Divine Majesty to rise for the help of the needy, with healing under his Wings'.[21] Lydia Hills had even believed that the age of miracles had ceased: 'I never expected to go without crutches more, except the Lord should work a miracle: But I said this was not a time for working Miracles; if it were, I would look for it.' It was, as we have seen, when she heard of Maillard's healing – 'the young Frenchwoman that was miraculously healed' – that she believed that God made miracles happen in her own day, and might even work one for her.[22] These women therefore had or developed a strong sense that Jesus Christ could still heal, just as he had cured the sick when living on earth. Susannah Arch wrote that her faith was fixed on Jesus Christ, 'who in the Days of his Flesh, when on earth, cured all Diseases and Sicknesses amongst the People; and I was confident, that he had the same Power now he was glorified in Heaven, as he had in the days of his Humiliation'.[23]

I. Signs for the Times? Miracles in the 1690s

Why the 1690s? Why did this rash of miracle events – or claims – occur in the 1690s? This was, undoubtedly, a significant decade in political and reli-gious terms: 1688 had seen the relatively smooth installation of the safely Protestant monarchs, William and Mary, in place of James II, a transition once called by historians the 'Glorious Revolution'. From that political settle-ment there followed, under the Dutch Calvinist William's steering, the offi-cial toleration of nonconformist worship in 1689, and this led – for the first time – to some form of 'truce' between Anglicans and nonconformists. But the religious and political situation was far from trouble-free. Non-jurors, those who felt they could not swear an allegiance to William and Mary because they had already done so to James II, were disaffected; almost as soon as James II had fled, there emerged a Jacobite following. And quickly after William and Mary's accession, there was William's waging of war against Roman Catholic France; this sharpened attitudes towards Roman Catholics at home. The 1690s also saw a growing and radical critique of institutional Christianity and central Christian doctrines from thinkers such as the deists and Socinians. Furthermore, many people believed that they were living in a socially dissolute age. The political, religious and cultural task of the 1690s was therefore to form a strong and safe Protestant nation.

In the midst of all this swift political and religious change, 'signs' were read in terms of the politics and other events of the day and as indicators of God's providence. William of Orange's safe and unchallenged landing on English soil had occurred on 5 November 1688 – Guy Fawkes day – and had therefore been interpreted as a sign of God's special favour. At a time when there was a strong sense amongst many that England had only averted an absolutist Roman Catholic monarch by such divine providence, there was concern that the nation should remain faithful. But when there was an earthquake in Jamaica on 7 June 1692, which destroyed the town of Port Royal, followed by an earthquake tremor in London on 8 September in the same year, these events were read as signs of God's displeasure with Londoners in particular, and the British generally; similarly, William's reversals of fortune in the war against France in the early 1690s were read as signs of God's anger and as warnings for the nation to repent of its sins, not least its lack of faith.[24]

Many commentators on these four miracle cases saw the miracles as public signs, imbued with great significance. Some observers read these miracle cases in apocalyptic terms. The 1690s, the last decade of a troubled century, gave rise to a variety of social and cultural anxieties, and so it should not surprise us that some people gave the miracles millennial overtones and expectations.[25] The Baptist minister, Elias Keach, wrote to a fellow minister, John Watts, on 20 December 1693, that the war was continuing and 'the Lord only knows what the event will be. We are full of expectation of great changes over the whole world.' For Keach, this meant that, 'Many are waiting for the coming and kingdom of our Lord Jesus Christ; and we are apt to conclude that it will be ushered in by the miraculous effusion of the holy spirit as in primitive times.' This 'miraculous effusion' had, he thought, already begun in Maillard. 'And the Lord Jesus to confirm the truth of his divinity hath begun already to work miracles among us; a very decrepid French girl (of about 14 years of age here in the city reading the gospel concerning the miracles of

Christ) was made to believe that Christ would cure her; and immediately there was heard a crackling, and she was made straight though she had been very crooked from a child.' He concluded: 'This was done this winter, and is an infallible truth.'

Keach also noted another miracle that had taken place in the same period, though a little out of London, which did not attract as much attention as the cases of Maillard and the other women. This was the healing of a shepherd in Hitchin in Hertfordshire, 'an infirm person much troubled with the painful swellings and ulcers of the king's evil' who, on hearing a sermon from 'an eminent gospel preacher' was converted and 'though lame went home from the meeting leaping and skipping and praising God and admiring his free grace, being cured at once in soul and body'. Here too, as in the cases of Arch and Hills, an analogy is drawn between the salvation (healing) of the soul and the cure of the body. In a pamphlet about this healed shepherd it was related, 'That he had faith given him for the cure of his Body the same time when the Spirit of God came upon him, and opened his heart, and gave him faith in Christ.'[26]

For Elias Keach, these events were a sign that 'Gospel light hath broke forth here [London] more of late in three or four years than, I believe, since the Apostacy.' The prevailing threats to godliness (which, interestingly, included Arminianism and the related theological idea that anyone could be saved) were regarded by the Calvinist Keach as ailing and failing: 'Arminianism and Socinianism begin to gasp for life. Universal redemption and falling from grace are almost heart sick.'[27]

The four miracle cases were given a millennial interpretation by a female prophet writing in the 1690s, variously known as M. M. and M. Marsin. Little is known about this author but in the late seventeenth and early eighteenth centuries, she published a number of prophecies concerned with the second coming of Christ.[28] In her *The Near Approach of Christ's Kingdom* of 1696, she wrote that while the nations have had 'awakening providences of God's displeasure, by the Earthquakes, and fires' that had recently occurred, 'so God in a wonderful manner hath appeared amongst us in the miraculous Cure of four women, which the like was never heard of since Christ's time'. These four women were, of course, Maillard, Savage, Arch and Hills, and it was deeply significant to Marsin that they were all *women*: 'For as the Lord came by a woman, so after he arose, he appeared first to the women. And now at the time of his second coming, he hath miraculously appeared in working of miracles on women.'[29] And in her book published the following year, *The Figurative Speeches*, she wrote of 'the Miraculous Cure of Mary Maillard', as one of the 'clear signs of the great jubilee' when 'it is said, the lame shall leap as an Hart'.[30]

Others were concerned with signs of Christ's coming. Thomas Beverly was Susannah Arch's minister, and he led a dissenting congregation that met at Cutler's Hall in London. He had strong millenarian beliefs, calculating that Christ would return to set up his kingdom on earth in 1697, and wrote many works arguing his case. We do not know whether he regarded the healing of his congregant, Arch, as one of the signs of Christ's coming, but it is likely that he did, as, in a *Discourse* he wrote just after the cures of Maillard and Savage and the shepherd near Hitchin, he described those events as 'Providential Awakenings, and Alarms of such Returning Power of Miracles', even if 'the Time of the Return of Miracles' was 'not yet'.[31] It is no surprise, then, that it was at Mr Beverly's meeting that Susannah Arch heard 'the People talk of a Miraculous Cure of one that was lame'[32] – the minister was interested in such cases. It is, perhaps, also significant that William Kiffin (whom we encountered in chapter 2, healing according to the instructions in James 5) was one of the witnesses of Arch's cure. He, too, may have taken a particular interest in the healing of Maillard, though we have no evidence of that. Interestingly, Beverly saw the removal of James II from the throne and the accession of William and Mary as part of the unfolding of events that would lead to Christ's return and the leading role England would play in the defeat of Roman Catholicism. By the mid-1690s he was also engaged in the debate about anti-Trinitarian ideas, challenging the Socinians (and in 1696 wrote a pamphlet refuting the deist John Toland's *Christianity Not Mysterious*). He was, then, a man much concerned with refuting the atheists of the day.[33]

Indeed, for some, the miracles were signs in an 'Atheistical Age', that is, 'a day wherein the Generation hath as much strained the Spirit of the Lord as any that were ever named by the House of Jacob', as the author of *Light in Darkness* put it. The miracles were signs that would lead others to faith: Maillard's miracle was described as a 'great Wonder at our Doors' by which God would 'rebuke our Atheism, and . . . awake the sleepers amongst us, to call upon God who is so near, easie to be found, ready to pardon, and a very present help in the time of Trouble'.[34] In a sermon on the deity of Jesus Christ, Deuel Pead, minister of St James Clerkenwell and chaplain to the Duke of Newcastle, likened the healing of Maillard to the curing of a lame man by Peter and John (in Acts 3) and described Maillard's cure as 'a Wonderful Work, a Signal Honour done to the Place and Age, as also a great Help (if rightly considered and well apply'd) to awaken the Obstinate Jew and the Vain and Dissolute Christian, who by Prophaneness, Hypocrisie and Infidelity, hath too long Blasphemed the Holy Name of Jesus'.[35] The writer of the Preface to the *Relation of the Miraculous Cure of Susannah Arch* wrote that the glorious design of God's miraculous works was 'to convince an athe-istical generation of men, that there is a God that acts above the Power of

Nature or natural causes' and 'that those who contemn and undervalue the Lord Jesus Christ . . . might be convinced that he was the true Messiah, yea God as well as Man'.[36]

In such an 'Atheistical Age' the healing of, and personal faith shown by, the four women who were miraculously healed were linked to God's relationship with the nation. The behaviour of individuals was connected to the fate of the nation, the individual body to the body politic. Earthquakes and bad luck in the war against France might be signs of God's displeasure at the sins of the individuals, but the miraculous healing of these women and their extraordinary faith might conversely be a sign of God's favour, as Marsin suggested. As the author of *Light in Darkness* put it, 'what greater things could be desired than the Lord's immediate hand in jointing the Bones of this poor Child, and what plainer demonstration could we have of his Ability to joynt together the broken members, both of Church and Nation . . . that he alone may be exalted in his day'.[37] The same author also thought it significant that Maillard came from a persecuted Protestant group: the Huguenots. Her healing was seen as a sign of hope that that community would one day be liberated from such persecution; her lame body a symbol of the broken body of the Huguenot church which would itself one day be made whole:

Consider her as a Member of a persecuted Church such as the Church of Christ, in France is this Day: And she may be looked on As a sign of its great Distress, which is persecuted but not forsaken, Perplexed but not in despair. Cast down but not destroyed, a burning Bush yet not consumed, . . . so may she not be set up as a sign of the Lords reviving of these dry bones of that persecuted Church? Are they broken to pieces? So was she: Are they bowed down? So was she; do they say we are cut off from our parts. So might she say. Are they out of joynt? And under many sad dislocations? So was she. Did bone come to bone? Was all jointed right again with her. Who knows but this same agent will as easily joyn all and put it together in his own time: let none despise the day of small things for you shall see greater.[38]

There was an urgent sense amongst a number of prominent Anglicans and dissenters in the 1690s that in this 'atheistical age', a reformation of manners was necessary in order to retain divine favour and atone for the nation's sins in an age of vice, debauchery and profanity; in D. W. R. Bahlmann's words, 'a moral revolution' followed the political revolution of 1688.[39] As John Spurr points out, the doctrine of providence was exercised not only to inculcate an ideology of order upon the nation, but also 'to associate the stability, even the fate, of the country with the reformation of national manners'.[40] In the autumn of 1690, a number of societies for the reformation of manners had been formed and they continued their work vigorously throughout that decade. They were most active in London, and their purpose was to combat sin by an assiduous keeping of the laws against vice and profanity. To this end, preachers encouraged members of their congregations to become informers, denouncing offenders before magistrates. These societies were a significant product of the toleration of dissenters, for they were pan-Protestant societies, involving both Anglican churchmen and moderate dissenters. They were religious in focus, but were also genuinely concerned to root out vice (breaking the Sabbath, drunkenness, lewdness, gambling, cursing, prostitution) in order to address the serious social problems of the city. For the pious Protestants who formed these societies, the cultivation of piety in an impious age would necessarily lead to better morals, the lessening of vice, and a more stable social order, as well as strengthened and renewed faith.[41]

Interestingly, these miracle cases were, at least implicitly, incorporated into this broader conversation about the reformation of manners. The healed women's firm daily religious practices (Bible reading; prayers; the observation of fast days) and strong faith fitted this milieu of practical Christianity. Despite all the Protestant hesitation about linking good behaviour to divine rewards, and works to faith, the underlying theme of these four stories was that faith and piety could result in rewards on this earth. These women served as models of faith who, enduring pain modestly and quietly, had faith and dared to trust and hope in God, and thereby came to receive a reward greater than they could possibly have imagined. Their experiences were the 'flipside' of stories of divine providence and punishment that were equally popular: narratives of people who engaged in vice and got their just desserts on this earth.[42] While the societies for the reformation of manners clearly made good use of the doctrine of providence, arguing that the nation must reform itself morally in order to avoid God's punishment, they also created a cultural and religious context in which these miracle cases could be used to the same effect. It seems that the distinction between providence and miracles was not, at this point and in this context, important in the way that it had been in 1660s Derbyshire when people tried to make sense of Martha Taylor's extraordinary survival without food, but used only the category of providence to do so. Nevertheless, miracle cases were used to do the same 'cultural work' of attempting to reform people's behaviour that the doctrine of providence had long done. We turn now to the examinations of these miraculous cases.

II. Miraculous Bodies/Bodies of Evidence

These miracle stories were widely circulated in London, both orally and in printed form. The healed women were the talk of the town or, as M. Marsin expressed it, 'these things being publickly known and attested in the City of London'.[43] The balladist writing about Marie Maillard reported: 'Thousands hath seen her walk alone, both Young and Old, nay Rich and Poor'.[44] Curious visitors came to see the miraculous results, and the interest in these women continued months after they had been healed. Samuel Jeake Junior, a nonconformist merchant and astrologer of Rye in Sussex (and son of the Samuel Jeake whom we encountered in chapter 2 who had clearly inherited his father's curiousity about these matters), recorded in his diary on 20 April 1694 that in the afternoon he had been to see Mrs Savage 'who had lately the miracle wrought on her of the Cure of her lame hand and side; the relation whereof I had seen before in print, with the affidavits taken before the Lord Maior'. Seeing Mrs Savage verified the truth of the case for Jeake: 'I met with her husband and her self both at home and had the truth thereof confirmed by their own Mouths.'[45] The Presbyterian Elias Pledger recorded in his diary his response to hearing of these cures, writing that he was 'much affected with the late miracles wrought upon Mary Malliard [sic] a French refugee, and Mrs Savage in Moorfields, and David Wright a Shepherd at Hitchin'.[46]

Soon after her cure, Marie Maillard was summoned by various prominent people, most notably, 'Dr Burnet, Bishop of Salisbury, and the Bishop of Worcester [who] both saw me, and examined me in one day. Amongst several other persons of Distinction that saw me was the Bishop of London, who order'd me, and several of my Friends, to attend him at Doctor's Commons; and there ... examined me before many witnesses upon my Oath, as well as several other Persons, who knew me during my lameness',[47] Lady Sunderland called for her, and the Bishop of Lincoln discussed her with Lady Sunderland; she was also sent for by Sir William Ashurst, the Lord Mayor, and examined by him upon oath. These examinations were very much 'scientific' examinations of her body, as indicated by the following description:

> Queen Mary sent four doctors to examine me, who having put everybody but my Mother and Father outside the Room, placed me in several postures to observe the motion of my Joints, and saw nothing but was perfectly in its right and proper place. The last posture was setting me on the ground, and then they measured my Legs, and perceived one Leg to be about the Thickness of a Crown-piece shorter than the other, ... and being asked the

Reason of it, they said, it might be necessary to remind me of my former Condition, of the great gladness of God in my miraculous cure.[48]

The account of Maillard's cure was published with the affidavits to the Lord Mayor and to the Bishop of London, and the testimonies of various key figures: Maillard's parents, Madame Laulan, her neighbours and James De Batt, the physician who had declared her lameness incurable.

Important, too, in the evidence supporting Maillard's miraculous healing, was the Letter of James Welwood, M.D. to Lady Ashurst, the Lady Mayoress, giving a medical explanation of Maillard's condition prior to the healing, and the unlikely odds of any cure being possible, which was published along with the various accounts of the healing and the multiple affidavits. In his Letter, Welwood established that Maillard probably suffered a dislocation of the thigh-bone as a young child, a condition difficult to fix at the best of times, 'but when the Dislocation is of long standing, as it was with this Maid, most surgeons and Anatomists look upon the case as deplorable, if not desperate'. Thus he concluded, he was 'not ashamed to own, that there is something in it [the cure] which I cannot well comprehend, and shall not be angry with anybody that ascribe to it something above or out of the Road of Nature'.[49] This is as close as Welwood got to any plain assertion that Maillard's healing was a miracle, but throughout the text he gave every suggestion that such was the case because his medical examination of Maillard identified no other possibilities. He thus admitted to the mystery of *both* religion and the laws of nature (or 'science'): 'If it is said why should God work such a Miracle, if it be any? (as I shall never determine) I must own to your Ladyship, that if I do not know all the secrets of Nature, I do much less know the secrets of the Author of Nature.'[50]

The gathering of evidence was, of course, vital to any proper investigation of such cases as these. This method of investigation had had thirty years to settle into the culture since Boyle and his colleagues had looked into the matter of Greatrakes' cures and applied their newly developing experimental methods. As Welwood cautioned, echoing Boyle and that earlier generation of Royal Society Fellows who had investigated Greatrakes, 'nothing is extraordinary, but upon very great and full evidence'.[51] The primary body of evidence was the miraculous body itself. Hence the examination of the healed body was an essential part of the investigation. Physicians and others who had treated the women medically were called upon to testify. Sometimes they commented that they felt this was a miracle. Thus Charles Nicholls, an apothecary, testified about Susannah Arch's cure:

On the 29th of September last, Susannah Arch coming to me on the behalf of another women, desired me to tell her what her distemper was? I gave it, as my Opinion, that it was a Leprosy, and could not be perfectly cured, but something might be given to check it, or keep it under. Furthermore, I coming this Day into Southwark, I saw this woman cur'd of her sad Distemper; and by what I heard her say, and is related in the foregoing Narrative, I do readily believe that it was done by the immediate Hand of God, as the Fruit and Effect of her Faith. I must say I stand in Admiration of beholding this Woman cured. In witness of all which I set my Hand this 1st day of January, 1694/5.

By contrast, another apothecary, Robert Hume, who had also treated Susannah Arch, was willing to say she had been healed – 'I do verily believe that she is wholly cured of it' – but he omitted any comments on whether he considered it a miracle.[52]

As much evidence as possible was sought from those who knew the women before and after their healings. The accounts of their miracles were therefore published with endless affidavits. Maillard had, of course, a wealth of illustrious witnesses, as well as her family members and neighbours. Elizabeth Savage's healing from the palsy attracted neither so many nor such elite witnesses as Maillard's cure, but nevertheless the account of her healing was published with eight affidavits from relatives, neighbours and friends who could witness to her condition before and after the healing, each also signed by the Lord Mayor, Sir William Ashurst, who testified to the credibility of these witnesses and their accounts. Two fellows of the Royal College of Physicians, Thomas Burwell and Richard Morton, also testified 'that upon diligent Search and Observation, we find Mrs Elizabeth Savage's Right Hand and Arm Strait and Useful as the other'.[53] The subtitle of the pamphlet about Mrs Savage advertised that the case had been 'Enquired into with all its Circumstances, by Noted Divines, both of the Church of England, and others: And by Eminent Physicians of the College: And many Persons of Quality, who have express'd their full Satisfaction.' The reputation of the healed women themselves was also commented upon, as it had been in the cases of Valentine Greatrakes and Martha Taylor. This was part of the context of the miracle events. Mr and Mrs Savage were described by the author of the preface to the account of Mrs Savage's healing as 'sincerely Devout and Religious People'.[54] Susannah Arch was described by the author of a similar preface to her narrative of healing as 'a woman of an holy conversation, [who] enjoys much communion with God, and is a Member of a congregation meeting in Devonshire Square'.[55] It was important, too, that just as Greatrakes had performed his cures out in the open, so Maillard's healing 'was done openly before witnesses, not in a corner, but in the Metropolis of the Nation'.[56] Writers describing and commenting on the case tried to reproduce this sense of the *transparency* of the matter, appealing to the bulk of evidence to support their case. The author of the first account of Maillard's cure (in 1693), claimed, 'I will give you a Plain and True Relation on the Matter of Fact without any Remarks, or Observations of my own, for the thing being undoubtedly true, needs nothing to set it off, or recommend it.'[57]

A seven-page discourse on miracles arguing for the continuation of miracles since New Testament times, and giving instructions on how to test miracles, was attached to the account of Elizabeth Savage's cure. The author of this appendix wrote:

> That miracles have Ceased, as to their Number and Greatness compared to what they were in Apostolical Times, seems very injudicious to deny. But that no miracle of any kind, or on any occasion whatsoever, hath been, or shall be performed, is every way as Ungrounded, and much more Irreligious.

Proper evidence for the miracle was vital, but if the miracle was proven true yet still denied, then the dangers of scepticism and irreligion were invited (a point to which we shall return shortly): 'So it would be very unchristian to Mock at the Miraculous Works of Christ wrought since the Establishment of the Christian Religion: when Sufficient Testimony is given of them.' The author then proceeds to tell the reader how to spot a hoax, and how to avoid false miracles. He instructs the reader 'to try Miracles as well as Spirits by the Word of God'. Here again the emphasis is on the Word, the scriptural basis of miracles. His practical instructions are that, 'The fact itself, and the Reputation of the Persons concerned, ought to be duly inspected.'[58] The reputation of the witnesses was, as always in this period, vital.

The question that this spate of miracle cases invites is this: why were so many people of 'Reputation' attracted to them and involved in them? What made these miracle cases such a live issue in the mid-1690s? Why did Queen Mary and the Lord Mayor of London and several bishops and fellows of the Royal College of Physicians get so intensely interested in what had happened to these women? The 1690s was the decade when those at the centre of power, those of the new Protestant court, were attempting to shape the identity of a new Protestant regime. It was also the decade when the great debate on miracles (as it has been called) began to 'break'. Some early deist texts, such as those by Charles Blount, had begun to broach the subject of miracles in the 1680s, but it was the 1690s that witnessed an intellectual crisis, not only about miracles, but also as a result of anti-clerical and Socinian (or anti-Trinitarian) challenges. Thus Anglicans and Presbyterians, Huguenots and Baptists, bishops and booksellers, physicians and apothecaries, and the poor neighbours and friends of four devout women of low social status as well as the Queen herself found themselves agreeing that miracles could still occur and, indeed, had (or might well have) occurred in the healed bodies of these four women. This sounds like a disparate group of people – and certainly they varied in social status and education – but when we look a little closer, we see that there were more connections between the various individuals who became involved in these cases than might appear at first glance.

The interest generated by these miracle stories in the mid-1690s, amongst such a seemingly disparate group of people, can be understood as part of a larger movement to create a 'Godly' nation. The involvement of Queen Mary should not surprise us: she was concerned to promote Godliness at the court, believing that a moral revolution could cement the 1688 revolution. Tony Claydon has pointed to the ways in which the combined tasks of consolidating William and Mary's authority and creating a godly court were achieved through a massive court propaganda machine, with, for example, the preaching of sermons, the minting of special coins and the observance of fast days monthly for divine assistance in the war against France. All of this was aimed at representing William and Mary's court as godly and Protestant, with God on its side.[59] Mary was a devout member of the Church of England; under her, royal chapel services became more frequent, as did preaching in them, and the subsequent publication of those sermons. She succeeded in transforming court culture – which had had the reputation of decadence under Charles II – largely by her personal example of piety and devotion. William had written in February 1690 to Henry Compton the Bishop of London about the 'overflowing of vice' and the need for 'a general reformation of the lives and manners of all our subjects'.[60] Mary, with William, supported the work of the societies for the reformation of manners, and shared their founders' belief in providence and the need for individuals to behave well for the ultimate good of the nation, so in July 1691, she issued a proclamation to the justices of the peace for Middlesex for the suppression of profaneness and debauchery at the prompting of Edward Stillingfleet, Bishop of Worcester.

Here, the significance of the involvement of particular bishops in Maillard's case is highlighted. In William's frequent absences abroad, Mary was responsible for appointing men to the bishoprics left empty by the nonjurors and she made sure they were filled with loyal clergy, usually Whigs. These men were some of the bishops who became interested in Maillard's case. Gilbert Burnet, Bishop of Salisbury, was perhaps the most important churchman at William and Mary's court, keenly active in both shaping and presenting the new Protestant ideology – for example, he had suggested a string of fasts and thanksgivings for the war that Mary organised while William was away at war – and was responsible for finding the churchmen who would support and promote it. He had become a royal chaplain and clerk of the royal closet almost as soon as William and Mary had come to the throne, and was soon afterwards, in 1689, appointed and consecrated Bishop of Salisbury. He and William never got on particularly well, but he got on exceptionally well with Mary and he was her preferred preacher. A Scottish man, he had come to London in the early 1660s and met the Cambridge Platonists Henry More and Benjamin Whichcote, the latitudinarians John Tillotson and Edward Stillingfleet (then at St Paul's Cathedral), as well as the natural philosopher and churchman responsible for setting up the Royal Society, John Wilkins. He must have made an impression as he was made a member of the Royal Society in 1664, and maintained an interested in both natural philosophy and chemistry all his life. He was also spiritual adviser to Boyle at the end of Boyle's life.

Henry Compton, Bishop of London, had been one of Mary's tutors when she was young, and had made sure her religious instruction was soundly Protestant (he was profoundly opposed to Roman Catholicism). Although he was disappointed not to be made Archbishop of Canterbury in 1691, and was in some matters increasingly allied with the Tories, his interest in the healing of Maillard in his own diocese is not surprising, not least because he was a supporter of the Huguenots.

Edward Stillingfleet, the Bishop of Worcester, and one of the leading intellectuals of his day was also one of the first men to be appointed to a bishopric under William and Mary, in 1689. He was closely involved in setting up the societies for the reformation of manners, which won him Queen Mary's affection; she remained ever after an ardent supporter of his. He was one of the outstanding intellectuals of his day (even John Locke responded to his criticisms of his work) and was an important influence in shaping a broad Anglican theology, outlining the parameters and core beliefs of the 'broad centre' of the Church of England. In his considerable work of natural theology of 1662, *Origines Sacrae*, he specifically addressed those who rejected the possibility of revelation, and outlined the ways in which he maintained there was sufficient evidence in point of reason to prove the existence of a deity; in that text, he also provided a standard account of the doctrine of the cessation of miracles.[61] As an old man in 1693, his involvement in Maillard's case suggested that he continued to show an interest in this question, though the extent of it is not recorded, and we do not know whether Maillard's case made him re-think his influential defence of the doctrine of the cessation of miracles. He was a man who had written, 'Wherever God requires us to believe anything as true, he gives us evidence that it is so.'[62] But he had also attacked Roman Catholic miracles as idolatrous.

Though there were differences between them, all of these bishops were, generally speaking, latitude men, and the shaping of a reasonable and yet orthodox theology was a key task for each of them. They were the heirs of the Great Tew Circle who, in the 1650s, had seen the synthesis of reason and faith as a vital path to peace and toleration. Burnet and Stillingfleet in particular were interested in the philosophy of the day, and had inherited the concern of those first members of the Royal Society, in the 1660s, to balance faith and reason. Stillingfleet, for example, believed that faith was a rational discursive act of the mind (not of the will) and accepted the traditional Anglican 'three-legged stool' of scripture, tradition and reason, as long as reason was not contradicted. On the other hand, in the 1690s, he attacked Hobbes' atheism, and Descartes' idea of motion and the mechanical laws of nature which he considered faulty (and potentially atheistical) because it explained the workings of the universe without the notion of God's providence.

The physicians who testified as to the healing of these women also had links to the court and Whig sympathies. James Welwood, who wrote the 'Letter' discussing Maillard's case and miracles generally, which was attached to one of the accounts of Maillard's healing, was a keen Williamite, promoted by Bishop Burnet at court, so that in 1691 he was appointed Physician to the Person (i.e., the king). In fact, although his qualifications as a doctor were entirely adequate (he had obtained an M.D. degree at Reims), and he had become a Fellow of the Royal College of Physicians in 1690, his commentary on the case of Maillard was his only medical publication, as he spent much of his time writing Whiggish political tracts.[63] Similarly, one of the medical witnesses of Mrs Savage's cure, Richard Morton, was a man with Williamite connections. He was a dissenter, a minister who had been ejected from his living in 1662, who – like many others in his situation – then trained in medicine. In December 1670, on the nomination of Prince William of Orange, he was created Doctor of Medicine at Oxford University; by the early 1690s, when Prince William had become King William, Morton had become Physician-in-Ordinary to the King.[64]

The publishers of the pamphlets about these women's cures also tended to be Whigs: Thomas Parkhurst, Richard Baldwin and John Dunton were all heavily involved in producing Whig propaganda. Dunton (who had been apprenticed to Parkhurst in the 1670s) had a particular connection to the court at just the time of Maillard's cure, as Queen Mary licensed him to print a translation of the *History of the Famous Edict of Nantes* in two volumes (1693–4) and in turn he promoted her drive for a moral reformation by publishing *Proposals for a National Reformation of Manners* (1694). Dunton was the son, grandson and great grandson of Anglican ministers, but had strong Presbyterian connections and even affiliations for at least part of his life and had good relations with dissenters generally; the bulk of his publishing was in the area of sermons, books of devotion and collections of 'wonder tales' – stories of prodigies, miracles, the supernatural and providential.[65] Others involved in the cases tended to share this religious and political sensibility, yet from very different angles. Sir William Ashurst, the Lord Mayor of London in 1693 when Maillard and Savage were cured, came from one of the most prominent Presbyterian families in the country, and was a part of the Whig establishment in the Corporation of London. Lady Sutherland, to whom Dr Welwood addressed his Letter about Maillard, was from a prominent Whig family.

What most of these participants had in common was a desire to promote a reasonable and moderate form of Christianity, which would lapse into neither enthusiasm nor 'atheism'. Many of them also had the strong desire to promote a Protestant form of manners and morals for the good of the nation. Their interest in these miracle cases was, therefore, part of their broader interest in steering a middle course in religion, balancing reason and revelation, shoring up the faith over and against the perceived twin threats of the enthusiast and the atheist, the one who believed too much and the other who believed too little. Welwood's Letter to Lady Ashurst illustrates this position well. He wrote of Maillard's cure, 'after all, if he [the Author of Nature] should think fit to do such an extraordinary thing in the Age in which we live, we must all confes there is occasion enough for it; since the very Existence of a Supreme Being, and his Power and Authority, is so much question'd'. Welwood identified two extreme positions held in response to an event such as Maillard's healing: there is the 'bigot', that is, the enthusiast or overly religious person who believes anything without testing it, and then there is the atheist who believes nothing. For Welwood, reason and revelation were not opposed; rather, he placed together those who took either to absurd lengths. The effect of either extreme was that men would 'degenerate into brutes'. Welwood therefore sought the middle way, which would synthesise reason and revelation:

> The Mean between these two, is to resolve on believing that nothing is extraordinary, but upon very great and full Evidence. In short, Men are apt to lye, or amplify . . . and therefore we have a right to suspend our Belief, and to examine well the fact when any strange thing is told us; and this is what every Wise Man ought to do. But when the Averment of the fact is

full, then every Enquirer into Nature, ought to consider how far the Powers of Nature may have co-operated to the Effect in question.[66]

Men such as Welwood wanted to test the plausibility of a miracle before declaring the truth or otherwise of it. The supernatural, the intervention of God, could be allowed as an explanation for occurrences such as the healing of these four women if, after testing all the evidence, it seemed the most likely and rational explanation. There are strong echoes of Boyle's position here.

The author of the appendix to the account of Mrs Savage's healing also sought this middle way. He wrote that it 'would be very UnChristian to mock at the Miraculous Works of Christ wrought since the Establishment of the Christian Religion, when sufficient Testimony is given of them'. Like Welwood, he believed it was in the extremes that danger lurked: 'It is an Extreme to deny all Miracles', he said, 'tho' it must be confest, the World has been extremely abused by false pretended Miracles, contrived to introduce and establish Superstition, and promote and enrich a Party: and 'tis no Point of Wisdom to be unjudiciously credulous.' Nevertheless the miraculous healing of both Maillard and Savage, about whom he writes in this appendix, were described by him as 'these late extraordinary Appearances of God' and he thought they might have important lessons in them, hoping they 'may be good Presages to the Godly of what God is about to do, and Monitors to the wicked, to awaken them to Repentance'.[67] As Dunton published this pamphlet about Mrs Savage, it is quite likely that he wrote this seven-page appendix. He had already been involved in discussions of the cessation of miracles in his highly successful *Athenian Mercury,* which he had started in 1691 (and which ran for seven years). Readers sent in their questions to an anonymous club of learned men, the Athenian Society, which met at Smith's Coffee House and formulated the answer to those questions.[68] This group included Samuel Wesley, who answered many of the religious questions, a number of which concerned miracles. For example, in April 1691, the following question and response were printed, and it bears the same hallmarks of trying to carve out a middle way:

Quest. 14. *Whether Miracles are ceas'd?*
Answ. Much of the controversie lies in the Definition of a Miracle, which I believe not so easie to fix as is commonly imaged. That which appears to me most full is – *A work beyond the ordinary power of Nature* produced by a Divine Agent, the Doubt recurs, How shall we know the Agent Divine? I answer, by comparing and examining what's thereby done, and the end it proposes with Reason and Revelation. To answer the Question espressly, I grant 'tis generally held in the Affirmative, and the Argument seems very

strong, *God does nothing in vain,* nor will make any Contradiction in Nature, unless for some weighty and even necessary Reason; none of which can now be pretended. But the truth of the last Assertion I am a little doubtful of. A warning given to any Person of impeding unavoidable danger by a Dream, or any thing of that Nature, comes up to the present Definition. I know not how to answer several undoubted matters of Fact of that Nature, nor therefore to affirm the total ceasing of Miracles on all Occasions. But thus far the forementioned Argument may hold, that we are to expect none such for the Confirmation of any ancient Doctrines, nor to receive any new one because attested by strange things, but rather suspect them.[69]

The inclusion of this question shows how much miracles – and in particular the question as to whether miracles had ceased or not, which this author was not willing to affirm – were a 'live' issue at the time.

What we do not have in the wealth of pamphlets and records about these four cases is any evidence of scepticism about the cases. We only have the fears of the major participants, in their defence of the possibility and plausibility of miracles in their own time, that too much scepticism was as dangerous as too little. As Michael Hunter has shown, the figure of the atheist was a general 'catch-all' used to describe sceptics, freethinkers, coffee-house wits and all others who appeared to pose a threat to serious Christianity. As Hunter remarks, 'people preferred to use the inclusive concept of "atheism" to encapsulate a range of phenomena that were believed to present a threat by sensationalising them in a single, pervasive stereotype'.[70] The atheist was regarded as foolish and irrational for denying the rational evidence presented for the truth of Christianity. The atheist was a person who misused his or her innate faculty of Reason, and thereby indulged in lax and immoral behaviour (over and against the correct use of the innate faculty of Reason which led both to the control of the will and to right belief and thus to right living); he or she was also a threat to the established church, in that a position of total scepticism would render the church unnecessary.[71] As is clear from the literature generated by these miracle cases, many people in the 1690s thought that 'atheism' – and all that that term encompassed – was an increased threat. Without dismissing that real threat, it is also necessary to recognise that the figure of the atheist was useful to the theologians, the popular publishers of wonder books, and anyone else who wanted to comment on the condition of society from a religious point of view. The spectre of the atheist was evoked and invoked as a warning to congregations and readers about the consequences of unbelief and immoral behaviour.[72]

Conclusion

These four miracle cases captured the public's imagination at many different levels. This suggests that miracles were themselves a 'sign' or a test case of what people were concerned about in the late seventeenth century. Two particular and intertwined concerns emerge from these stories. The first was to do with the morals of individuals and thus, it was perceived, the fate of the nation; the second was to do with the proper relation between reason and revelation. These concerns were large enough that any Protestant scepticism about miracles could be forgotten or bracketed; or, to put it another way, Protestant worries about miracles were overridden by greater considerations. In shaping a theological middle way and a distinctly Protestant morality and piety, a range of people thought it perfectly proper to harness these miracle stories for their own use. They were, after all, stories of piety and they were perfectly Protestant miracles, extraordinary transformations of the body through God's holy Word and without the intervention of a theologically tricky intermediary figure.

In accepting these miracles – or at least the *possibility* that the healings were miracles – churchmen and physicians and booksellers of a Whiggish and Protestant persuasion realised that they had to balance reason and revelation. To go too far in either direction was to court danger. To this end, the experimental methods of the Royal Society, which were fast becoming culturally embedded, and the new philosophy, were harnessed to the purposes of theology. Religious experience therefore became an object of investigation in this period. J. Samuel Preus argues that the seventeenth century was the 'generative context' for the term 'religious experience'. Preus writes, 'we witness . . . a novel reification of inner religious events, of the innermost reaches of religious life'. This reification is 'not a signal of alienation from religion, but, on the contrary, an aspect of its intensification, featuring relentless analysis and answering to specific, identifiable religious needs'. Preus focuses on the reification of *inner* religious events in Puritan sermons, pamphlets and books, but this notion of reification is applicable to the ways in which religious phenomena such as miracles were examined and discussed. By the end of the seventeenth century, John Locke's philosophy was influential: knowledge of God was a truth to be discovered by reason, and reason could and should judge whether something is a divine revelation. God's works should be investigated for they would in turn provide further knowledge and proof of the nature of God; one's innate faculty of reason enabled that testing.[73] Such testing, as we have seen, required reliable witnesses, neutral public spaces and 'objective' prose.

The investigations of miracle claims in the public sphere of conversation, sermon, print and coffeehouse provided the places and spaces in which understandings of 'reason', 'revelation' and other contested terms could be defined and debated. That is one explanation for why these miracle claims attracted so much attention: they provided a means by which people staked their theological epistemological claims at a time of rapid intellectual, political and religious change. What is interesting about these four miracle cases is that men and women from all levels of society were involved in that debate; this conversation was not the exclusive domain of philosophers or churchmen. These debates allowed the mixing and mingling of people of varying social status, both genders and different religious affiliations, as a wide range of people ventured to understand and explain what these miracles meant for their own times and circumstances. Furthermore, while it is tempting to see these miracle stories along typically gendered lines − women's bodies being examined by male experts − it is nevertheless the case that these women's bodies were the bodies of evidence, and their own narratives and expressions of strong religious faith were central to the discussions that occurred. While there are in these women's descriptions of their 'pre-miraculous' states faint echoes of the theme of female suffering that we encountered in Sarah Wight, Anna Trapnel and Martha Taylor, these healed women told their narratives within a different paradigm, as stories of God's grace and new life. Furthermore, while all of these women's cures occurred inside their homes − and that factor contributed to the Protestant nature of these miracles − their narratives and the investigation of their miracle claims took them into the public spheres of print, court culture and ecclesiastical debate.

These four miracle cases occurred at another significant moment in the Enlightenment debate about miracles, for the terms of the debate were about to shift. If Greatrakes in the mid-1660s marked the turning point into a particular mode of miracle investigation, representing a particular theological stance, then Maillard and the other healed women in the mid-1690s marked a turning point out of it. Those churchmen and others like Welwood who tried to steer a middle course through enthusiasm and atheism were by the 1690s beginning to fight a rearguard action against the logical outcome of two Protestant attitudes to miracles. Ultimately, both of those attitudes would lead to forms of Enlightenment scepticism. Those Protestants who had declared the cessation of miracles, while not questioning God's ability to work miracles, nevertheless provided the foundation for a key Enlightenment question: did God work miracles at all? Those Protestants who so readily took up miracles in the 1650s and afterwards provided ammunition for the sceptics who said that there were too many miracles for anyone to take any of them seriously (like the boy who cried wolf). This caused problems for those 'middle way' Anglicans and reasonable dissenters who wished to balance reason and revelation, perceiving that such a balance was essential to a stable religious situation and thus to the stability of the nation. This 'middle way' remained an essential line of argument in the Enlightenment philosophical and theological debate about miracles, but it took something of an intellectual battering; it is to that eighteenth-century debate, and some of the formative miraculous 'episodes' of the early eighteenth century, that we now turn.

CHAPTER 7

Miracles and the Philosophers

Accounts of the philosophical debate on miracles in the eighteenth century tend to focus exclusively on the arguments of the philosophical and theological texts, without contextualising them in any way. In short, ideas are not related to practice or lived religion.[1] Idea is seen to flow naturally into idea; idea is refuted by idea. Of course, thinkers influenced one another: John Toland, for example, in *Christianity Not Mysterious* was (amongst other things) trying to refute John Locke's claim that even within reasonable Christianity there was a place for revelation; as the debate proceeded, thinkers responded to one another, generating a large amount of literature on the topic of miracles in the first five decades of the eighteenth century.[2] But such a narrative, which focuses only on the relationship of idea to idea, argument to argument, the natural methodology of intellectual historians or philosophers, cannot take account of the ways in which the activities of the religiously faithful and specific religious events and claims, as well as the intertextual discussion of those events, might have had an impact on *how* the issue of miracles was discussed and argued about in the philosophical debate. I have already made the case that far from the eighteenth-century philosophical debate being the *opening* of a discussion about miracles, it was the *end result* of a discussion that had been taking place for at least the preceding fifty years, and also a consequence of shifting Protestant attitudes towards miracles and the claims of some Protestants that they were experiencing miracles. In this final chapter, I do not attempt a full survey of the eighteenth-century philosophical debate on miracles – and thereby to repeat the work of intellectual historians and philosophers who have already ably done this – but rather to illustrate two endpoints of my overall argument in this book.[3] First, I discuss two contrasting texts which were published in the mid 1690s, on the eve of the philosophical debate on miracles. Secondly, I indicate the ways in which miracle claims – particularly those of the French Prophets who were active in London at the end of the first decade of the eighteenth century – were used by the deists and sceptics to undermine any appeal to evidence, especially testimony, which was a key plank in their argument against the Christian apologists. Thirdly, I look at how the apologists responded to this, sharpening their 'evidentialist' position. Thus, I indicate how, even in the *philosophical* debate on miracles, idea and practice, doctrine and lived religion, were intertwined; and that, furthermore, the less esteemed partner of the two (namely, lived religion, in the form of miracle claims and events) influenced the philosophers and theologians in what they said and how they said it. Finally, I briefly consider the ways in which the philosophical debate in the early eighteenth century opened up and discussed the question which had been threatened or 'prepared' for some time – but which had been thus far held back: namely, was the Christian God a god who could or would work miracles at all?

I. On the Eve of the Philosophical Debate: Two Texts

In late 1695, John Toland published (anonymously) his *Christianity Not Mysterious*, a work that has often been taken to mark the start of the deist 'onslaught' on orthodox Christianity.[4] In it, Toland declared that true Christianity consisted of no doctrines that were above or beyond reason. All those doctrines that relied upon contradictions – transubstantiation being the most obvious example – were absurd; mystery had no part in Toland's rational Christianity. He was, therefore, highly sceptical about miracles: 'When all other shifts prove ineffectual, the Partizans of Mystery fly to Miracles as their last Refuge.'[5] Toland argued that no miracle could be contrary to reason; therefore, 'all those miracles are fictitious where there occur any Contradictions, as that Christ was born without opening any Passage out of the Virgin's Body; that a Head spoke some days after it was sever'd from the Body, and the Tongue cut out; with the Multitudes of this kind that may be met with among the Papists, the Jews, the Bramins, the Mahometans, and in all Places where the Credulity of the People makes 'em a Merchandize to their Priests'. Furthermore, Toland stated, 'God is not so prodigal of Miracles, as to work any at random.'[6] While miracles were not the primary focus of *Christianity Not Mysterious*, Toland was opening up two questions that had thus far been avoided in (English) discussions of the Protestant doctrine of the cessation of miracles and in the debates that had occurred in response to the miracle claims and events in England over the preceding four decades. First, if contemporary miracles were to be dismissed, as they were in the doctrine of cessation, why not question the biblical miracles too? Were the biblical miracles true? This was related to a second, much larger question: was the Christian God a god who worked miracles at all, who altered the course of nature, rather than a god who had simply stopped working miracles when they were apparently no longer needed, as the Protestant doctrine of cessa-tion had all along maintained? Both of these questions were central to the deist or sceptical side of the debate about miracles as it proceeded through the eighteenth century.

Toland was not the first to open up such questions: Spinoza had done so in chapter 6 of his *Tractatus Theologico-Politicus*, published (anonymously) in 1670. This work was not unfamiliar to those in England who were concerned with these questions: the freethinker Charles Blount had published (again, anonymously) a translation of chapter 6 of the *Tractatus* and other chunks of Spinoza (along with some Hobbes) in his *Miracles, No Violation of the Laws of Nature* in 1683.[7] But it was Toland's book that immediately caused contro-versy on publication, even though it may have been neatly timed to appear just after the expiry of the Licensing Act, in 1695, and thus avoid that act's censorial powers. Nevertheless, the book was denounced and burnt by both the English and Irish parliaments, and Toland returned to his native Ireland for a while to avoid the controversy.[8] Published in the mid-1690s, Toland's book appeared at just that moment when the Williamite Court was pressing for the reformation of manners and was raising questions about the relation-ship of private belief and devotion to public behaviour and morality, as demonstrated in the previous chapter.

In 1696, the same year that an imprint of Toland's explosive *Christianity Not Mysterious* was published, identifying him as its author, Moses Pitt, a bookseller and printer who had published the work of members of the Royal Society, including Robert Boyle and Gilbert Burnet, and in 1683 the Society's *Transactions*, published a pamphlet about his former childhood servant, Ann Jeffries. According to Pitt, Jeffries had been fed by fairies for six months and had performed 'strange and wonderful cures' with 'salves and medicines she received from them, for which she never took one Penny of her Patients', as the pamphlet's title page informed the reader. Pitt also included on that title page a quotation from a sermon preached by one Samuel Barton before the House of Commons on 16 April 1696: 'All the works of Providence are not alike. Sometimes for wise and good Reasons God has been pleased quite to alter the course of Nature, as it were, to shew himself to have a Power above it.' We do not know if either Barton or Pitt was explicitly refuting Toland's suggestion that God was not a god who altered the course of nature. It is certain, however, that the story of Ann Jeffries' encounter with fairies would have been dismissed by Toland as one of the 'celebrated Feats of Goblins and Fairies', which, he argued, 'must be accounted fictitious, idle, and superstitious Fables, for in all these there appears no End deserving a Change in Nature'. For Toland, such things 'evidently contradict our idea of God, and quite subvert his Providence'.[9]

So why did Moses Pitt publish this account of Ann Jeffries' apparent interaction with fairies, an encounter which had occurred some forty years before?
The motivation seems to have come from Edward Fowler, the Latitudinarian
bishop of Gloucester, one of William and Mary's key episcopal appointees,
and a strong supporter of the societies for the reformation of manners, who
believed that 1688 had heralded a providential call for a spiritual and moral
renewal in the nation.[10] Fowler had corresponded with Henry More about
ghosts and spirits in the 1670s, and passed on to him several stories of the
supernatural, which More included in his *Sadducismus Triumphatus, or, Full
and Plain evidence Concerning Witches and Apparitions* (1681). Pitt's pamphlet
was dedicated and addressed to Bishop Fowler who, according to Pitt, had
earlier, in 1696, reminded him of the story of Ann Jeffries that Pitt had related
to him some eighteen or nineteen years before. This reminder had urged Pitt
to publish the narrative, giving the usual reason – 'that atheists may believe'.
As he wrote in the preface to Fowler:

> Moreover, my Lord, if Men would give themselves time to think, they
> cannot but remember that the Great God has done as great and marvellous
> works in our Age, both in Judgement and in Mercy, as he did in the days
> of old. By which the greatest Atheist may be convinc'd, not only of the
> Being of a God, but also that his Power and his Goodness are as manifest
> now as of old; and therefore it's the Duty of all that do by personal knowl-
> edge know any extraordinary works of Providences of God, which are
> uncommon, to publish them to the world, that the Great God may be
> glorified, and mankind edified; which is purely and truly the Design of
> publishing the following Narrative.[11]

Although Ann Jeffries was still living in 1696, she would not give her own
account, influenced by neighbours who thought she might fall into trouble
again about it as she told Pitt, or, as Pitt's brother-in-law Mr Humphrey
Martyn claimed she told him, because, 'Pitt would make either Books or
Ballads of it and . . . that she would not have her name spread about the
country in books or ballads'. Her fears that she might get into further trouble
were not unreasonable: when the 'fairy story' had become known in mid-
1640s Cornwall, she had been questioned before justices of the peace, arrested
by John Tregeagle, a Justice of Peace, and taken to Bodmin Gaol; she was then
questioned at the Sessions and by the judges at the Assizes, kept in prison for
some time and even held prisoner in John Tregeagle's house for a while. It was
no surprise that she did not want to give her account. Pitt therefore had to
rely on his own memories of the events, which had occurred when he was a
small boy (he had been born in 1639).

As Pitt remembered it, Jeffries had said that she first encountered the fairies in 1645 when she was knitting in an arbour in the garden; six persons 'small in stature, all clothed in green' hopped over the garden hedge to see her, at which point she was so surprised that she had a convulsion-fit. The illness lasted a while but when she recovered, she was able to heal Moses Pitt's mother's leg (which Mrs Pitt had hurt when she had been walking home) by stroking. At this point, she broke the news of the fairies, and the gift of healing they had bestowed upon her, to the Pitt family. Jeffries also claimed that she survived on food the fairies gave her; 'she forsook eating our victuals', reported Pitt. As a small boy, Moses Pitt was full of curiosity about the fairies and one day he looked through Ann Jeffries' key-hole and saw her eating some special bread: she opened the door and gave him a piece, 'the most delicious Bread that ever I did eat either before or since', he recalled. The stories of her healing and the fairies' provisions became well known, so that 'People of all Distempers, Sicknesses, Sores and Agues came not only so far off as the lands-end, but also from London, and were cured by her'.[12] However, this public knowledge of Jeffries' story brought her to the attention of magistrates and ministers who were suspicious that evil spirits had affected her. She was arrested and examined; she survived without food in gaol (fed by the fairies, she said), and when Moses Pitt and his mother were commanded to appear for questioning at Sessions, the first question young Moses was asked was whether he had anything (i.e., food) in his pocket for the family's servant, Ann. He emptied out his pockets to prove he had nothing. Released, finally, Ann was not allowed to return to the Pitt household, and therefore went to work for Moses Pitt's aunt, where she continued to perform her cures, before leaving to live with her brother and, later, marry. In this 'plain relation of these very strange passages', Moses Pitt repeated two of the main ingredients of these sorts of pamphlets about wonders and miracles. First of all, he emphasised Jeffries' piety: 'she constantly went to church to pay her Devotions to our great and good God, and to hear his Word read and preached . . . she took mighty delight in devotion, and in hearing the Word of God read and preach'd, although she herself could not read'. This was to indicate – over and against the magistrates – that this was a story of the miraculous rather than the demonic, though the link between the fairies and the Christian God was, frankly, rather tenuous. Pitt's comment was that he could not 'give one *Natural* Reason for any one of these passages that happened to this poor Woman' (my italics). Secondly, he attempted to offer a 'plain relation' of the events, relating the story as 'only matter of fact', without 'observations or reflections upon any one passage'.[13] He also hinted to the reader that, while Ann Jeffries would no longer tell her story, there were witnesses who would verify Pitt's narrative, should anyone wish to investigate the truth of it.

It was an odd little story to publish, hardly one that would persuade an 'atheist' of the truth of Christianity; but one designed to suggest that miracles still occurred. Its publication, at the end of the seventeenth century, at the prompting of a latitudinarian bishop, is nevertheless significant, for it marked the end of a period in which Latitudinarian bishops might take such stories seriously. As the philosophical debate proceeded in the early and mid-eighteenth century, it became increasingly tricky for the Latitudinarians and their like – those who sought a middle way between the 'atheist' and the enthusiast – to investigate current miracle claims in the way that they had done since the 1660s. This was in part because their reliance on evidence – and all the related technologies, such as reliable witnesses, that went with the scientific investigations proposed by Boyle and his followers and adopted at local level by the investigators of Martha Taylor and Marie Maillard – came under fierce attack in the philosophical debate on miracles. The weaknesses of an appeal to evidence, and especially the use of testimony, were relentlessly probed and exposed by the deists. But it also became more difficult for those seeking a middle way – the apologists in the debate that was opening up – to investigate and refer to recent miracle claims and events because deists and sceptics themselves started to employ those examples of 'lived religion' in their own arguments. James Herrick has indicated the ways in which ridicule was a key method employed by the deists in the philosophical debate on miracles.[14] For the deists, there was nothing better suited to ridicule than a current or recent example of a miracle claim or 'wonder', illustrating, they believed, the continuing credulity of the masses. Furthermore, the deists also used recent accounts of miracle claims and investigations in their critiques of any appeal to evidence, by questioning the credibility of witnesses in the past in comparison with the credibility of those in the present. That is, they argued that recent, well-attested accounts were better than those less well-attested accounts of miracles in the Bible, thereby attacking the belief amongst the orthodox – who accepted an appeal to testimony but were less likely to believe in current-day miracles than in biblical miracles – that the biblical miracles were unquestioningly true. They had the opportunity to employ all these modes of attack when the French Prophets arrived in London in the first decade of the eighteenth century.

II. The French Prophets and the Philosophers

The Earl of Shaftesbury in the opening pages of his 'Letter Concerning Enthusiasm' (written in September 1707 and published in 1708) made a dig at Bishop Fowler's connection to Moses Pitt in the publishing of Ann Jeffries' story:

Even a good Christian, who would needs be over-good and thinks he can never believe enough, may, by a small inclination well improved, extend his faith so largely as to comprehend in it not only all scriptural and traditional miracles, but a solid system of old wives' stories. Were it needful, I could put your Lordship in mind of an eminent, learned, and truly Christian prelate you once knew, who could have given you a full account of his belief in fairies.[15]

In fact, it was not fairies but prophets that prompted Shaftesbury to write the 'Letter' – the French Prophets (Durand Fage, Elie Marion and Jean Chevalier) who had come to London in the previous year, 1706, and had soon begun to make English converts.[16] Shaftesbury had indeed even met one of their most prominent English converts, a London merchant and Presbyterian named John Lacy, who became 'inspired' and began frequent prophesying.[17] The French Prophets had already made a stir in the Cevennes in the south of France where they had come into conflict with the Roman Catholic authorities when they had made detailed prophecies while writhing, twisting, shouting and displaying numerous other embodied manifestations of their ecstatic state. It was too obvious a target for Shaftesbury to resist: his witty, elegant prose embodied the method of ridicule that was so central to the deists' means of attack. 'I am told, for certain,' he wrote, 'that they are at this very time the subject of a choice droll or puppet-show at Bartholomew Fair.' He continued, 'And while Bartholomew Fair is in possession of this privilege, I dare stand security to our national Church that no sect or enthusiasts, no new vendors of prophecy or miracles, shall ever get the start or put her to the trouble of trying her strength with them, in any case.'[18] Since the beginning of the seventeenth century, monsters, prodigies and wonders had regularly been displayed at Bartholomew Fair as spectacles that attracted crowds of onlookers.[19]

The French Prophets also claimed that they could work, and that they did indeed experience, miracles. This gave Shaftesbury the opportunity to attack not only the belief that miracles were occurring in his own day but also, implicitly, the notion that such belief might be plausible if the evidence and testimony were sufficient. He described this as 'a sort of enthusiasm of second hand'. He wrote, 'when men find no original commotions in themselves, no prepossessing panic which bewitches them, they are apt still, by the testimony of others, to be imposed on and led credulously into the belief of many false miracles'.[20] He presented the idea, which would recur frequently in the writings of the deists and sceptics (and is discussed in greater length below), that such testimony was *necessarily* partial. Referring to a 'most signal' miracle amongst the prophets, which occurred in front of many hundreds of people, 'who actually give testimony to the truth to it', he asked 'whether there were present, among those hundreds, any one person who, having never been of their sect or addicted to their way, will give the same testimony with them?'[21] This idea – that people only support the miracles of their own group or sect – also recurred in the deist arguments, as did the notion of 'enthusiasm' being infectious. Of the witnesses of such a miracle, Shaftesbury wrote that:

I must not be contented to ask whether such a one had been wholly free of that particular enthusiasm but whether, before that time, he was esteemed of so sound a judgment and clear a head as to be wholly free of melancholy and in all likelihood incapable of all enthusiasm besides. For otherwise, the panic may have been caught, the evidence of the senses lost as in a dream, and the imagination so inflamed, as in a moment to have burnt up every particle of judgment and reason.[22]

Shaftesbury was, of course, reflecting changing ideas of 'enthusiasm' in which it was being re-cast in medical terms.[23]

The French Prophets nevertheless went out of their way to make their accounts of their miracles as believable as possible, with clear prose and reliable witnesses. Several of their most prominent members were scientists who knew the rules of the experimental method and therefore what would be judged trustworthy evidence. Sir Richard Bulkeley, who became involved with the group late in 1706, had been educated at Trinity College, Dublin and Christ Church, Oxford, was a member of the Royal Society and had been a Fellow of Trinity College, Oxford. He was an inventor, experimenter and horticulturist whose inventions (which included an air pump for ships) and experiments (which involved the planting of maize and propagating elm trees from seed) were discussed in the *Transactions* of the Royal Society. Nicholas Fatio was a mathematician and natural philosopher, with extremely wide-ranging interests and abilities, a Fellow of the Royal Society, who was, for a time, a close friend of Isaac Newton. He encountered the French Prophets in the summer of 1706, soon becoming a follower and one of their scribes. Hillel Schwartz notes that the 'concern for accuracy, which did not end when the Scientists became French Prophets, characterised their religious pursuits as much as their inventions'.[24] So, for example, when John Lacy cured another follower, Elizabeth Gray, of her temporary blindness, the timing of the event and the conditions of the cure were noted with exceptional precision.[25]

When Lacy, the main healer amongst the prophets, related the stories of the cures he had effected, he did so in plain prose, giving the exact details of the condition of the person before and after they were cured. For example, this is the account he gives of the healing of Hugh Preston, the first person to be cured (and who was not a believer beforehand) on 29 November 1707:

> Mr Preston, lodging in the Underground Room, No. 2 of the New Square, Lincoln's-Inn, aged about 77, in November last too, having a Carbuncle on the Nape of his Neck, about five inches diameter, and two high; after a Prayer, the Spirit said touching him in my mouth, *I command away the Tumour:* which accordingly went clear away, without any application but a Bladder (to keep it from the Linen) in about ten days after.

The method of healing was the same in most cases that Lacy described, with the Spirit (the Holy Spirit – which enabled Lacy to prophesy) giving words of healing to the sick person through Lacy: that is, Lacy said a prayer and/or commanded the sickness to be gone while he was 'inspired'. For example, Mrs Mary Moor had a deep consumption and had been in bed for a month; Lacy visited her and 'after a prayer, under the operation of the spirit, words of healing were pronounc'd. The effect was that the very next day she rose at tea, and sat up till eleven at night; and has since continu'd in a good degree of health'.[26] But as these cures were occurring in private, usually in the home of the sick person, there remained the problem of witnesses – at least, reliable witnesses. Sir Richard Bulkeley, a baronet, was considered, at least amongst the French Prophets, a significant and trustworthy witness. He therefore often gave his own accounts of these healings, designed specifically to answer the criticisms of those that 'are not willing to admit of any thing of miraculous Operation, that shall surpass nature and Reason'.[27] He acted as eyewitness to the healings effected by the 'inspired' Lacy, often providing more details, as he did in the following account of the healing of Preston's carbuncle. While Lacy described very simply and briefly the carbuncle on Preston's neck, Bulkeley described the boil in detail:

> at length it broke, and while it was running, no body having the Care to dress it but his Wife, by very ill managery, it grew so bad, spreading upward and toward each Ear, that when I saw it, it was as big as a large Turnip of five inches Diameter, and above two inches high; all of dead Flesh, black and livid; but having diverse Orifices in it, out of which Corruption was continually running; and all sides of it, all around, very much inflam'd.

According to Bulkeley, it was Preston who requested that 'Mr Lacy would pray for a Command from God to come and heal him; who, upon Prayer, was sent thither.' Ten people went with Lacy to Preston's house, and the boil 'was open'd to all our view' and then covered again, after which 'we had Prayers and an Inspiration from two of the Inspir'd'. After about an hour and a half, Lacy asked that the sore be opened up again, at which point Preston reported an ease from the burning and shooting pain, and the eyewitnesses thought 'it seem'd to be diminsh'd about a sixth part'. Lacy said the witnesses could come and see it in a couple of days; Bulkeley returned, and saw 'it had lost above a third part' and remarked that it looked 'like a flat dry'd Apple'. In about a fortnight's time, 'it was as smooth and level as the back of one's hand, and has been ever since perfectly well'. Thus, Bulkeley reported, 'upon all occasions' Preston 'magnifies and blesses the Name of God'.[28] In fact, Preston became a believer, and in that sense miracles could be a missionary tool.[29]

The French Prophets may have gained some new adherents through their miracles, but they did not garner much respect, nor were their miracle claims seriously investigated by outsiders, despite the attempts by Lacy and Bulkeley to create trustworthy, well-attested accounts of them. In fact, the French Prophets represent something of a turning point in the investigation of miracle claims in Enlightenment England. In the preceding forty years or so, claims of miracles and similar extraordinary episodes had attracted attention from a wide range of people – philosophers, scientists, Anglican and dissenting clergymen, printers and booksellers, as well as neighbours and crowds, many of whom wished to investigate the truth of those miracle claims, as we have seen. But this was now no longer the case. The French Prophets certainly received plenty of attention, but much of it was highly critical: between 1707 and 1710, Hillel Schwartz has calculated, ninety books, pamphlets, journals and newspaper articles were published against them.[30] Why, then, were their miracle claims not investigated with the seriousness accorded to the cures wrought, for example, by Valentine Greatrakes? Why were they not 'sound' enough to be taken up by the orthodox in the wider debate about miracles?

There are several reasons – I suggest five here, two *ad hominem*, three evidentialist – why the French Prophets' miracle claims were not deemed credible. There were two *ad hominem* arguments meant to discredit the alleged miracle-workers. One was the behaviour of the French Prophets themselves, particularly when they were inspired, which meant that the miracle-workers themselves were considered disreputable (compare that with the lengths to which supporters of Greatrakes went to portray him as pious, orthodox and believable). The crying, shaking, burping, whistling, gulping, tumbling, writhing and other bodily manifestations of their 'inspiration' made them deeply suspect. This activity did not go down well in the emerging age of politeness. As Schwartz discusses, different hypotheses were offered for the Prophets' behaviour, none particularly flattering. Some, such as Edward Fowler (responding to Shaftesbury's 'Letter Concerning Enthusiasm'), thought the

Prophets were 'acted upon' as they claimed – but by demonic spirits rather than the Holy Spirit. He wrote that he believed there was 'more of Possession, than intended Imposture or delusion, in them'.[31] Others thought they were mad or deluded, while yet others, such as the broad churchman Benjamin Hoadly, offered medical explanations: the French Prophets were the victims of natural forces ('vapours' or 'hysteric fits') in their bodies. Medical explanations could therefore be used to explain the miracles. For example, the clergyman Francis Hutchinson suggested that Lacy had glided ten feet across the floor because he had all the extraordinary strength of a mad man. Miraculous cures resulted from the imagination, not least the imagination of one person governing that of another. This relates to the notion, discussed by Shaftesbury, that religious enthusiasm was infectious. It was a disease of the individual but also, potentially, of the body politic, endangering church and society.[32]

A second *ad hominem* reason for scepticism about the French Prophets amongst their contemporaries was the make-up of the group. Ironically, perhaps, the gentlemanly status of some of the group's most prominent adherents, far from giving the group status, made its beliefs and activities all the more surprising, even discredited. It was shocking to men of like status and intellect that gentlemen should be involved in such a form of religious 'enthusiasm'; it was thought that women were far more prone to such excessive religiosity.[33] Interestingly, given that the involvement of *women* in such groups usually gives rise to acerbic comment, accusations of a lack of respectability and even scandal (one might think of the Montanists in the early Church or the Quakers in the seventeenth century), the activities of female French Prophets caused much less comment. Indeed, the French Prophets provide us with a rare example of a woman who prophesied and healed miraculously: Sarah Wiltshire, a former Quaker. She was active in the group towards the end of its time in London (which may be another reason why she was little discussed). Richard Roach, an Anglican clergyman and Philadelphian,[34] described her as one who 'speaks in the Person of God; but without Agitation; and has Answers given directly from the Lord upon occasions'. In January 1710/11, it was claimed that she cured a clergyman's daughter, Mary Heath, who had been in Bedlam in 'a deep, sullen melancholy' and had lost the use of her legs.[35] Her own account of this was remarkably sober, and the healing presented as extremely discreet, with others in the room not fully aware of what she was doing. She said a short prayer for healing; the group sang a hymn; Wiltshire felt Mary Heath's legs, which were hard; after about a quarter of an hour, she felt 'an unusuall warmth in my right hand which caused a throbbing like the motion of a Puls' and then she heard 'a soft still voice pronounce these words, Do thou touch, and I will heal'. Wiltshire related that she put her hand on the hardest part of the leg, and,

I lift up my heart to God and said, Lord let thy Power be manifest, be it unto her according to thy holy word and the Answer of the Spirit was be unto her according to my word. I keep my hand on some time; wch Mrs Laughton took notice of, telling me at that instant she had known miracles perform'd by the Healing operation. But I gave her no answer, nor did not mention any thing of what I had secretly manifested on this occasion felt. I had an opportunity with Mr Roach and in private I related the whole matter to him. A Day or two after I heard she could walk across the Room without a cane or other Assistance.[36]

This healing was not published or broadcast around. Whether this was because a woman performed it, or because it came towards the end of the French Prophets' time of popularity in London, or because it did not have the flamboyance of other 'miracles' claimed by the group, or for some other reason, is not known. The private circumstances of the cure and lack of 'neutral' eyewitnesses may have made it less than credible to outsiders. But in its form and content it bears a closer resemblance to the cures quietly effected by the Baptists, discussed in chapter 2, than the emotional, exuberant miracles of the male French Prophets. If more of the French Prophets' miracle claims had been of this sort, they may well have aroused much less hostility.

Then there were the three objections, relevant to evidentialist issues, which cast doubt on the evidence for the miracle itself. First, the circumstances of the French Prophets' miracles were not ideal, in terms of the conditions for an impartial investigation: the cures often took place in people's homes, and therefore in a private space. This was a problem for Protestants whose piety often occurred in the domestic sphere. The Protestants had always criticised Roman Catholic 'pretended miracles' because, they claimed, they were performed in private (Greatrakes was quick to compare his public, open healings by touch, with Roman Catholic miracles, 'which they pretend to do in cells'[37]). It is no surprise therefore that the Anglican priest and political writer, Richard Kingston wrote of the French Prophets, 'They are as expert in the Art of Shifting, Doubling and Equivocating as any Society of Jesuits in Christendom.' But there was a particular Protestant spin to their privacy, said Kingston: their own private inspiration: 'Ask them why they work their Miracles in private, and they will tell you, because they have no Authority from the Spirit to perform them publickly.'[38]

Secondly, the witnesses were partial, usually being followers of the French Prophets themselves. Some of the people who were cured were not followers, but became so after they experienced healing, and therefore became 'tainted' as witnesses. Although Sir Richard Bulkeley considered himself a 'believable' witness, being a baronet and a gentleman of independent means, he had dependencies in other ways. He claimed to have had numerous afflictions (headaches, recurring fevers, kidney stones, a hernia, rheumatism) cured after being blessed by the prophets, and he interpreted his healing as a sign of their spiritual powers. He gave a long account of his healings, and John Lacy gave a shorter one, stating that Bulkeley had been cured 'by the merciful Hand of God, without means, soon after a Promise thereof made him thro my mouth, under the Operation of the Spirit'.[39] This meant he was seen as a less reliable witness. The deist Peter Annet made exactly this point in criticism of the French Prophets many years later, echoing Shaftesbury's concerns: 'Mr Lacy, one of the French Prophets, published a Book in London, entitled *A Cry from the Desart,* in which is an Account of a Famous Miracle, done by Mr Clary at Cannes near Sevignan, in France, August 1703, and by them said to be attested by a Thousand; which I do not know was ever contradicted though nobody but themselves believed it, if themselves did.'[40] Critics of the French Prophets, at the time they were active in London, jumped on this point. Kingston discounted some of Lacy's claims of miracles because 'there were no other Witnesses than themselves . . . and they were necessitated to engage the Learned Pen of Sir Richard Bulkeley, to put it into the best Dress that so foul and gross an Imposture would admit of'.[41]

But the third and most spectacular 'evidentialist' reason for the widespread scepticism about the French Prophets generally, and their miraculous gifts in particular, was their failed prophecy, proven false in the case of the resurrection of Dr Emes. Thomas Emes was a medical practitioner who joined the French Prophets in 1706. As Emes was dying in late 1707, Lacy predicted that Emes would be raised from the dead; when Emes did not come to life again after his death (despite his corpse being kept in the bed for some time[42]) he was buried at Bunhill Fields in London on 25 December. A week after Emes' burial, the Prophet John Potter set a specific date for the resurrection, 25 May 1708, saying in the voice of the Spirit, 'By the same Power that I have raised Jesus, will I raise that Body now asleep, More fat, and more fair, than ever he has been.'[43] This prediction, along with another prediction for 25 March, that the city of London would see fire and brimstone falling down on its buildings, and the various missions of the French Prophets to Enfield, Colchester and Ipswich where the 'inspired' prophesied to Quaker and Baptist meetings, meant that the group was much talked about in early 1708. Of course, any claim to raise someone from the dead caused gossip, controversy, idle curiosity and chatter: it had been the same with the Quaker James Nayler, when he had made such claims some sixty years earlier. In the case of the French Prophets, it was a particular turning point in their reputation: as these spectacular miracles were not realised, they and their followers were mercilessly lampooned and ridiculed in numerous pamphlets. Of course, they

had an answer: that the world was not prepared for such a miracle, and therefore it could not happen; or, as the Holy Spirit reportedly put it into the
mouth of one of the inspired: 'you had had a greater Manifestation of my
Work, but your Unbelief hinder'd. . . . I call for more Sanctity than is now
amongst you'.[44] *The Flying Post* reported that on 25 May great crowds flocked
to Emes' grave in Bunhill Fields, 'to see whether the pretended Prophets
would come to raise Dr Emmes from the dead, according to their predictions,
but none of them thought fit to appear, so that 'tis hoped there's an end of that
unaccountable Infatuation which has made so much noise of late, since they
themselves own'd before, that this would be decisive whether it was real
Inspiration or a Delusion they were under'.[45] But, as Schwartz reports, on 26
May, with no resurrection, the French Prophets and their followers were unre-
pentant and, far from there being 'an end of that unaccountable Infatuation',
their numbers continued to increase as their reputation suffered.[46]

All of this meant that the Latitudinarians, who wished to carve out a
reasonable path forward, did not wish to associate themselves with the French
Prophets, even though they shared some of the same concerns. Both Lacy and
Bulkeley were keen supporters of the societies for the reformation of manners;
several on the side of the orthodox were genuinely interested in prophecy; and
the French Prophets, just like the orthodox, characterised this as an age of
unbelief. But none of those on the orthodox side of the debate on miracles
wished to be thought in any sympathy with the French Prophets: Schwartz
records that Edward Fowler and his wife were listed as followers by them, but
he does not record the reaction of this bishop and his wife – which was probably either embarrassment or horror. George Hickes, a high Anglican and
non-Juror, summed up the difficulty of all on the orthodox side of the debate
when he noted that the spirit of delusion in the French Prophets meant that
no possible fresh revelations could now be taken seriously, for the prophets'
'Pretensions to the Holy Spirit, and his miraculous Gifts, have given occasion
to those common Enemies of Revealed Religion, the Atheists, Deists, and
Sceptics, to blaspheme God.'[47] Shaftesbury summed up the dilemma for the
orthodox in his essay 'The Moralists' when, in a dialogue on miracles in that
essay, one speaker maintains that 'the giving up of miracles for the time
present would be of great advantage to the atheists' and his companion immediately questions this, asking 'whether the allowing them might not be of as
great advantage to the enthusiasts and sectaries against the national church,
this of the two being the greatest danger both to religion and the state'.[48] In
the first part of the eighteenth century, the majority of the orthodox came to
agree with the opinions of the second speaker. In short, the French Prophets,
arriving as they did just when the sceptical assault on orthodox Christianity
was warming up, had dealt the deists and sceptics a winning card.

III. The Deists' Objections

The deists took advantage of the reputation of the French Prophets and used criticisms of the modern prophets' miracle claims to mount a broader attack on evidentialist arguments supporting both contemporary miracle claims and biblical miracles. They did this in several ways, four of which are discussed here. First of all, they proposed that past testimony in favour of past miracles does not have as much evidential weight as present testimony in favour of present miracles. Shaftesbury, for example, wrote that, 'The attestation of men dead and gone in behalf of miracles past and at an end can never surely be of equal force with miracles present'.[49] Obviously what was at stake here was not so much present miracles, but past miracles, namely, biblical miracles. The French Prophets' miracles had been so discredited that the argument that their miracles were more believable, on evidentialist grounds, than the biblical miracles, was clearly ridiculous. The deists therefore used this idea to suggest that if evidence in favour of current-day miracles is not credible, then biblical evidence for past miracles cannot be credible either. By discrediting the biblical miracles they were unpicking not only the doctrine of the cessation of miracles but any belief in miracles whatsoever.

Secondly, it was proposed that one person's testimony that there were many first-hand witnesses to a miracle could not augment the evidential weight first-hand unless testimonies from those witnesses themselves also existed. Again, deists used the French Prophets' miracle claims to attack biblical miracles, attacking the evidence for the New Testament miracles by attacking the evidence for the miracles of the French Prophets. Thomas Chubb was a candle-maker from Salisbury who, about 1711, became interested in religious controversy after reading the historical preface to William Whiston's *Primitive Christianity Revived* of 1710, and became increasingly sceptical over the next three decades. In his *Discourse on Miracles* of 1741, Chubb discussed the case of 'Brother Clary', one of the French Prophets in France who, in August 1703, 'stood upon a pile of wood, when set on fire, and remaining upon it till it was consumed, without receiving any harm thereby'.[50] This story was the one cited by Shaftesbury and Peter Annet, as we have seen. In that sense the story took on its own *textual* life, being used and re-used, told and re-told, for various purposes. Chubb used the French Prophet John Cavalier's[51] own account of the events, in which the Spirit commanded 'a fire to be immediately made. And I say to thee, my child [Clary] I will that thou put thyself into the midst of the flames, and they shall have no power to hurt thee.' The troops surrounding the large audience that had gathered, the immediate group involved, along with Clary's wife and her father and two sisters, all witnessed the event, reported Cavalier: 'Every one in the assembly might see him stand surrounded with flames, that rose much above his head.' Cavalier reported that 'I was one of the first who embraced our precious brother Clary; I took notice of his clothes and hair, which the flames so much respected also, that no mark could be discerned of fire on them.'[52]

Chubb took this 'miracle or fact, which is said to have taken place in our own times' and stressed that it 'was declared and attested by John Cavalier of Sauve, on January 31, 1706, at London' and published in Lacy's book *A Cry from the Desert*, which was, Chubb noted, subtitled, *Testimonials of the Miraculous Things lately come to pass in the Sevennes, verified upon Oath, and by other Proofs*.[53] He further noted: 'This fact, or miracle, was performed before a great number of witnesses, by computation not less than one thousand.' These witnesses had suffered for their faith, had 'great piety', were 'persons of reputed honesty and integrity' and 'could not possibly have any worldly advantages in view to dispose them to engage in, or to countenance a fraud, as the government they lived under was very much against them, and greatly opposed that new dispensation they were believers in'. This 'fact or miracle took place, or at least is said to have taken place in our own times, and in our neighbourhood . . . and before a great number of witnesses who were well qualified to discern and judge of its reality'. All of this emphasis on attestation and testimonial, oaths and proofs, was deliberate on Chubb's part because he was about to take the rug out from under it. The difficulty was that, although the claimed miracle was seen 'by a multitude of spectators', the story 'rests wholly on the authority of Mr Cavalier's testimony', a 'single testimony', because none of those spectators gave accounts of what they had seen.[54]

Chubb translates this problem back onto the New Testament. Simply put, the (presumably many) witnesses to the miracles in the New Testament *had not given their own accounts* of what they had seen or heard. The testimony of the gospel writer was not enough, just as the single testimony of John Cavalier was not enough. There had to be other reliable testimonies. It was Chubb's contention that in order to 'try' the witnesses of any fact or miracle, three things were needed: 'first, the testimonies of those witnesses; secondly, their ability to know the truth of what they testified; and thirdly, whether there be sufficient ground for presuming that they would, or did testify the truth of what they knew.' And it was the first that was the most significant: in any court of law, 'the words of the witnesses themselves' and 'not the words of an artful commentator' would be required. Thus he concludes,

If Simon, and Andrew, and Philip, are to be considered as witnesses of the resurrection of Christ, and if these witnesses are to be tried, then upon such trial, the testimony of Simon must be produced in the words of Simon himself, and the testimony of Andrew in the words of Andrew himself, and the testimony of Philip in the words of Philip himself, and not in the words of another. . . . It is quite ridiculous to pretend to try a witness, without producing the testimony of that witness; seeing a witness without a testimony is like a body without a soul, that is dead and useless.[55]

Chubb and Annet brought forward a third philosophical (if controversial) principle: testimony in favour of miracles (past and present) is not as credible as testimony in favour of ordinary (past or present) events. Do 'miracles stand upon as good a foot of credibility as any other facts of which our publick histories are composed?', Chubb asked;[56] or in Annet's words, are miracles 'as capable of the same Evidence as other historical facts'?[57] Annet's answer to this question was a resounding no. The orthodox Christian, believing in the experimental method and the reliability of evidence would say, 'Miracles are as capable of the same evidence, and have equal Right to be believed upon human credible Testimony, with any other historical Facts'. In opposition, the deist maintains that 'Testimony cannot be credible which relates Incredible Things; therefore the Relaters of such have not an equal Right to be believed, as those that relate any other historical Facts.' This proposition was partly grounded in a fear of deception. Human beings are not good enough judges, by our senses, to distinguish deception. Annet gave the following hypothetical example:

Suppose for instance that a Miracle-monger and dexterous Juggler both perform alike Things to Appearance, though the one be real, and the other delusory, while the Evidence of the Facts seems to be equal on both sides, who but those that are skilled in the one, or the other, can distinguish the one from the other? How many juggling Tricks of heathen and popish priests are recorded in History for miracles?[58]

Chubb and Annet were anticipating a fourth argument: Hume's claim that natural regularities constitute a decisive evidential presumption against miracles. In his 1748 text 'Of Miracles', at the end of the whole philosophical debate on miracles,[59] Hume swept in and attacked head-on the very notion of using eyewitness testimony to establish the credibility of miracles. While the deists had shown that the evidence for contemporary miracles (which were generally dismissed by the evidentialist apologists) was weak, and therefore, using the same criteria, for biblical miracles it was even weaker, Hume proposed that the quality of the evidence did not matter because no evidence was ever good enough in the case of miracles because, by his definition, a miracle was a violation against nature: 'A miracle may be accurately defined, a transgression of a law of nature by a particular volition of the Deity, or by the interposition of some invisible agent.' Armed with this definition, which made any miracle impossible, Hume targeted the appeal to testimony by the apologists. In the first part of his essay, he argued against miracles from probability – which had been the underpinning of the approach of Boyle, Sprat and those who came after them in steering a middle way between 'enthusiast' and 'atheist'. He wrote, 'that no testimony is sufficient to establish a miracle, unless the testimony be of a kind that its falsehood would be more miraculous than the fact which it endeavours to establish.'[60] In the second part of his essay, he went on to look at three examples of well-attested post-biblical miracles where the evidence fulfilled all the criteria of the evidentialists: the healings performed by the Emperor Vespasian, recounted by Tacitus; a story told by Cardinal de Retz of the doorkeeper at Saragossa cathedral, whose missing limb was regenerated when he rubbed holy oil into it; and finally, the stories at the tomb of the Jansenist Abbé Paris in France, in the early part of the eighteenth century. He wrote, 'Many of the miracles were immediately proved upon the spot, before judges of unquestioned integrity, attested by witnesses of credit and distinction, in a learned age.' Hume's point was that one could have as much good evidence and as many reliable witnesses as possible, but 'no testimony for any kind of miracle has ever amounted to a probability, much less to a proof'.[61] The problem for Hume was that a miracle broke the established laws of nature and the evidence for the laws of nature would always be greater than the evidence for a miracle; 'therefore we may establish it as a maxim, that no human testimony can have such force as to prove a miracle, and make it a just foundation for any such system of religion'.[62] This is a point to which we shall return.

These writers were not just attacking evidentialism and the attempt to carve a middle way where miracles could be regarded as plausible and even sometimes probable, they were also attacking biblical miracles generally, and therefore the idea that Christianity could be founded on a supernatural foundation, a notion that the Protestant doctrine of the cessation of miracles had necessarily maintained. Biblical miracles were therefore explained in natural terms by the deists. John Toland, for example, wrote in *Tetradymus*, 'that several transactions generally understood to be miraculous, were in reality very natural'. Focusing on the Old Testament, which he described as 'very hyperbolical', he asserted: 'Everything therefore that's hyperbolical is not strait to be counted supernatural, not what's onely magnificent to be admir'd as miraculous.'[63] In 'Hodegus', the first of the dissertations in *Tetradymus*, Toland discusses the pillar of light that guided the Israelites in the wilderness, so often considered 'the most durable of miracles' and explains it as a beacon described in literary terms.

The definitive attack on biblical miracles came from Thomas Woolston, a scholar of the early church, an ordained cleric and Fellow of Sidney Sussex

College, Cambridge, who wrote six *Discourses* between 1727 and 1729, questioning the gospel accounts of Jesus' miracles, and providing natural and figurative explanations for them. Woolston's aim, as he spelt it out at the beginning of his first *Discourse*, was to 'prove that the literal story of many of Jesus's Miracles, as they are recorded in the Evangelists and commonly believed by Christians, does imply Improbabilities, and Incredibilities and the grossest Absurdities, very dishonourable to the name of Christ; consequently, they were never wrought, but are only related as Prophetical and Parabolical Narratives of what would be Mysteriously and more Wonderfully done by him'.[64] For example, in the first discourse, he analysed three of Jesus' miracles: the singlehanded clearing out of the temple; the casting of the spirits into the herd of pigs; and the Transfiguration. His study of Jesus' casting out the devils from the madman, and permitting the devils to enter the swine, has all the hallmarks of his approach. He questioned the credibility of the story, asking, for example, whether there could even have been any swine when 'the Jews are forbidden to eat swines flesh'; he asked whether Jesus would have even done this sort of miracle – 'where was the Goodness and Justice,' he asked, 'in permitting devils to enter a herd of swine to their destruction?'[65] And, finally, he provided his own mystical or figurative reading of the miracle, by introducing the patristic writers: in this case, he turned to St Hilary, and understood the madman to stand for mankind 'under the Rule of Diabolical sins' at Christ's coming while Jesus' exorcism was taken to stand for the conversion of those former sinners to the faith.[66] Origen was another favourite of Woolston, to whom he often appealed, not least because of his figurative exegesis of the biblical texts.

It might be that Woolston's argument that miracle stories are allegories was only designed to counter the arguments of those who believed that biblical miracles were evidence of the truth of Christianity. But it might also be that Woolston wished to use his argument to 'save' the Bible while maintaining that no literal interpretation of the biblical miracles is possible and no testimony is sufficient to establish a miracle. Certainly, the reception of Woolston's work was, in his own day, and has since been, mixed. His enemies declared he was not a Christian and this point was debated by the many who responded to his work. Thomas Ray, in his tract on Woolston, writing in the dedicatory preface to the Bishop of London who had accused Woolston of being an infidel, wrote that 'I really don't well know what to take Mr Woolston for if not for an Unbeliever of the Scriptures.'[67] Woolston's sarcastic style added to this reputation, even though it is possible to read his work as mystical at heart. He appealed time and again to the fathers in order to give an allegorical and mystical interpretation to events often interpreted as miraculous, such as the Transfiguration. Voltaire, visiting England, summed up the difficulties over interpreting Woolston's work, and the reception of it. Voltaire declared that 'no one ever before had gone such lengths of rashness and scandal' in their treatment of the miracles of Jesus Christ. He added that Woolston 'solves all this, however, under favour of a mystical sense, saying, that these miracles are pious allegories. All good Christians do not the less hold his works in detestation.' Voltaire also reported an incident that indicates how despised Woolston was, and Woolston's calm response to the event: 'One day, that a woman, heated with devout zeal, met him in the street, she spit in his face; he wiped it off very coolly, and said, *It is thus that the Jews treated your God.*'[68] Over a century later, Leslie Stephen described Woolston's treatment of the biblical miracles thus: 'Through six straggling discourses, Woolston attempts to make fun of the miracles. There are, at intervals, queer gleams of distorted sense, and even of literary power, in this midst of his buffoonery.'[69] By contrast, James Herrick describes Woolston as 'between 1720 and 1729, . . . the single most troublesome enemy of the Church of England'.[70] Certainly, the six *Discourses* were relentless in their treatment of the New Testament miracles, and the result was that they sold in the thousands. Voltaire noted that 'there were three successive copies of it, of ten thousand copies each.'[71] It was read widely, and many copies were sent to the American colonies. Ultimately, the *Discourses* led to Woolston being found guilty of blasphemy before the jury of the King's Bench. He died in poverty, unable to pay his fine.[72]

IV. The Apologists' Response

How, then did the Christian apologists respond to all of this? If *ad hominem* and evidentialist considerations discredited present and recent miracles, such as those of the French Prophets, then the apologists needed to show that biblical miracles were different with respect to the features criticised in the French Prophet cases: they needed to refute the idea that past testimony in favour of past miracles does not have as much evidential weight as present testimony in favour of present miracles and to show that as mainline believers they were more reasonable than the 'enthusiasts'. This strategy meant that they had to join with the deists in discrediting the French Prophets' miracle claims with both *ad hominem* arguments against the miracle-workers and against the eyewitnesses, and in using evidentialist criteria. So, in some sense, they conceded that their opponents had the right criteria but they also had to argue that biblical miracles held up under those criteria. This was a tricky (even ironic) strategy but it was perhaps the only way forward because the apologists needed to present a convincing case in favour of the New Testament miracles, especially those of Jesus, 'for a Confirmation of a particular Doctrine or Message from Heaven', as the Huguenot refugee Abraham Le Moine put it in his 1747 *Treatise on Miracles*, a response to Thomas Chubb's work of 1741.[73] In particular, the miracles of Jesus were regarded as vital confirmation of his divinity, and thus an important intellectual weapon in the apologists' defence against the Socinian threat.

Edward Fowler was one of the first of the apologists to address the problem of the French Prophets, in a reply to Shaftesbury's *Letter Concerning Enthusiasm*, in which he himself had been ridiculed. Both Shaftesbury and Fowler were writing while the French Prophets were still active in London, and were a 'live' issue. Fowler's concern was to distinguish between the false prophecies and miracles of the French Prophets and the true prophecies and miracles of the biblical texts. He did this by pointing to the *form* of the modern prophets' activities:

> In the reading of Mr Marion's Prophecies &c. I always thought there was something little and mean, and far below the Majesty of the spirit of Prophecy, such as contain'd in Holy Writ. . . . I do firmly believe, that there never was, nor ever will be any Vain Signs, or False Inspirations; but that, in a little time, there will appear sufficient Symptoms, and abundant Characteristicks, whereby to discern them from the true, or such as are really Divine.[74]

Later apologists, responding especially to Chubb's and Woolston's work, had to go one step further than this and demonstrate the weakness of the French Prophets' *claims* and *evidence*. Le Moine directly addressed Chubb's use of the story of the French Prophet Clary surviving the fire into which he walked in 1703, by dismissing it as 'one of the most stupid Things that ever was published'. Le Moine also needed to make it clear that he was not siding with the sceptics themselves, in his critique of the French Prophets; he therefore criticised Chubb for relating the story in such a way as 'to shew that it has all the Circumstances required in a true Miracle'. Chubb's mistake, Le Moine maintained, was to assume that 'a Believer and credulous enthusiastic Person is much the same', for Chubb had asked: 'Who is there that thinks he has proper and sufficient Ground to justify his giving Credit to this Fact, supposing it has, or should come within his Notice? . . . Or can shew sufficient Reason why he should not?' Le Moine therefore set out to 'shew . . . that nothing is more easy, even at this Distance of Time and Place, than to satisfy one's-self of the Falsity of this Pretended Miracle'. Le Moine did this in an entirely evidentialist way, first of all quizzing all aspects of the original story, picking holes in the details so that the whole might fall apart. For example, if 'Clary had put himself on top of the pile of wood, straight up right, with his

Hands joined and lifted above his head', how could he have set fire to himself as was claimed?

Secondly, Le Moine attacked the character of the original author of the story, John Lacy, whose account Chubb had used; quite simply, Lacy was not a credible writer, being:

> a very weak Man, addicted to Enthusiasm, as appears by the Character he bore in the World, by his joining with the French prophets when they came over to England, and indeed by his very Book; for whoever will take the trouble to read it, will discover throughout such a Credulity and visionary Turn of Mind, as is utterly inconsistent with a sound Judgement, the chief Qualification of a good historian.

Thirdly, he attacked the eyewitness whose account of events Lacy had used, John Cavalier: 'a cousin of Colonel Cavalier, the Leader of the Cevennois . . . but when he joined their Troop, he had so bad a Name, the Name of an idle, debauched, pilfering young Fellow, that his own cousin was at first against admitting him; and afterwards he behaved so ill amongst them, that he was several Times publicly reprimanded, and at last ignominiously expelled'. Furthermore, after joining the French Prophets in London, Cavalier went to Paris 'where he turned Papist'.

Fourthly, Le Moine – being of French descent himself and therefore with a good network of contacts amongst the French refugee population of London – found himself a more reliable witness, a Mr Mairargues, 'a Gentleman of an unexceptionable Character, who lives at Hoxton near Moorfields, and will, if required, make his Affidavit, having given me leave to acquaint the Public with the same'. Mairargues testified that the soldiers used to light fires to keep themselves warm at night, and 'once Clary, in order to persuade his Countrymen that he was truly inspired, said he would stand on a Pile of Wood set on fire, till it was consumed, without receiving any Hurt; but that, instead of putting himself upon it, he only jump'd over it, or run swiftly round it'. All of this was ratified by other documents from eyewitnesses that Le Moine managed to acquire, including a letter that he had received in 1741 from the Revd David Durand, the Huguenot Minister of the united French chapels in Soho and St Martin's Lane in London, who had been chaplain of a regiment of Camisards in France. Le Moine employed the experimental approach as it had emerged and developed in the second half of the seventeenth century: reliable accounts and reliable witnesses were at the heart of this method. He replaced the unreliable evidence taken unthinkingly from the French Prophets by the sceptics, and replaced it with reliable evidence, according to the methods tested and tried by his late seventeenth-century precursors; thus he ended by asking the 'impartial Reader' to 'judge whether Mr Chubb has acted the Part of a fair Inquirer after the truth'.[75]

This evidentialist approach was seen by many of the apologists as the best line of defence, even though it was constantly attacked by the sceptics (the most devastating of these attacks came from Hume). The result was, if anything, a more hardened evidentialist line, in which probability – so favoured by the late seventeenth-century natural philosophers – became less significant. As we have seen in chapter 4, the experimental method of the natural philosophers and the legal approach to evidence were related. What seems to have happened in the eighteenth-century debate was that, as the apologists took a more starkly evidentialist stance, less and less room was left for probable judgments, and thus the experimental method of the seventeenth-century natural philosophers gave way to a more hard-edged legalistic approach. This was apparent in the Bishop of Bangor, Thomas Sherlock's 1729 response to Woolston's critique of the biblical miracles, *Tryal of the Witnesses*, in which he took a legal approach to the evidence for the biblical miracles. In the rhetorical opening of his text he described a scene in which, soon after the trial of Woolston for blasphemy, he was in conversation with some gentlemen of the inns of court when one of the more orthodox conversation partners asked one who approved of Woolston's discourses against the miracles of Christ and thought Woolston's arguments unanswerable: 'I wonder that one of your abilities, and bred to the profession of the law, which teaches us to consider the nature of evidence, and its proper weight, can be of that opinion: I am sure you would be unwilling to determine a property of five shillings upon such evidence, as you now think material enough to overthrow the miracles of Christ.'[76] Sherlock's argument was then laid out in the style of a trial with the cross-examination of witnesses (the Apostles making especially reliable witnesses) and the gathering of historical evidence in support of the biblical miracles, focusing on the resurrection of Jesus.

Sherlock's text was influential on the orthodox side, and went through many editions. His approach took the mystery out of the biblical miracles and looked for clear and certain evidence in their favour so that they could be used as physical proofs of Jesus' claims about himself. The influence of this work can be seen in numerous subsequent apologetic texts, such as George Wade's *Two Discourses* of 1729; that miracles were being discussed amongst a range of people is indicated by the fact that Wade, Vicar of Gainsborough, originally delivered the discourses to his parishioners (though of course we do not know if the parishioners ever discussed their vicar's words). The strongly evidentialist method of Sherlock, Wade and others relied on refuting the sceptics' claims about the details of the story, either by asserting there was historical evidence in favour of the miracles or by questioning whether the sceptical opponents, such as Woolston, had any evidence for their own non-miraculous explanations of the biblical miracles. For example, in the long-running debate about the resurrection of Jesus, the sceptics claimed that the guards had fallen asleep at the tomb, so the disciples had been able to come along and steal the body. Wade responded by describing this claim as 'the ridiculous Story of the Sleeping Watch, the merest Dream, the most idle and inconsistent tale, that ever was invented' and for which there was no evidence or authority.[77]

Much was made of the reliability of the disciples as witnesses (as it was in Sherlock's work); precisely because they were Jesus' disciples, their accounts were deemed trustworthy. Wade wrote of the historical evidence in favour of the resurrection of Jesus that it was 'founded on the Testimony of such witnesses, whose Honesty, and Knowledge in the affair, cannot reasonably be doubted of'. Furthermore, the (male) disciples were not overly eager to believe; they were not, for Wade, first-century enthusiasts. When the women told them the story of the empty tomb, the angel and the appearance of Christ himself, 'they wanted farther and better Evidence of so marvellous a thing'; this they received that very day when 'Christ himself takes care to give it them by personally appearing' on the road to Emmaus. When Thomas would not believe in the resurrection of Jesus without 'such and such Evidence' then 'the blessed Jesus condescends to him' and asked Thomas to 'reach his finger, and examine his hands; and reach his hand, and thrust it into his side, and not be faithless, but believing'. Wade comments, 'Could the most squeamish Infidel in the World make a doubt of this? Thomas, it is plain, with all his Scepticism, could not.'[78] Herrick writes of Wade that he made Jesus an evidentialist just as the deists made Jesus a rationalist, and this comment sums up the style of this particular apologetic approach.[79]

The anonymous author of *An Answer to the Jewish Rabbi's Two Letters Against Christ's Resurrection*, responding to Woolston, made many of the same arguments, poking holes in the sceptics' case against the resurrection of Jesus by asking questions – such as, how many guards were by Jesus' tomb? – to which there were no certain answers but which threw doubt on his opponents' argument. He also appealed to the disciples as reliable witnesses: 'educated by Jesus to a Life of Piety, and in all the Precepts of Virtue and Morality', they were the first-century equivalent of the eighteenth-century believable gentleman. This author also attacked head-on the possibility of any parallel between the resurrection of Jesus and the episode, earlier in the century amongst the French Prophets, of Dr Emes's supposed resurrection. He argued that the sceptics had got their facts wrong – 'Dr Aymes himself did not pretend to predict anything of his being to rise again'. The author discredited those who had made the claim, calling them 'idle imposters' and made clear that any witnesses were unreliable, being nothing 'above the Rank of the Mob'. He also noted that the expectation of Emes' resurrection fizzled out in the darkness, whereas 'our Saviour's Ascension . . . was done at Noon-Day, in the Face of the Sun, and before Five hundred Witnesses'.[80]

The old Protestant doctrine of the cessation of miracles was attacked by the French Prophets – who obviously believed that miracles were still happening – and by the deists and sceptics who argued that there could never be reliable evidence that any miracles had ever occurred or could occur in the present. But some late seventeenth- and early eighteenth-century apologists who wished to avoid belief in current-day miracles continued to appeal to the idea that miracles had ceased after biblical times. Several of the early Boyle lecturers argued this. John Williams, Bishop of Chichester, said in his 1694/5 Boyle Lectures that, 'There is no need of any Farther Revelation' and that 'we cannot suppose that God will work Miracles, and break through the standing Laws of Nature, when there is no Occasion for it, nor Necessity to require it'.[81] Offspring Blackall, Bishop of Exeter, in his Boyle Lectures, argued that new miracles were not necessary because the miracles of the past, the biblical miracles, should be enough to convince people towards belief. Furthermore, he warned that too many miracles could even be counterproductive.[82] But after the attacks on the biblical miracles by Woolston in the late 1720s, it was difficult for apologists to appeal so simply to the biblical miracles as 'true'. The doctrine of cessation had become a problematic line of argument. The majority of eighteenth-century apologists, adherents of biblical miracles, found themselves having to reject both of these lines of argument and thus most came to rely on weaker evidentialist principles.

There were a few who took a different position. William Law, in *The Case of Reason* (1731), coming from a more mystical position, thought that to approach miracles as problems in evidence was be too thoroughly rationalist. Writing in response to the deist Matthew Tindal's *Christianity as Old as Creation*, Law believed that there was a gap between God's reason and human reason; the deists' notion of universal human reason was impossible. The miracles should not, then, be seen as instances of evidence in the overall case for God (which he regarded as a dangerous approach) but rather as part of God's revelation, vital for human beings' moral and theological guidance. At the heart of his argument was the mystical notion that God is ultimately mysterious to human beings, for our minds cannot grasp the workings of God's mind. Law's approach was not widely taken up; furthermore, it was satirised by Henry Dodwell in his *Christianity Not Founded on Argument* (1741), though a number of apologists rushed to respond to Dodwell.[83]

Joseph Butler, then Rector of Stanhope (later Bishop of Bristol, and at the end of his life, Bishop of Durham) in his *Analogy of Religion* (1731) presented an important apologia for the use of probability in assessing miracle claims. Proof was not decisive, he argued. A high degree of probability 'will amount even to moral certainty'. Within this remit, 'nothing can destroy the evidence of Testimony in any Case, but a Proof or Probability, that Persons are not competent Judges of the Facts to which they give Testimony'. This led Butler to suggest: 'Upon the whole: As there is large historical Evidence, both direct and circumstantial, of Miracles wrought in Attestation of Christianity, collected by those who have writ upon the Subject; it lies upon Unbelievers to shew, why this Evidence is not to be credited.'[84] While the deists and sceptics had confronted the believer in miracles with a crushing burden of proof, Butler blithely shifted the burden back onto the opponents of miracles: the burden of proof was on the unbeliever to show why the evidence in favour of miracles was discredited.

However, the sceptics' use of current-day miracles to discredit the evidence for the biblical miracles, and the activities of the French Prophets themselves, meant that many apologists found it difficult to make the case for the *probable* evidence for current or recent miracles without looking foolish. Arthur Ashley Sykes, Rector of Rayleigh in Essex, a man who entered into many of the controversies of the day, looked back to Valentine Greatrakes in his work on miracles. Despite the testimonies of the great and the good, Sykes could not quite bring himself to say that Greatrakes' cures were miraculous:

> There was, not very many years ago in England, a Man very famous for the strange Cures by him perform'd; and every fact comes to us so well attested by the Best, and Ablest, and most Judicious men then in this kingdom, that their Truth cannot be doubted: I mean such men as Bishop Wilkins, Dr Cudworth, Dr Patrick, Dr Whichcot, Dean Rust, Dr Evans, Mr Boyle, and a great many more, who have attested the Truth of Mr Greatrak's Cures. . . . But yet, I am inclined to believe that Mr Greatrak's stroking, which produced such extraordinary Effects, was not properly miraculous.[85]

In fact, Sykes did not want to dismiss the idea of probability in assessing miracles; he simply noted that, 'miracles in general are unlikely or improbable'. Therefore, doubt should be exercised before belief, though he did not want to reject the biblical miracles. However, in defending his belief in Jesus' miracles, the stumbling block was, in the wake of the sceptics' attacks, the question of why anyone should believe those miracles any more than the claims of the French Prophets. Writing in 1742, Sykes was still trying to answer the following question:

Whether there be any material circumstance attending the Miracles done by the Founder of the Christian Religion and his First Disciples which may make them more to be regarded than those done by the French Prophets, or by the Abbé Paris, or any other who pretend to work Miracles, and which may determine any honest man to believe the one to have been done, at the same time that he is justifiable in disbelieving, or in not being at all solicitous about the other.

This question had been rumbling on for nearly half a century, and still the apologists found it hard to answer. Sykes' criteria for believing only in the biblical miracles cannot have been convincing to his opponents, relying as they did on intra-biblical evidence of a prophetic spirit amongst the miracle-workers, and the fulfilment of prophecies which occur 'in the sacred scriptures'.[86] By linking prophecy to miracles, and arguing that the former gave credibility to the latter, Sykes had to assume that the context and authority of the biblical text carried more weight than any current-day contexts or evidence. The fact was, that by the mid-century point, the deists had questioned biblical authority, and the apologists could only defensively reassert it.[87]

V. Did God Work Miracles?

At the heart of the whole debate was a further question: did God work miracles? There were two refinements of the question. First, *would* God violate the laws of nature? And secondly, *could* God violate the laws of nature? And if people were to discuss these questions, they had to define what a miracle was. William Fleetwood, at the time chaplain to the king (later Bishop of Ely), published *An Essay Upon Miracles* in 1702, in part responding to Toland's *Christianity Not Mysterious*. He defined a miracle as 'an extraordinary operation of God, against the known course, and settled Laws of Nature, appealing to the senses'. This was quite consistent with seventeenth-century definitions of a miracle. The quotation from a sermon preached by one Samuel Barton in 1696, which Moses Pitt had included on the title page of his pamphlet about Ann Jeffries and the fairies maintained that God could and did violate the laws of nature: 'Sometimes for wise and good Reasons God has been pleased quite to alter the course of Nature, as it were, to shew himself to have a Power above it.' But how, Fleetwood asked, does one recognise the 'known course' and therefore how can one perceive the exceptions? The answer, for Fleetwood, was to appeal to the experimental method; you will know the settled laws of nature 'by your experience, observation, and by the Use of your Senses, concurring with the experience, observations of other People'. The purpose is to know 'the operations that are constant, certain, and expected, . . .

those we call the ordinary ones. And that is the known course of Nature, which is the common and the usual one, with which we are all well acquainted, and which causes no wonder in us, and those are the settled laws'. Recognising those settled laws, by the same methods of experience, observation and the use of your senses, one will know when something is a miracle. This was simply the employment of the experimental method. It was exactly what Boyle and the other seventeenth-century virtuosi had thought: once men knew and understood all the laws of nature, they would be able to know clearly whether something was a miracle or not. What was radical about Fleetwood's argument was his assertion that, 'None but God, and those commissioned by him, can work true miracles.' Thus he dismissed earlier ideas that 'false' miracles might be worked by demonic powers. This argument, that only God could work miracles, was related to Fleetwood's definition of a miracle: 'No power less than that of God, can unsettle the establish'd Course of Nature, which no Power less than his could settle and establish.' Fleetwood's idea that only God could work miracles was challenged,[88] but the notion that because God created the laws of nature he *could* break them was a cornerstone in the arguments of many of the apologists.

In response, the deists and sceptics claimed that God simply would not or could not alter or break the rules of nature. To suppose that God *would* not violate the laws of nature was to make an argument from divine character and purpose: that God is of consistent purpose, God thinks through what kind of world he wants to begin with, and then opts for the natural laws he wants. To suppose that God *could* not violate the laws of nature was to develop Spinoza's argument, that it was metaphysically impossible for those laws to be contravened. The deist Matthew Tindal, in his *Christianity as old as the creation* (1730), took the first line, arguing for the impossibility of miracles from the nature of God. God is 'a kind and beneficent being' and thus 'the Divine Precepts can't vary'; they are 'the permanent Voice of God'. This points Christians towards their duty: to love God because he is a consistent God. By contrast, 'tis not in our Power, though ever so often commanded, to love the Deity, while we conceive him an arbitrary Being acting out of Humour and Caprice'.[89] Writing in the next decade, the deist Peter Annet, in his *Supernaturals examined* (1747) took the second line of argument, that God could not violate the laws of nature: 'To suppose that God can alter the settled Laws of Nature, which himself formed, is to suppose his Will and Wisdom mutable; and that they are not the best laws of the most perfect Being; for if he is the Author of them, they must be as immutable as he is; for he cannot alter them to make them better, and will not alter them to make them worse.' Miracles were *a priori* impossible. In order to say this, Annet had to make sure his definition of a miracle was entirely about the contravening of the laws of nature. He argued, 'Nature has no Power to act Contrary to her invariable Rules of Action.' Furthermore, 'Miracles must be by a supernatural power, or they cannot be at all.' And finally, 'to change the course of Nature is inconsistent with the Attributes of God.' Indeed, for Annet and other deists, the very notion of God changing the laws of nature was paradoxical, and indeed inimical to the nature of God.[90]

Interestingly, by the time Annet was writing, it was the deists and other sceptics who were especially insisting on this very fixed definition of a miracle as breaking the laws of nature. They defined a miracle in terms of the reversal or breaking or suspension of the laws of nature. Annet's list of sample miracles illustrates the point:

> The raising the Dead to Life; the constant Motion of the Sun or Earth standing still at the Word of Command; the Sun's going back fifteen Degrees, when requested; a Sea parting, and making two Walls, of a broad Road betwixt for a nation to go through between them on dry Ground; . . . A man's living three days in the Belly of a Fish in the Sea; making Bread and Fish faster than ten thousand hungry People could eat them; . . . Such Facts are inconsistent with, and some of them plainly contrary to the general Course of Nature.[91]

Hume, in his essay 'Of Miracles' defined a miracle as 'a transgression of a law of nature by a particular volition of the Deity, or by the interposition of some invisible agent'.[92] Hume may not have said that the laws of nature could not be broken; he did, however, think it is not reasonable for us to believe a law of nature can be broken.

One reason for this insistence, amongst the deists and sceptics, on this very particular definition of a miracle was that a new position had emerged amongst the apologists, most notably the Newtonians – men like Samuel Clarke, Richard Bentley and William Whiston; they began to define miracles differently in order to try and accommodate their scientific understanding of the world. As Peter Harrison has noted, 'If the operation of gravity was, as Whiston indicated, a supernatural and miraculous occurrence in terms of the prevailing definition, then a new understanding of miracle was required, for without such a definition, gravitation, and the whole mechanical system it supported, would be deemed miraculous.'[93] Thus, this group of Newtonians revived the Augustinian notion of a miracle – as something unusual. Harrison argues that men such as Clarke and Whiston simultaneously held different understandings of the same phenomena: they had a philosophical definition that understood a 'miracle' as something distinct only in its unusualness, and they had a theological definition that understood a miracle as a violation of the laws of nature by God. Using this approach, Whiston and others such as Thomas Burnet and Nehemiah Grew argued that various events in the Bible, presumed to have resulted from miraculous interventions, were in fact in the ordinary course of nature. Nevertheless, they held in reserve the more traditional notion of a miracle as a violation of a natural law so that they could retain their position as Christian apologists believing in miracles. All of this meant that they tackled the deists' arguments against biblical miracles from a different angle. They explained many of the biblical miracles – especially those in the Old Testament – as consistent with the laws of nature, and pointed to their 'unusualness' or their timing as significant. Nevertheless, they were able to retain a traditional understanding of miracles for the big events – the creation of the world, the resurrection of Christ – upon which orthodox Christian doctrine relied for proof. This preserved the role of revelation, whilst allowing current knowledge to explain much that was apparently supernatural, over and against the deist insistence that reason was sovereign – a position which, for many apologists, left no place for God all.[94] For the Newtonians, God had to intervene from time to time in order to keep the solar system stable. The apologists and sceptics did not only disagree on the nature of God, then; they also disagreed on the immutability or mutability of the natural order. For many of the deists and sceptics, God was bound by the laws of nature, which he had created. For the apologists, God as the creator of those laws of nature was free to break them or work within them as he pleased.

CHAPTER 8

Conclusion

The deist Peter Annet wrote in 1747, 'thank God, since the French Prophets, there have been among us no Fools great enough to profess foretelling future Events'.[1] Hume's contribution to the philosophical debate on miracles, a year later in 1748, injected a note of utter scepticism into the discussion. This did not mean, of course, that miracle claims stopped. It is certainly the case that the French Prophets had both been received into and, by their extraordinary activities, contributed to a climate of increasing scepticism about miraculous phenomena; they marked a turning point in the investigation of miracle claims, and how contemporary miracle claims could be employed in theological argument. But in the world of lived religion, people were still sick and hoped for healing; extraordinary feats were still thought miraculous. In September 1748, the same year that Hume published his essay 'Of Miracles', the *Gentleman's Magazine* carried a report of a female healer, Bridget Bostock, who had come to prominence that month in Cheshire:

> There is risen up in this country a great doctress, and old woman, who is resorted by people of all ranks and degrees, to be cur'd of all diseases; . . . she has several hundred of patients in a day out of all the country round for 30 miles: I went to see her yesterday out of curiousity, and believe near 600 people were with her.[2]

She healed by stroking with fasting spittle and the prayer, 'God bless you with faith.' She was about seventy years of age, and her dress was very plain: 'she wears a flannel waistcoat, a green Lindsey apron, a pair of clogs, and a plain cap, tied with a half-penny lace'. Her minister, the Revd William Harding (curate of Coppenhall), reported that she was of good character and faith, and was 'a constant frequenter of his church'.[3] She was healing about six hundred to seven hundred people a day by early September, and later – seeking neither fame nor fortune – decided that she would only see those she had treated before. 'She cures the blind, the deaf, the lame of all sorts. The rheumatic, king's evil, hysteric fits, falling fits, shortness of breath, dropsy, palsy, leprosy, cancers, and, in short, almost everything except the French disease, which she will not meddle with.' Nor did she simply attract the poor and credulous, as the deists would have suspected. It was reported: 'so many people of fashion come to her, that several of the poor country people make a comfortable subsistence by holding their horses. In short, the poor, the rich, the lame, the bind, and the deaf, all pray for her, and bless her; but the doctors curse her.'[4] She was even asked by one man, Sir Richard Price, of Buckland, Brecon, if she would raise his wife from the dead. With a wisdom possessed by neither James Nayler nor John Lacy, she declined to try. John Bennett, who was a Methodist minister, visited her twice and recorded in his diary his impressions and the reports of others, ultimately declaring himself unable to account for her cures.[5]

Reactions to her were mixed. While for one reporter, 'the country are gone stark mad', a correspondent to the *Gentleman's Magazine* noted that Mrs Bostock, like Christ, required a great degree of faith in her patients, and therefore suggested that 'perhaps, the chief reason why instantaneous cures are not so frequently performed as formerly, is, because we have not faith to be healed'. A hostile article was published in the *General Evening Post* on 18 October (and reproduced in the *Gentleman's Magazine*), in which the writer said firmly: 'I can assure you 'tis an imposition, and downright falsehood; and though most in the neighbourhood may be willing to abet the cheat, for the sake of the advantages they receive from such numbers continually flocking thither, yet many of them are so honest as to confess the truth, and own they believe her to have no just claim to any extraordinary healing power.'[6] His opinions were based on a visit to Bridget Bostock, with a friend. At this stage, at the end of the philosophical debate on miracles, when those trying to steer a middle way (and treat miracles as plausible) had been so roundly attacked, no one from the Royal Society made the trek to Cheshire to witness Bostock's healing, to investigate whether it was miraculous or natural. Or at least if they did, they did not write a letter into the Society about it.

It is tempting to see the mid-century point providing evidence of an increasing split between 'elite' and 'popular' culture – or at least of a split between intellectual debate and lived religion. At about the same time that there were continued reports and comments about Bostock in the *Gentleman's Magazine*, in 1749,[7] there were also discussions of (and excerpts from) Conyers Middleton's *A Free Enquiry into the miraculous powers, which are supposed to have subsisted in the Christian Church*, which had made a critique of the miracles of the early church, and thereby attacked the doctrine of the cessation of miracles. The work had made quite a splash. Bridget Bostock had attracted hundreds of visitors and had become well known. But no connections were made between the two. Nevertheless, interest in Bostock continued into the next century, as evidenced by some articles in the *Monthly Magazine* in 1808.[8]

Certainly the deists had made their own contribution to the cultivation of an elite/popular split, at least at an intellectual level, in the preceding decades. By claiming to demystify Christianity by taking it down to its barest essentials, refuting Jesus' miracle stories and concentrating on his ethical message, the deists were, in effect, trying to create a 'natural religion'. They were also being thoroughly elitist. Their critique of miracles – and indeed, their critique of all that they considered 'superstition' and 'enthusiasm' – were based on their idea of the credulity of the masses. John Toland wrote in his *Pantheisticon* (1720): 'We shall be in safety if we separate ourselves from the Multitudes; for the Multitude is a Proof of what is worst.'[9] As Frank Manuel puts it, the deists believed that 'there were two religions in every society, one for the men of reason, and one for the fanatics, one for those who comprehended the marvellous order of the world and one for those who relied on gods for every event, the ignorant men full of terrors which they allayed with ludicrous rituals.'[10] The French Prophets had seemed to fulfil exactly what they thought about the religion of fanatics, and they used the examples of their miracle claims to attack both the doctrine of the cessation of miracles and the apologists' evidentialist line of argument. In this sense, they relied on the French Prophets – though they would have hated to think of it like that – just as the members of the Royal Society and the Latitudinarians had relied on miracle claims to make their point in the preceding decade. Steven Connor, in his history of ventriloquism, puts it like this: 'If the manifestations associated with these religious movements were in one sense the unacknowledged object of the debates about magic, miracle and reason, they were in another sense a participant in those debates.'[11]

The broader culture added an attitude of spoof and lampooning to the intellectual scepticism of the deists. When Mary Toft claimed she could give birth to rabbits in 1726, she was seriously examined by doctors who – on the whole – thought that her claims were true: it was only when a lawyer threatened her with a nasty examination that she confessed to the hoax. The popular press, meanwhile, had a field day. The wide discussion of such a case, and of other wondrous or strange events throughout the eighteenth century, such as the mysterious disappearance of Elizabeth Canning in 1753 for a month and her survival (she claimed) on half a jug of water and a loaf of bread during that time, or the Cock Lane ghost episode, so thoroughly investigated by Dr Johnson in 1762 (who believed in the apparent ghost but was discredited when it turned out to be a hoax),[12] illustrates the ways in which the boundary between the ordinary and the extraordinary, the natural and the supernatural, was a constant talking point. There was even a national memory of such episodes, each one remembered as a new case arose. This is illustrated by William Hogarth's print 'Credulity, Superstition and Fanaticism' (1762), which visually documents the claims from the seventeenth and eighteenth centuries of the extraordinary, miraculous and supernatural that had been unmasked as impostures, and by numerous satires such as the following 'Ghost Catechism', which appeared in *The Universal Magazine*: 'I believe in signs, omens, tokens, dreams, visions, spirits, Ghosts, spectres and apparitions. And in Mary Toft, who conceived and was brought-to-bed of a couple of rabbits. And in Elizabeth Canning, who lived a whole month, without performing the usual offices of nature, on six crusts of dry bread and half a jug of water . . . And in all the miracles of the Holy Roman Church.'[13] Despite such a spoof as this, it is significant that few people gave these cases *religious* interpretations. William Whiston stands out: he gave Mary Toft a millenarian spin, when he maintained that Toft's rabbit births portended the apocalypse, fulfilling the prophecy of Esdras.[14]

The essential point about mid-eighteenth-century Britain is that a range of ideas and opinions on the miraculous and the wondrous, the ordinary and the extraordinary, existed. The series of slight earthquakes in London in 1750, and the seriously devastating Lisbon earthquake of 1755, which led to widespread fear about God's wrath amongst all sorts of people, demonstrated that ideas about providence were alive and well.[15] The first shock in London on 8 February 1750 caused little stir, but after the second on 8 March, people began to get nervous, and Thomas Sherlock, by now Bishop of London, published a letter to his clergy and people on 17 March, claiming that the recent shocks were a divine warning for Londoners to examine their shortcomings. He especially criticised the constant craving for entertainment that he saw in the capital city.[16] Some ridiculed his letter, but it sold in great numbers and was reprinted several times. Many preachers expounded on the earthquake from the pulpit. The timing of the two shocks, exactly four weeks apart, led a man named Mitchell (a lifeguard) to prophesy that a third was to be expected on the evening of Wednesday 4 April or the morning of Thursday 5 April. Clergymen spoke out against the prophecy, but Londoners were worried and left town. The ever-observant and ever-scoffing Horace Walpole wrote to Horace Mann, 'This frantic fear prevails so much that within these three days seven hundred and thirty coaches have been counted passing Hyde Park.'[17] The shocks of 1750 in London were sobering enough to Britons that when they heard the news of the severe damage caused by the Lisbon earthquake of 1755, there was again widespread preaching on the topic and much moralising. A solemn fast day was held in February 1756, and a masquerade, advertised to take place at the Haymarket Theatre in late January, was cancelled by the king at the request of the Bishop of London and Archbishop of Canterbury.[18]

These responses to the earthquake were cast in terms of a theology of providence, rather than of the miraculous, and J. C. D. Clark argues that while 'publications on miracles were much less frequent after the 1750s; works on Providence continued in full flood'.[19] This is largely true of the intellectual arena; the eighteenth-century philosophical debate on miracles carried on into the next few decades, but only sporadically and slowly. Nevertheless, other forces were at work at the mid-century point, which continued into the latter part of the century and which would see the continuation of miracle claims, and the examination of them. There were singular cases, such as that of Bridget Bostock, but more significantly for the wider culture, there was the rise of Methodism and John Wesley's clear belief in miraculous healings as well as providence, visions, witchcraft, ghosts and the spiritual significance of dreams. He catalogued all such events in his Journal. Henry Rack has calculated that Wesley recorded over sixty such incidents in his Journal from 1739 to 1742, and about ten a year in the 1750s.[20] And yet, for Wesley to believe in such incidents, the testimony of credible witnesses was required. Wesley was, as Rack has put it, a 'reasonable enthusiast: rational in form but enthusiast in substance'.[21] In a letter to Thomas Church in June 1746, Wesley wrote:

And I acknowledge that I have seen with my eyes and hear with my ears several things, which, to the best of my judgment, cannot be accounted for by the ordinary course of natural causes, and which I therefore believe ought to be ascribed to the extraordinary interposition of God. If any man choose to study these miracles, I reclaim not. I have diligently inquired into the facts. I have weighed the preceding and following circumstances. I have strove to account for them in a natural way. I could not without doing violence to my own reason. . . . I must observe that the truth of these facts is supposed by the same kind of proof as that of all other facts is wont to be – namely, the testimony of competent witnesses; and that the testimony here is in as high a degree as any reasonable man can desire. Those witnesses were many in number: they could not be deceived themselves; for the facts in question they saw with their own eyes and heard with their own ears, nor is it credible that so many of them would combine together with a view of deceiving others.[22]

Despite the deist attack on testimony and the credibility of witnesses, Wesley still adhered to an important strand of the Enlightenment tradition in negotiating the potential division between reason and revelation: the investigation of miraculous and supernatural phenomena along the lines of the experimental method.

Perhaps the main conclusion to be drawn from all of this is not so much that there was a distinct elite–popular split, but rather that a range of views on and attitudes towards the miraculous – and all the related questions that had been thrown up by the debates about miracles – co-existed by the middle of the eighteenth century. Susan Juster in her work on prophets in the late eighteenth century has argued that the Age of Reason was oxymoronic: it was a time when prophets tried to make sense of religious beliefs and experiences in the light of rational philosophy.[23] The same might well be said of miracles and those who tried to make sense of them. Through a wide range of religious practices and experiences, the responses to them, and the writings of philosophers and theologians, the Enlightenment opened up a series of questions about experience, reason, the miraculous and the nature of God, which were not resolved in the eighteenth century. Both intellectual debate and lived religion led to a questioning of the category of experience, for example – the French Prophets through their activities, the deists and Hume in their argument that experience and testimony were unreliable. Hume himself, by the very nature of his sceptical argument, suggested that these matters might not be resolved.

The Enlightenment can, then, be described as a watershed with regard to these questions. But the Enlightenment did not provide closure; it did not solve the problem of how the relationship between reason and revelation might be negotiated. It did, however, set the terms for how people thought about that problem in the future. This book has explored three streams of thought and practice within Protestantism, with regard to miracles: first, the doctrine of the cessation of miracles; secondly, the miracle claims that occurred within various Protestant groups and churches, and the responses to them; and thirdly, the attempt to negotiate a middle way between an excessive rationalism or a too-ready 'enthusiasm', by using the experimental method to investigate the evidence for contemporary miracle claims, and appealing to probability rather than certainty. While all three of these 'streams' were attacked and challenged by the deists and sceptics in the philosophical debate of the first half of the eighteenth century, all three remained key ingredients in the lively debates about miracles which ensued in the nineteenth century, as theologians and philosophers returned to those seventeenth- and eighteenth-century themes and arguments and reworked them, and new generations of Christians claimed that they too had experienced miracles.

John Henry Newman, for example, when a young man, believed in a limited age of miracles. He later revised his views, arguing for the important role of probability in assessing modern miracles. He saw this as a way of rescuing the biblical miracles. In his *Essay on Ecclesiastical Miracles* (1843), he drew on Joseph Butler's *Analogy of Religion* (which by the 1830s was in the Oxford curriculum) to suggest that the believer had to assess the evidence for both the biblical and ecclesiastical (post-biblical) miracles in order to decide the probability of their occurrence. Crucially, Newman, first as a high Anglican, and then (after his conversion) as a Roman Catholic, revised his ideas when engaging with the lives of the saints, and their miraculous feats, in the compilation of *Lives of the English Saints*.[24] In this sense, religious practices – albeit the practices of others – influenced ideas. The wider culture repeated this pattern. For Protestants, there were plenty of contemporary claims of miracles, new revelations and manifestations of the supernatural. From the wealth of new religious groups in the nineteenth century – Spiritualism, Theosophy, Christian Science, the Irvingites – many of them heterodox in their beliefs and appealing to a wide range of people, there emerged a wide range of such claims. Furthermore, science was brought in to 'test' them, just as it was in the case of Valentine Greatrakes two centuries before. The Society for Psychical Research, founded in 1882 in the wake of the great popularity of parlour seances, promised to examine paranormal phenomena in a scientific and unbiased way; for many people this was the promise of real evidence of God's intervention in the world, if there was any to be had. In the end, people argued, it would not be intellectual debate that would settle the question but evidence.

Over the hundred-year period covered by this book, attitudes to miracles changed, though not always in the direction we might expect: that is to say, there was not a steady and inevitable progress towards a more sceptical approach. This is, in part, because the motors of change were not only intellectual. The political upheaval of the mid-seventeenth century was, for example, the context in which independent churches and radicals began to claim divine healing and miracles. The political context of the Restoration meant that Charles II had a great deal at stake in touching for the King's Evil, in defining his own kingship. The perceived need to create a godly nation, in the aftermath of the 1688 revolution, led church and court alike to take the case of Marie Maillard seriously, and harness it to a larger movement for the reformation of manners. But even the intellectual shifts that occurred in this period, most especially the growth of experimental philosophy, do not lead us to conclusions that – retrospectively – many historians have assumed in the past. Rather, the experimental philosophers wanted to try and know enough about the natural world so that they could, with enough evidence, assess what was mystery or miracle, and what was not.

While there prevailed in mid-eighteenth-century England a sceptical and scoffing tone, this was not universal, nor did it necessarily point in a teleological way towards ever-increasing scepticism. It is important to remember the sociologist David Martin's argument that 'instead of regarding secularization as a once-for-all unilateral process, one might think rather in terms of successive Christianizations, followed or accompanied by recoils'.[25] There was no easy resolution of the question of miracles. Intellectuals continued to debate the question in the terms set in the second half of the seventeenth century, and developed in the first half of the eighteenth century. Moreover, individuals and groups still sought, and believed they received, evidence of God's existence, God's activity in the world and God's love for them in the working of miracles. As long as that occurred, the debate could not be closed: in that sense, lived religion would always affect the ideas of intellectuals.

Notes

Chapter 1 Miracles, Protestantism and the Enlightenment: An Introduction

1. Thomas Sprat, *The history of the Royal-Society of London for the improving of natural knowledge* (London, 1667), p. 362.
2. See, for example, *God's Great and Wonderful Work in Somersetshire: Or, The Charitable Farmer Miraculously Rewarded* (London, 1674); *The Wonderful Recompense of Faith: Or, Strange News from Dursly in Gloucestershire* (London, 1675).
3. See, for example, J. Paul Hunter, *Before Novels: The Cultural Contexts of Eighteenth-Century English Fiction* (New York: W. W. Norton & Company, 1990) who argues that wonder literature 'held sway over the popular imagination in England from the last quarter of the seventeenth century until the novel emerged as a cultural force.' p. 209. On the rise of cheap print and its relationship to religious practice in the period preceding this, see Tessa Watt, *Cheap Print and Popular Piety, 1550–1640* (Cambridge: Cambridge University Press, 1991) and Ian Green, *Print and Protestantism in Early Modern England* (Oxford: Oxford University Press, 2000).
4. For other examples of this approach, see Anne-Marie Korte, ed., *Women and Miracle Stories: A Multidisciplinary Exploration* (Leiden: Brill, 2001).
5. On the emergence of the public sphere in post-Restoration England, see Jürgen Habermas, *The Structural Transformation of the Public Sphere* (trans. Thomas Burger) (Cambridge, MA: MIT Press, 1989) (translated from *Strukturwandel der Öffentlichkeit*, 1962). Habermas's notion of the public sphere has been much debated by historians. For late seventeenth-century England, the literature is considerable; Brian Cowan provides a useful, recent survey of that literature in his: 'What was Masculine about the Public Sphere? Gender and the Coffeehouse Milieu in Post-Restoration England,' *History Workshop Journal*, 51 (2001), pp. 127–57. It has been noted that Habermas did not tease out the implications of the public sphere for religion; see David Zaret, 'Religion, Science and Printing in the Public Spheres in Seventeenth-Century England', in Craig Calhoun, ed., *Habermas and the Public Sphere* (Cambridge, MA: MIT Press, 1992), pp. 212–35.
6. Brian Cowan, *The Social Life of Coffee: The Emergence of the British Coffeehouse* (New Haven and London: Yale University Press, 2005), p. 91.
7. Cowan, *The Social Life of Coffee*, p. 91.
8. See Adrian Johns, *The Nature of the Book: Print and Knowledge in the Making* (Chicago and London: University of Chicago Press, 1998), pp. 553–60, and Cowan, *The Social Life of Coffee*, chapter 4.
9. Joseph Glanvill, *A Blow at Modern Sadducism* (London, 1668), p. 106.

10. On Molyneux and Toland, see Cowan, *The Social Life of Coffee*, pp. 111–12.

11. On the link between printers and coffeehouses, see Johns, *The Nature of the Book*, pp. 111–13; on the showing of curiosities in coffeehouses, see Cowan, *The Social Life of Coffee*, chapter 5.

12. See Cowan, 'What was Masculine about the Public Sphere?'

13. See, for example, Bernard Capp, 'Separate Domains? Women and Authority in Early Modern England' in *The Experience of Authority in Early Modern England*, eds Paul Griffiths, Adam Fox and Steve Hindle (London: Longman, 1996), especially pp. 127–30.

14. Robert Shoemaker, 'Gendered Spaces: Patterns of Mobility and Perceptions of London's Geography, 1660–1750' in *Imagining Early Modern London: Perceptions and Portrayals of the City from Stow to Strype, 1598–1720*, ed. J. F. Merritt (Cambridge: Cambridge University Press, 2001), pp. 144–65.

15. Adam Fox, *Oral and Literate Culture in England 1500–1700* (Oxford: Clarendon Press, 2000), p. 400.

16. Alexandra Walsham has shown how earlier print genres were appropriated for a providentialist literature which combined didactic moral messages with narrative entertainment. See her *Providence in Early Modern England* (Oxford: Oxford University Press, 1999).

17. Green, *Print and Protestantism in Early Modern England*, p. 502.

18. Tony Claydon, 'The sermon, the "public sphere" and the political culture of late seventeenth-century England' in *The English Sermon Revised: Religion, Literature and History 1600–1750*, eds Lori Ann Ferrell and Peter McCullough (Manchester: Manchester University Press, 2000), pp. 208–34.

19. Quoted in Claydon, 'The sermon, the "public sphere" and the political culture of late seventeenth-century England', p. 208.

20. Johns, *The Nature of the Book*, p. 446; see chapter 7 for the establishment of that 'accreditation' of experiences through print.

21. J. Paul Hunter writes, 'We can now say with confidence what intuition and nineteenth-century social history only guessed: that literacy in the English-speaking world grew rapidly between 1600 and 1800 so that by the latter date a vast majority of adult males could read and write, whereas two centuries earlier only a select minority could do so', *Before Novels*, p. 65. See also David Cressy, *Literacy and the Social Order: Reading and Writing in Tudor and Stuart England* (Cambridge: Cambridge University Press, 1980).

22. See Green, *Print and Protestantism in Early Modern England*, pp. 24–7, and Fox, *Oral and Literate Culture in England 1500–1700*, especially pp. 46–50.

23. See, for example, Peter Burke, *Popular Culture in Early Modern Europe* (New York: New York University Press, 1978); the concluding chapter of Keith Thomas, *Religion and the Decline of Magic: Studies in Popular Beliefs in Sixteenth- and Seventeenth-Century England* (Harmondsworth: Penguin, 1971); and Owen Chadwick, *The Secularization of the European Mind in the Nineteenth Century* (1975) (Cambridge: Cambridge University Press, 1990); Chadwick writes: 'Enlightenment was of the few. Secularization is of the many' (p. 9). Evidence for the religious practices and beliefs of 'the people' in this period has often been drawn from the work of nineteenth-century folklorists, such as Andrew Lang, and anthropologists, such as Edward Burnett Tylor, who worked with an evolutionary model of society, collecting what they described as 'the legends, customs, beliefs of the Folk, of the people, of the classes which have been least altered by education, which have shared least in progress'. Lang, 'The Method of Folklore' in his *Custom and Myth* (London: Longmans, Green and Co., 1884), p. 11.

24. See especially David D. Hall, ed. *Lived Religion in America: Towards a History of Practice* (Princeton, NJ: Princeton University Press, 1997); see also Robert A. Orsi, *The Madonna of 115th Street* (New Haven and London: Yale University Press, 1985);

Robert A. Orsi, ed. *Gods of the City: Religion and the American Urban Landscape* (Bloomington: Indiana University Press, 1999); Colleen McDannell, ed. *Religions of the United States in Practice*, Volumes I and II (Princeton, NJ: Princeton University Press, 2001).

25. M. J. Ingram, 'From Reformation to Toleration: Popular Religious Cultures in England 1540–1690', in *Popular Culture in England c.1500–1850* ed. Tim Harris, (Basingstoke: Macmillan, 1995), pp. 95–123.

26. In recent years, historians have begun to look at how a wider cast of characters might have been agents in the Enlightenment, and in some areas (such as the French Revolution) this has been especially fruitful. For a good example of this, see Carla Hesse, *The Other Enlightenment: How French Women Became Modern* (Princeton, NJ and Oxford: Princeton University Press, 2001). For a general text that takes this approach, see Thomas Munck, *A Comparative Social History 1721–1794* (London: Arnold, 2000). S. J. Barnett, in his recent book on the Enlightenment and religion (looking at England, France and Italy), calls for historians to 'broaden Enlightenment studies out from the few canonical texts which have traditionally formed its core' and criticises the fact that 'in Enlightenment studies, research into interaction between the elite and the "lowbrow" still remains marginal'; but he largely fails to redress this himself. He takes the political and social context of elite texts into account, but does not broaden his canvas to look at how the 'lowbrow' thought about theology, or to incorporate an analysis of religious practices. S. J. Barnett, *The Enlightenment and Religion: The Myths of Moderntiy* (Manchester: Manchester University Press, 2003), pp. 218, 64.

27. Peter Brown points to the dangers of taking at face value elite descriptions of who was associated with what practices and beliefs; in his book on the fourth-century cult of the saints he looks at the ways in which the eighteenth-century two-tiered system of polite/vulgar or elite/popular, as applied to religion in the work of David Hume for example, affected the historiography of the early church from Edward Gibbon onwards. In re-evaluating the fourth-century evidence apart from those suppositions, Brown demonstrates that historians mistakenly assumed that the cult of the saints was a 'popular' practice. Peter Brown, *The Cult of the Saints: Its Rise and Function in Latin Christianity* (Chicago: University of Chicago Press, 1981), especially pp. 18–20.

28. Henry More, *Enthusiasmus Triumphatus, or, a Brief Discourse of the Nature, Causes, Kinds and Cure of Enthusiasm*, ed. M. V. Porte (2nd edn, 1662, facsimile) (Los Angeles: University of California Press, 1966), p. 2. These ideas have been reproduced in the secondary literature. R. A. Knox treated 'enthusiasm' as an error that has blighted all of Christian history; see his *Enthusiasm: a chapter in religious history with special reference to the XVII and XVIII Centuries* (Oxford: Clarendon Press, 1950). More nuanced historical discussions of the problem and the use of the term in this period can be found in D. W. Dockrill, 'Spiritual Knowledge and the Problem of Enthusiasm in Seventeenth-Century England', *The Concept of Spirit, Prudentia* (Auckland: University of Auckland, 1985) and Michael Heyd, *'Be Sober and Reasonable': The Critique of Enthusiasm in the Seventeenth and Early Eighteenth Centuries* (Leiden: E. J. Brill, 1995).

29. David Hume, 'Of Superstition and Enthusiasm' (1741) in *Essays Moral, Political and Literary*, ed. Eugene F. Miller (Indianapolis, IN: Liberty Classics, 1987), p. 78.

30. Paul Langford, *A Polite and Commercial People: England 1727–1783* (Oxford: Clarendon Press, 1989), p. 282.

31. Jan Albers writes, 'Religious stereotyping was one of the rhetorical foundations of Georgian discourse, and the popular shorthand of the street. It can be found every-where – in government documents, newspapers, sermons, letters, diaries, novels.' See her '"Papist Traitors" and "Presbyterian Rogues": Religious Identities in Eighteenth-Century Lancashire' in *The Church of England c. 1689–c. 1833: From Toleration to*

Tractarianism, eds John Walsh, Colin Haydon and Stephen Taylor (Cambridge: Cambridge University Press, 1993), p. 317.

32. Rob Iliffe argues that 'the way in which the new philosophy was pursued in seventeenth-century England was in some measure a response to a number of earlier fears about ubiquitous sources of error, imposture and delusion'. See Rob Iliffe, 'Lying Wonders and Juggling Tricks: Religion, Nature and Imposture in Early Modern England' in *Everything Connects: In Conference with Richard H. Popkin, Essays in his Honour*, eds James E. Force and David S. Katz (Leiden: Brill, 1999), p. 189.

33. There are, of course, numerous histories of these intellectual developments. See especially Charles Webster, *The Great Instauration: Science, Medicine and Reform 1626–1660* (London: Duckworth, 1975), and Michael Hunter, *Science and Society in Restoration England* (Cambridge: Cambridge University Press, 1981).

34. Michael Hunter, *The Royal Society and its Fellows 1660–1700* (Chalfont St Giles: The British Society for the History of Science, monograph 4, 1982), p. 12.

35. Paul Hazard, *The European Mind: The Critical Years, 1680–1715* (1935), translated from the French, *La crise de la conscience européenne, 1690–1715* by J. Lewis May (Cleveland and New York: Meridian Books, The World Publishing Company, 1964), p. xvii.

36. My thinking about the relationship between philosophy and the experience of lived religion has been shaped by Marilyn McCord Adams's book, *Horrendous Evils and the Goodness of God* (Ithaca, NY: Cornell University Press, 1999); Adams addresses the relationship as a philosopher who wishes to take the *particular* experiences of horrendous evil seriously in her analysis.

37. R. M. Burns, *The Great Debate on Miracles from Joseph Glanvill to David Hume* (Lewisburg: Bucknell University Press, 1981), p. 12.

38. Burns, *The Great Debate on Miracles*, p. 11.

39. Burns, *The Great Debate on Miracles*, p. 13.

40. Historians' use of the term 'Enlightenment' has been questioned in recent years. J. C. D. Clark, in a recent article, writes: 'It is taken as axiomatic in this article that 'the Enlightenment' is a polemical term devised in the nineteenth century to place interpretations on what happened in the eighteenth: the term did not therefore correspond to any clearly-demarcated eighteenth-century phenomena, and could be made to mean whatever its nineteenth- and twentieth-century users wished. Its use here attends to, without endorsing, the meanings conventionally ascribed to the term in recent discourse.' J. C. D. Clark, 'Providence, Predestination and Progress: Or, Did the Enlightenment Fail?', *Albion*, 35: 4 (Winter 2003), p. 559.

41. See, for example, Peter Gay, *The Enlightenment, an Interpretation: The Rise of Modern Paganism* (1966) (New York: Vintage Books, 1968).

42. Roy Porter, *Enlightenment: Britain and the Creation of the Modern World* (London: Allen Lane, 2000), p. xvii.

43. See, especially, Roy Porter and M. Teich, eds, *The Enlightenment in National Context* (Cambridge: Cambridge University Press, 1981).

44. J. G. A. Pocock, *Barbarism and Religion* Volumes 1 and II (Cambridge: Cambridge University Press, 1999); see also B. W. Young, *Religion and Enlightenment in Eighteenth-Century England: Theological Debate from Locke to Burke* (Oxford: Oxford University Press, 1998).

45. See Peter Harrison, *'Religion' and the Religions in the English Enlightenment* (Cambridge: Cambridge University Press, 1990), and J. A. I. Champion, *The Pillars of Priestcraft Shaken: The Church of England and its Enemies 1660–1730* (Cambridge: Cambridge University Press, 1992).

46. Both evangelical and Anglo-Catholic historians of the nineteenth century wished to show their own reforms in the best light, as significant innovations in a moribund church, and therefore portrayed the eighteenth-century church in a negative light.

Agnostics – as we have seen in the case of Leslie Stephen – also brought their own agenda to bear on the intellectual history of the period.

47. J. C. D. Clark, *English Society, 1688–1832: Ideology, Social Structure and Political Practice During the Ancient Regime* (Cambridge: Cambridge University Press, 1985).

48. Norman Sykes pioneered this research in 1950s – see, for example, his *From Sheldon to Secker: Aspects of English Church History 1660–1768* (Cambridge: Cambridge University Press, 1959) – but his work had a limited impact for the next few decades, until there was a revival of interest in the eighteenth century in the 1980s. An important volume which published the first fruits of this recent wave of research was John Walsh, Colin Haydon and Stephen Taylor, eds, *The Church of England* c. *1689–*c. *1833: From Toleration to Tractarianism* (Cambridge: Cambridge University Press, 1993). Many doctoral theses and monographs have been published in this area since. For a full bibliography of this work, and an assessment of the development of the research in this field in the last ten years, see Jeremy Gregory and Jeffrey S. Chamberlain, eds, *The National Church in Local Perspective: The Church of England and the Regions, 1660–1800* (Woodbridge: Boydell Press, 2003). Review articles charting the shift in scholarship on religion in this period include: Jane Shaw, 'The Long Eighteenth Century' in *A Century of Theological and Religious Studies in Britain*, ed. Ernest Nicholson (Oxford: Oxford University Press, for the British Academy, 2003), pp. 215–36; Jonathan Sheehan, 'Enlightenment, Religion, and the Enigma of Secularisation: A Review Essay', *American Historical Review*, 108: 4 (October 2003), pp. 1061–80; Robert Sullivan, 'Rethinking Christianity in Enlightened Europe', *Eighteenth-Century Studies*, 34: 2 (Winter 2001), pp. 298–309.

49. Amos Funkenstein, *Theology and the Scientific Imagination* (Princeton, NJ: Princeton University Press, 1989). However, Funkenstein's claim that for 'many seventeenth-century thinkers, theology and science merged into one idiom, part of a veritable secular theology such as never existed before or after' (p. ix) has been criticised. For example, Charles Webster writes that Funkenstein 'makes little effort to substantiate this claim, which might be correct in a trivial sense, but at the more fundamental level . . . faces serious problems of definition . . . his assertion is falsified by evidence of the pervasive unity of religious and natural philosophical speculation in the Western intellectual tradition'. Charles Webster, Book Review, *Journal of Ecclesiastical History*, 39 (1988), p. 597.

50. Michael J. Buckley, *At the Origins of Modern Atheism* (New Haven: Yale University Press, 1990); Alan Charles Kors, *Atheism in France, 1650–1729. Volume I: The Orthodox Sources of Disbelief* (Princeton, NJ: Princeton University Press, 1990).

51. Champion, *The Pillars of Priestcraft Shaken*.

52. Jonathan Sheehan, *The Enlightenment Bible: Translation, Scholarship, Culture* (Princeton, NJ: Princeton University Press, 2005), p. 1.

53. David Martin, *On Secularization: Towards a Revised General Theory* (Aldershot, England and Burlington, VT: Ashgate, 2005), p. 3.

Chapter 2   Protestantism and Miracles

1. On medieval miracles, pilgrimages and shrines, see Benedicta Ward, *Miracles and the Medieval Mind: Theory, Record and Event 1000–1215* (London: Scolar Press, 1982) and Ronald C. Finucane, *Miracles and Pilgrims: Popular Beliefs in Medieval England* (London: J. M. Dent & Sons, 1977).

2. Ward, *Miracles and the Medieval Mind*, pp. 89 and 101.

3. Valerie Flint makes the case that the Church deliberately borrowed, harnessed and adapted for its own purposes an older tradition in which supernatural power was seen as inherent in water, other elements and particular places. See Valerie I. J. Flint, *The*

Rise of Magic in Early Medieval Europe (Oxford: Clarendon Press, 1991), especially chapter 9. Thanks to Barbara Harvey for this reference.

4. John Calvin, *Institutes of the Christian Religion*, I, trans. Ford Lewis Battles, ed. John T. McNeill (London: SCM Press, 1961), pp. 14–15, 16.

5. Calvin, *Institutes*, I, pp. 16, 17.

6. Martin Luther, 'Lectures on Genesis, Chapters 1–5' in *Luther's Works*, Volume I, trans. George V. Schick, ed. Jaroslav Pelikan (St Louis: Concordia Publishing House 1955–86), p. 140.

7. John Calvin, *Commentary on the Gospel according to St John 11–21 and the First Epistle of John*, transl. T.H.L. Parker, eds David W. Torrance and Thomas F. Torrance (London and Edinburgh: Oliver and Boyd, 1961), p. 213.

8. Martin Luther, 'Sermons on the Gospel of St John, Chapters 14–16' in *Luther's Works*, vol. 23, ed. Pelikan, pp. 74 and 75.

9. Calvin, *Institutes*, I, p. 17.

10. John Calvin, *Commentary on the Acts of the Apostles*, Volume I (1552), trans. John W. Fraser and W. J. G. McDonald, eds David W. Torrance and Thomas F. Torrance (Carlisle: The Paternoster Press and Grand Rapids, Michigan: Erdmans, 1965), pp. 63, 64.

11. For further details of the destruction of shrines and relics at the English Reformation, see Eamon Duffy, *The Stripping of the Altars: Traditional Religion in England 1400–1580* (New Haven and London: Yale University Press, 1992), especially chapter 11. See also Helen L. Parish, *Monks, Miracles and Magic: Reformation Representations of the Medieval Church* (London and New York: Routledge, 2005) and Peter Marshall, 'Forgery and Miracles in the Reign of Henry VIII', *Past and Present*, 178 (2003), pp. 39–73.

12. This was influential in Elizabeth I's reign with editions in 1581 and 1584.

13. John Hooper, 'A Brief and Clear Confession of the Christian Faith' in *Later Writings of Bishop Hooper*, ed. Charles Nevinson for The Parker Society (Cambridge: Cambridge University Press, 1852), pp. 44–5.

14. D. P. Walker, 'The Cessation of Miracles' in *Hermeticism and the Renaissance: Intellectual History and the Occult in Early Modern Europe*, eds Ingrid Merkel and Allen G. Debus (Cranberry, NJ: Associated University Presses, 1988), p. 113. Lipsius's text *Diva Virgo Hallensis* was first translated into English in 1688 but it would have been read in England before that in the original Latin (or in French or Dutch, into which it was translated earlier).

15. For a longer discussion of the development of the doctrine of the cessation of miracles in the early seventeenth century, see Walker, 'The Cessation of Miracles'.

16. Alexandra Walsham, 'Miracles and the Counter-Reformation Mission to England', *The Historical Journal*, 46: 4 (2003), p. 781.

17. See Samuel Harsnet, *A declaration of egregious popish impostures* (London: I. Roberts, 1605).

18. Thomas Stapleton, *A fortresse of the faith first planted among us Englishmen* (Antwerp, 1565).

19. D. P. Walker, *Unclean Spirits: Possession and Exorcism in France and England in the Late Sixteenth and Early Seventeenth Centuries* (London: Scolar Press, 1981).

20. In recent years, historians have shown that use of the term 'Anglican' before the Restoration period (1660) is problematic because it was anachronistic.

21. Article 72, *Constitutions and Canons Eccleasiasticall . . .* (London, 1604), sig. M4r–v.

22. See David Harley, 'Explaining Salem: Calvinist Psychology and the Diagnosis of Possession', *American Historical Review*, 101: 2 (April 1996), p. 310. For further details of John Darrell's case, see D. P. Walker, *Unclean Spirits*, especially chapters 3 and 4. For further examples of Puritan and Roman Catholic cases of exorcism in the late sixteenth and early seventeenth centuries, see Michael MacDonald, 'Religion, Social

Change and Psychological Healing in England, 1600–1800' in *The Church and Healing*, Studies in Church History, vol. 19 (Oxford: Basil Blackwell, 1982), pp. 101–29; and Thomas, *Religion and the Decline of Magic*, chapter 15.

23. Walsham, 'Miracles and the Counter-Reformation Mission to England', p. 801. See also the analysis of the Darrell case by Thomas Freeman in 'Demons, Deviance and Defiance: John Darrell and the Politics of Exorcism in Late Elizabethan England' in *Conformity and orthodoxy in the English Church, c. 1560– c. 1660*, eds Peter Lake and Michael Questier (Woodbridge: Boydell Press, 2000), pp. 34–63.

24. Walker, *Unclean Spirits*, p. 73.

25. John Jewel, *The Works of John Jewel, Bishop of Salisbury, The Third Portion*, ed. John Ayre for the Parker Society (Cambridge: Cambridge University Press, 1848) p. 197.

26. Others wrote in this vein. For example, Harsnet, *A declaration of egregious popish impostures*; John Gee, *The foot out of the snare* (London 1624); William Crashaw, *The Jesuites Gospel* (London, 1610) and Robert Tynley, *Two learned sermons* (London, 1609).

27. William Fleetwood, *An Essay upon Miracles in Two Discourses* (London, 1701).

28. For a fuller discussion of Calvin's doctrine of providence, see William J. Bouwsma, *John Calvin: A Sixteenth-Century Portrait* (Oxford and New York: Oxford University Press, 1988), chapter 10.

29. Walsham, *Providence in Early Modern England*, pp. 2–3.

30. Quoted in Henry Cadbury's 'Introduction' to his edition of *George Fox's 'Book of Miracles'* (Cambridge: Cambridge University Press, 1948), p. 18.

31. For a fuller discussion of this, see Ward, *Miracles and the Medieval Mind*, chapter 1. See also John A. Hardon, 'The Concept of Miracle from St Augustine to Modern Apologetics', *Theological Studies* 15 (1954), pp. 229–57.

32. See Alexandra Walsham, 'Reforming the Waters: Holy Wells and Healing Springs in Protestant England' in *Life and Thought in the Northern Church c.1100 – c.1700: Essays in Honour of Claire Cross*, ed. Diana Wood, Studies in Church History Subsidia, vol. 12, (Woodbridge: Boydell Press, 1999), pp. 236 and 244.

33. Brad S. Gregory, *Salvation at Stake: Christian Martyrdom in Early Modern Europe* (Cambridge, MA: Harvard University Press, 1999), p. 182. See also, Diarmaid MacCulloch, *Thomas Cranmer* (New Haven: Yale University Press, 1996), pp. 603–4. For a similar point about French Protestant martyrdom accounts, see David Nicholls, 'The Theatre of Martydom in the French Reformation', *Past and Present*, 121 (1988), pp. 49–73.

34. This is carefully documented by Thomas Freeman in 'Texts, Lies and Microfilm: Reading and Misreading Foxe's 'Book of Martyrs', *The Sixteenth Century Journal*, 30: 1 (Spring 1999), pp. 36–8. See also Thomas Freeman, '"Great searching out of bookes and authors": John Foxe as an Ecclesiastical Historian' (PhD thesis, Rutgers University, 1995), pp. 205–27 and Patrick Collinson, 'Truth, Lies and Fiction in Sixteenth-Century Protestant Historiography' in *The Historical Imagination in Early Modern Britain*, eds Donald R. Kelley and David Harris Sacks (Cambridge: Cambridge University Press, 1997), pp. 55–6.

35. Walsham, *Providence in Early Modern England*, pp. 230–2, also suggests this was the case.

36. *The Life and Death of Mr. Vavasour Powell, That Faithful Minister and Confessor of Christ* (London, 1671), p. 15.

37. The context of the civil war as the *occasion* when miracle claims were triggered, experienced and articulated will be discussed in the next chapter.

38. Thomas Edwards, *Gangraena: Or a Catalogue and Discovery of many of the Errours, Heresies, Blasphemies and pernicious Practices of the Sectaries of this time, vented and acted in England in these four last years* (London, 1646; first edition), p. 32.

39. Edwards, *Gangraena*, p. 56.

40. Edwards, *Gangraena*, p. 104.

41. For details of Knollys and Jessey, see later sections of this chapter.
42. Thomas Edwards, *The Third Part of Gangraena or, A new and higher Discovery of the Errors, Blasphemies, and insolent Proceedings of the Sectaries of these times; with some Animadversions by way of confutation upon many of the Errors and Heresies named* (London, 1646), p. 19.
43. Anthony Sparrow, *A Rationale or Practical Exposition of the Book of Common Prayer* (London: 1657), pp. 346–7. Sparrow was one of those at the Savoy Conference in 1661, who reviewed the Book of Common Prayer (and also decided to keep the Presbyterians out of the Church of England).
44. John Gilbert, *An answer to the Bishop of Condon (now of Meaux) his Exposition of the Catholick faith etc. wherein the doctrine of the Church of Rome is detected and that of the Church of England expressed, from the publick acts of both churches* (London, 1686), pp. 63–4.
45. General Baptists were the earliest Baptists, developing out of late sixteenth- and early seventeenth-century separatist groups. The Calvinist or Particular Baptists emerged as a self-conscious group in the 1640s. For details about their theological and ecclesiological differences, see B. R. White, *The English Baptists of the Seventeenth Century* (London: The Baptist Historical Society, 1983), chapters 1 and 2.
46. T. W. W. Smart, 'A Biographical Sketch of Samuel Jeake Senr. of Rye', *Sussex Archaeological Collections* 13, (1861), pp. 67–8.
47. Hanserd Knollys and William Kiffin, *The Life and Death of that old Disciple of Jesus Christ . . . Mr Hanserd Knollys . . . Written with his own Hand to the Year 1672, and continued in General, in an Epistle by Mr William Kiffin* (London, 1692), p. 32. Knollys had been imprisoned in May 1670, having been taken at a meeting in George-Yard. The Lord Mayor had committed him to the Compter in Bishopsgate, where the keepers had looked favourably on him and had allowed him to preach twice a week to the other prisoners in the common hall.
48. Knollys and Kiffin, *The Life and Death of . . . Mr Hanserd Knollys*, pp. 33, 34, 35, 36.
49. Calvin, *Institutes*, II, p. 1466.
50. Calvin, *Institutes*, II, p. 1467.
51. Thomas Grantham, *Christianismus Primitivus* (London, 1678), Book 2, pp. 38–9. This was Grantham's principal work (and contained reprints of some of his earlier works) and was designed as an exposition and defence of Baptist theology. It is therefore significant that in it he defends the possibility of miracles in his own age. Throughout his life, Grantham engaged in debates with many people (Baptists and others) on the key theological issues of the day.
52. See, for example, the essays in *Religion Medici: Medicine and Religion in Seventeenth-Century England*, eds Ole Peter Grell and Andrew Cunningham (Aldershot: Scolar Press, 1996).
53. See, for example, the career of the Presbyterian John Reynolds discussed in chapter 5 who practised medicine when he was expelled from his living in Wolverhampton at the Restoration.
54. Henry Jessey was pastor of a congregation in London from 1637 until his death in 1663. The congregation practised 'open membership' – that is, had members who had not been baptised as believers – and therefore remained rather on the fringes of the seventeenth-century London Baptist world. This is not surprising given Jessey's links to the radical, millenarian group, the Fifth Monarchists. For more details of that group, see chapter 4. See also *The Life and Death of Mr Henry Jessey* (London, 1671).
55. Henry Jessey, *The Exceeding Riches of Grace Advanced, By the Spirit of Grace, in an Empty Creature, viz. Mris. Sarah Wight* (London, 1647), p. 56.
56. Jessey, *The Exceeding Riches of Grace Advanced*, pp. A3–A4. For a discussion of some of the medical and religious aspects of Jessey's account of Wight, see Barbara Ritter

Dailey, 'The Visitation of Sarah Wight: Holy Carnival and the Revolution of the Saints in Civil War London', *Church History*, 55:4, especially pp. 445–7. For an expanded discussion on fasting women as miraculous, including Wight, see chapter 5.

57. Christopher Blackwood, *Expositions and Sermons upon the Ten First Chapters of the Gospel of Jesus Christ, According to Matthew* (London, 1659), pp. 609–10.

58. There is an alternative version of the story in Matthew 17:14–21.

59. Stevan Davies draws on recent anthropological and psychological work on spirit possession to analyse Jesus' role as exorcist in the healing miracles in the gospels. See Stevan L. Davies, *Jesus the Healer: Possession, Trance and the Origin of Christianity* (London: SCM Press, 1995).

60. Roger Hayden, ed. *The Records of a Church in Christ in Bristol, 1640–1687* (Bristol: Bristol Record Society, 1974), pp. 139–41.

61. Hayden, ed. *The Records of a Church of Christ in Bristol*, p. 142.

62. See M. F. Snape, *The Church of England in Industrialising Society: The Lancashire Parish of Whalley in the Eighteenth Century* (Woodbridge: Boydell Press, 2003) and M. F. Snape, '"The Surey Impostor": Demonic Possession and Religious Conflict in Seventeenth-Century Lancashire', *Transactions of the Lancashire and Cheshire Antiquarian Society*, 90 (1994), pp. 93–114.

63. Thomas, *Religion and the Decline of Magic*, p. 586.

64. Snape, 'The Surey Imposter', p. 112.

65. Smart, 'Biographical Sketch of Samuel Jeake Senr. of Rye,' pp. 68–9.

66. Blackwood, *Expositions and Sermons*, p. 607.

67. Smart, 'Biographical Sketch of Samuel Jeake Senr.', pp. 68–9.

68. Blackwood, *Expositions and Sermons*, p. 109.

69. Norman Glass, *The Early History of the Independent Church at Rothwell, alias Rowell in Northamptonshire* (London, 1871), p. 38. Glass was a nineteenth-century minister of Davis's old church. He summarises the charges against Davis and the events surrounding them. For the criticism of Davis, see Rehakosht, P. (pseud.), *A Plain and Just Account of a Most Horrid and Dismal Plague . . .* (London, 1692). Davis's reply is recorded in his *Truth and Innocency Vindicated* (London, 1692).

70. Glass, *Early History of the Independent Church at Rothwell*, p. 37.

71. The dispute arose from the implication that gifts were passed to the ordained person by the ritual of laying on of hands *only*. Baptists were of course opposed to the Catholic notion of apostolic succession. For some details of this controversy, see White, *The English Baptists of the Seventeenth Century*, especially pp. 42–5.

72. Charles Doe, *Narrative of the Miraculous Cure of Anne Munnings of Colchester, by Faith, Prayer, and anointing with Oil, on New Year's Day, 1705* (Totham: Charles Clark, 1848), unpaginated. E. Spurrier, the author of the history of the Colchester Baptist Church, described Charles Doe as 'a very public man in the Borough, London' who printed the narrative by leave of the 'persons immediately concerned who forbore to do it themselves, to prevent thoughts of boasting or assuming vain glory. When he printed it he said the maid had resided in London several months, and many had talked with her to their satisfaction'. Spurrier, *Memorials of the Baptist Church Worshipping in Eld Lane Chapel, Colchester* (Colchester: F. Wright, 1889), p. 15. The printed narrative contains the names of fifteen men and eight women who attested to the truth of the story. Doe was himself a Baptist and author of several other books and pamphlets, including a defence of believers' baptism, written in the 1690s. See also William Rawlins, *A true copy of a letter from a minister of a dissenting congregation at Colchester, to a friend in London: concerning the miraculous cure of the daughter of Mrs Muliner* (London, 1706).

73. Doe, *Narrative of the Miraculous Cure of Anne Munnings*.

74. Doe, *Narrative of the Miraculous Cure of Anne Munnings*.

75. It is also quite different from the story of Marie Maillard's healing, related in chapter 6, in which Maillard's private reading of the Bible and strong faith were the means to her miraculous cure.

76. Rawlings does not seem to have received any criticism for his role in Anne Munning's healing, at least none that has been recorded. He went on to become a minister of a church in London. Anne Munnings was baptised after her cure and became a member of the Baptist Church in Colchester. Spurrier, *Memorials of the Baptist Church Worshipping in Eld Lane Chapel, Colchester*, pp. 13–16.

77. Hayden, ed. *Records of a Church in Christ in Bristol, 1640–1687*, p. 141.

Chapter 3   Miracle Workers and Healers

1. Quoted in Cadbury, 'Introduction', *Book of Miracles*, p. 10.

2. *Journal of George Fox*, Volume I (Cambridge University Press, 1911) pp. 140–1. See also Cadbury, *Book of Miracles*, p. 125.

3. *Journal of George Fox*, I, p. 107. Myers appears to have died nine months later; Fox thought this was a punishment because Myers disobeyed a command of the Lord to go to York with a message. See Cadbury, ed. *Book of Miracles*, pp. 130–1.

4. *Journal of George Fox*, I, p. 45. See Cadbury, ed. *Book of Miracles*, p. 121.

5. *Journal of George Fox*, I, p. 140.

6. William C. Braithwaite, *The Beginnings of Quakerism* (London: Macmillan, 1923), p. xxvi.

7. Both Coornhert and Allen are quoted in Rufus Jones, 'Foreword', Cadbury, ed. *Book of Miracles*, p. vii. For a fuller account of the Seeker background to the Quakers, see Rufus M. Jones, *Studies in Mystical Religion* (London: Macmillan, 1909), pp. 452–66 and Christopher Hill, *The World Turned Upside Down: Radical Ideas During the English Revolution* (London: Penguin, 1972), chapters 9 and 10.

8. See Braithwaite, *Beginnings of Quakerism*, pp. 25–7 and 58–9.

9. According to Thomas Ellwood's *Journal* (1694), Jay or Gay was a planter of Barbados, a companion of Fox, probably Irish, and died in Dublin in 1674.

10. *Journal of George Fox*, II, pp. 226–7 (p. 16 of original *Book of Miracles* MS). The Bodleian *Journal* MS says that the accident occurred at Porback near Shrewsbury. An earlier version (Bristol MSS v, 37ff) omits the words 'and broke his neck as they say' near the beginning, and omits at the end 'and many hundreds of miles afterwards'. A twentieth-century surgical view of the episode is given in *Journal of Friends Historical Society*, VIV, 1917, p. 84. See Cadbury, ed. *Book of Miracles*, p. 110.

11. See Braithwaite, *Beginnings of Quakerism*, pp. 247–8.

12. John Deacon, *The Grand Impostor Examined* (London, 1656), p. 18.

13. Deacon, *The Grand Impostor Examined*, p. 39.

14. Quoted in Cadbury, 'Introduction', p. 13.

15. *A Declaration from Oxford, of Anne Greene . . . that was lately . . . hanged . . . but since recovered* (London: T. Clowes, 1651), pp. 1, 4.

16. R. Watkins, *Newes from the Dead. Or a True and Exact Narration of the Miraculous Deliverance of Anne Greene, who being executed at Oxford afterwards revived* (Oxford, 1651), p. 1.

17. See William Petty, *The Petty Papers: some unpublished writings of Sir William Petty*, ed. H. W. E. P. F. Landsdowne (London, Constable, 1927), pp. 157–8. For a description of the case, see Laura Gowing, 'Greene, Anne (c.1628–1659)', in *Oxford Dictionary of National Biography*, eds H. C. G. Matthew and Brian Harrison (Oxford: Oxford University Press, 2004), hereafter *DNB*, http://www.oxforddnb.com/view/article/11413.

18. *The Diary of John Evelyn*, ed. E. S. De Beer (London: Oxford University Press, 1959), pp. 608–9.

19. *A Miraculous Proof of the Resurrection: Or, The Life to Come Illustrated. Being a Strange Relation of What Hapned to Mris Anna Atherton* (London, 1680) [two-page pamphlet, unpaginated]. Care had obviously been taken with the production of this pamphlet and readers were warned against 'a Cheat of This true Original Relation, from the Doctor, the maids own brother, is Ap'd and ridiculously counterfeited in a little trivial penny book; be not abused with that which invades Propriety'.

20. William Turner, *A compleat history of the most remarkable providences, both of judgement and mercy, which have hapned in this present age* (London, 1697), part 2, chapter 34, p. 34.

21. Thomas Underhill, *Hell Broke Loose: or An History of the Quakers both old and new* (London, 1660), pp. 17, 44. Underhill noted that this claim was to be found in *Truth's defence against the refined subtilty of the serpent held forth in divers answers to several queries made by men (called ministers in the North)* by George Fox and Richard Hubberthorn.

22. N. Dorcastor, *The Doctrine of the Masse Booke concerning the making of holye water, salt, breade, candels* (London, 1554), p. Aiii. Dorcastor described these material ritual objects associated with the Roman Catholic mass as 'superstitious trumpery' (p. Aii).

23. Richard Blome, *The Fanatick History, or An Exact Relation and account of the old Anabaptists and new Quakers* (London: J. Sims, 1660), p. 137. James Nayler and Richard Hubberthorn replied for the Quakers in a pamphlet, *A Short Answer to a Book called the Fanatick History: published by Richard Blome, against the Quakers* (London, 1660), that Nicholas Kate, the man mentioned by Blome was not known by the Quakers and therefore the accusation against him was none of their concern.

24. Ephraim Pagett, *Heresiographie* (London, 1654, 5th edn), p. 40. Pagett was Rector of St Edmund the King, Lombard Street, London and stood firmly in the Calvinist tradition within the Church of England. He died in 1646 and it was his bookseller who updated and oversaw the several later editions of *Heresiographie*, including the fifth edition. See S. C. Dyton, 'Pagett, Ephraim (1574–1646)', in DNB http://www.oxforddnb.com/view/article/21125.

25. Richard Baxter, *Reliquiae Baxterianae* (1696), Lib 1, part 1, p. 116.

26. Jonathan Clapham, *A Full Discovery and Confutation of the wicked and damnable doctrines of the Quakers* (London, 1656) pp. 45–6.

27. Clapham, *A Full Discovery*, pp. 46–8.

28. George Whitehead, *The Christian Progress of that ancient servant and minister of Jesus Christ, George Whitehead* (London, 1725) pp. 55–6.

29. Whitehead, *The Christian Progress*, p. 57.

30. For an account of the place of miracles in the spread of early Christianity, see Ramsay MacMullen, *Christianizing the Roman Empire: A.D. 100–400* (New Haven and London: Yale University Press, 1984).

31. Samuel Eaton, *The Quakers Confuted, being an answer to nineteen queries* (London, 1654), p. 14.

32. J. Camm, *An Answer to a Book which Samuel Eaton put up to Parliament* (London: Giles Calvert, 1654) p. 16.

33. George Fox, *The Great Misery of the Great Whore* (London, 1659), p. 3.

34. T. L. Underwood, *Primitivism, Radicalism and the Lamb's War: The Baptist–Quaker Conflict in Seventeenth-Century England* (New York and Oxford: Oxford University Press, 1997), pp. 86–7.

35. See the entry for scrofula in *The Cambridge World History of Disease*, ed. Kenneth F. Kiple (Cambridge: Cambridge University Press, 1993), pp. 998–1000. The Oxford English Dictionary defines scrofula as 'a constitutional disease characterized mainly by chronic enlargement and degeneration of the lymphatic glands'.

36. *Journal of George Fox*, Volume II, p. 310; *Book of Miracles*, Cadbury, ed. p. 117.
37. Sir William Lower, *A Relation in the form of journal of the voyage and residence which the most mighty Prince Charles the II king of Great Britain, & c. hath made in Holland* (The Hague, 1660), p. 78.
38. *By the King, A Proclamation for the Better Ordering of Those Who Repair to the Court for the Cure of the Disease Called the Kings-Evil* (London, 1662). Proclamations continued to be published to this effect by all the monarchs who touched for the King's Evil – that is, by all the English monarchs until the Hanovers, except for William who would not practise it.
39. 'A register of the numbers touched by Charles II at the public healings in London was . . . kept, first by the Serjeant of the Chapel Royal down to September 1664, and afterwards from May 1667 to May 1682, by the Keeper of the Closet. In the former period of four years, the register shows that 22,982 persons were touched: then followed a suspension of public healings owing to the plague. In the latter period of fifteen years no less than 67,816 were touched, making a total number of 90,798 for the whole nineteen years of active operation.' Raymond Crawfurd, *The King's Evil* (Oxford: Clarendon Press, 1911), p.112. The surgeon John Browne, who wrote about the King's Evil in Charles II's reign, states that over 6,000 were touched by Charles II in one year, and also gives the total number of healings for Charles II's reign as 92,107. He states that from 1660–4, the numbers are 'taken from a Register kept by Thomas Haynes Esq. Serjeant of His Majesties Chappell Royal' and then for 1667–82 they are 'taken from a Book or Register thereof, kept by Mr Thomas Donkley. Keeper of His Majesties Closet belonging to His Majesties Royal Chappell'. See John Browne, *Adenachoiradelogia: or, An anatomick-chirurgical treatise of glandules & strumaes. Together with the royal gift of healing. [3 pt., the 2nd and 3rd entitled respectively, Chæradelogia and Charisma basilicon.]* (London, 1684), part 3, p. 79; Part 3 (pp. 197–207; pages not numbered after p. 196).
40. Harold M. Weber, *Paper Bullets: Print and Kingship under Charles II* (Lexington, KY: The University Press of Kentucky, 1996), p. 61.
41. Lower provides a description of the ceremony as Charles performed it *Voyage and residence*, pp. 74–8.
42. Browne, *Adenachoiradelogia*, part 3, pp. 101–2. His description of the ceremony can be found on pp. 94–101.
43. Thomas Allen, *Cheirexoke. The Excellency or Handy-Work of the Royal Hand* (London, 1665) pp. 14, 6.
44. Browne, *Adenachoiradelogia*, part 3, pp. 76–7.
45. Allen, *Cheirexoke*, pp. 9–10.
46. Allen, *Cheirexoke*, pp. 1, 11.
47. For various examples of such seventh son healers, and the controversy they caused, see Thomas, *Religion and the Decline of Magic*, pp. 237–9.
48. Anonymous letter from London, dated 8 October 1603, in the Vatican archives. Quoted in M. Bloch, *The Royal Touch, Sacred Monarchy and Scrofula in England and France*, trans. J. E. Anderson (London: Routledge and Kegan Paul, 1973), p.188. A larger extract is translated in Crawfurd, *The King's Evil*, p. 83.
49. Bloch, *The Royal Touch*, p. 188.
50. John Aubrey, *Miscellanies* (London, 1696), p. 98.
51. Henry Clark, *His Grace the Duke of Monmouth Honoured in his Progress in the West of England in an Account of a most Extraordinary Cure of the Kings Evil: Given in a Letter from Crookhorn in the County of Somerset from the Minister of the Parish and many others* (London, 1680), pp. 1–2.
52. See *A True and Wonderful Account of a Cure of the King's Evil, by Mrs Fanshaw, Sister to His Grace the Duke of Monmouth* (London, 1681) and *An Answer to a Scoffing and Lying Libell, put forth and privately dispersed under the title of A Wonderful Account of the*

Cureing of the King's-Evil, by Madam Fanshaw the Duke of Monmouth's Sister (London, 1681).

53. Aubrey, *Miscellanies*, pp. 98–101, 95.
54. Samuel Werenfels, *A Dissertation Upon Superstition in Natural Things. To which are added, Occasional Thought on the Power of Curing the King's Evil Ascribed to the Kings of England* (London, 1748), p. 51.
55. See Crawfurd, *The King's Evil*, pp. 157–8.
56. Bloch, *The Royal Touch*, p. 219.
57. See Paul Kleber Monod, *Jacobitism and the English People 1688–1788* (Cambridge: Cambridge University Press, 1989), p. 128.
58. William Beckett, *A Free and Impartial Enquiry into the Antiquity and Efficacy of Touching for the Cure of the King's Evil* (London, 1722), p. 37.
59. Weber argues that it was the investigation of Greatrakes that 'accelerated a technological discourse that within fifty years would challenge the royal touch, claiming for the medical profession alone the power to police the body and heal disease'. Weber, *Paper Bullets*, p. 67.
60. Monod, *Jacobitism and the English People*, p. 131.
61. For a summary and discussion of this shift in historiographical debate, see Steven Shapin, *The Scientific Revolution* (Chicago and London: University of Chicago Press, 1996). Shapin characteristically and provocatively begins the book by declaring 'There was no such thing as the Scientific Revolution, and this is a book about it', p. 1.

Chapter 4   Valentine Greatrakes and the New Philosophy

1. *A Short and Plain Narrative of Matthew Coker, touching some mistakes and misrecitals in reference to his gift of Healing &c.* (London, 1654), pp. 5, 6.
2. *The Conway Letters*, ed. Marjorie Hope Nicholson, rev. Sarah Hutton (Oxford: Clarendon Press, 1992) pp. 98–104. Gell was interested also in astrology and was accused of unorthodox views by some. See: Louise Hill Curth, 'Gell, Robert (1595–1665)' in *DNB*, http://www.oxforddnb.com/view/article/10510.
3. Anne Conway certainly knew about Greatrakes as early as July 1665, as Lord Conway wrote to his brother, Sir George Rawdon, about Greatrakes on 26 July, 1665. See *Conway Letters*, p. 261.
4. *The Correspondence of Henry Oldenburg 1663–1665*, Volume II eds and trans. A. Rupert Hall and Marie Boas Hall (Madison, Milwaukee and London: University of Wisconsin Press, 1966) pp. 512–13, 556; see also p. 560.
5. For a discussion of the term Latitudinarian, and a sceptical approach (which I do not share) to its usual usage, see John Spurr, '"Latitudinarianism" and the Restoration Church', *The Historical Journal* 31:1 (March 1998), pp. 61–82.
6. For a discussion of the differences between English (Protestant) and European (Roman Catholic) scientific methods as they developed in the seventeenth century, with a particular focus on how this affected discussions about miracles, see Peter Dear, 'Miracles, Experiments, and the Ordinary Course of Nature', *Isis* 81 (1990), pp. 663–83.
7. Robert Boyle to Henry Stubbe, 9 March 1666, *The Correspondence of Robert Boyle*, eds Michael Hunter, Antonia Clericuzio and Lawrence M. Principe (6 vols, London: Pickering and Chatto, 2001), vol. 3, p. 94.
8. On Boyle and miracles see J. J. MacIntosh, 'Locke and Boyle on miracles and God's existence' in Michael Hunter, ed. *Robert Boyle Reconsidered* (Cambridge: Cambridge University Press, 1994), pp. 193–214. MacIntosh points out that unlike Boyle, John Locke 'did not seriously consider contemporary reports of miracles, even if they were uncontested', p. 205. Richard S. Westfall, in his *Religion and Science in Seventeenth*

Century England (New Haven: Yale University Press, 1958) argues that Boyle's views on miracles were in conflict with his scientific ideas (see pp. 83 ff.); R. M. Burns convincingly refutes this idea. See Burns, *The Great Debate*, pp. 51–7.

9. See Walter Pagel, *New Light on William Harvey* (Baseland NY: S. Karger, 1976), p. 50. Thanks to Charles Webster for this reference. While Harvey and Boyle gave a natural explanation to this cure, it is worth remembering that the dead body parts of martyrs were regarded as relics by Roman Catholics, and were used for healing. The most well-known example from the seventeenth century was Father Arrowsmith's hand: Edmund Arrowsmith was a Jesuit priest who was martyred in 1628; his hand was preserved and used for healing by stroking well into the eighteenth and nineteenth centuries. See Rushworth Armytage, 'Father Arrowsmith's Hand' in *Bygone Lancashire*, ed. Ernest Axon (London, Manchester and Hull, 1892).

10. Joseph Glanvill, *Sadducismus Triumphatus* (London, 1689), p. 73.

11. *The Conway Letters*, pp. 98–9.

12. Dear, 'Miracles, Experiments, and the Ordinary Course of Nature', pp. 664–5, 674.

13. Sprat, *History of the Royal-Society*, p. 352.

14. K. Theodore Hoppen, 'The Nature of the Early Royal Society', part 1, *The British Journal for the History of Science*, 9 (1976), p. 5. See also Katherine Park and Lorraine Daston, 'Unnatural Conceptions: The Study of Monsters in Sixteenth- and seventeenth-Century France and England, *Past and Present* 92 (1981), pp. 20–54, and Katherine Park and Lorraine Daston, *Wonders and the Order of Nature 1150–1750* (New York: Zone Books, 1998).

15. Sprat, *History of the Royal-Society*, pp. 214, 215.

16. Greatrakes described the beginning of his healing career in *A Brief Account of Mr Valentine Greatraks, and Divers of the Cures by him lately performed. Written by himself in a letter addressed to the Honourable Robert Boyle Esq.* (London, 1666), p. 22.

17. For details of these political connections and other biographical information, see Peter Elmer, 'Greatrakes, Valentine (1629–1683)', *DNB*, http://ww.oxforddnb.com/view/article/11367.

18. Henry Stubbe, *The Miraculous Conformist; or An Account of Severall Marvailous Cures Performed by a Stroaking of the Hands of Mr. Valentine Greatraik with a Physicall Discourse thereupon, In a Letter to the Honourable Robert Boyle, Esq.* (Oxford, 1666), pp. 6–7.

19. Joseph Glanvill reproduced the letter in his *A Blow at Modern Sadducism* (London, 1668), p. 106. Rust was here, presumably, using apostle in the first-century sense; later, in the 1750s and 1760s, the term had a double meaning, being used (ironically) also to signify Roman Catholics. Chambers in his 1751 *Cyclopedia* defined it thus: '*Apostolici, Apostoli*, or *Apostles*, was a name assumed by two different sects of heretics, on account of their pretending to imitate the manners and practice of the apostles.' Quoted in the *Oxford English Dictionary*, 2nd edition (Oxford: Oxford University Press, 1989).

20. *The Great Cures and Strange Miracles performed by Mr Valentine Gretrux* (London, 1666), p. 6.

21. Greatrakes, *A Brief Account*, p. 29.

22. Greatrakes, *A Brief Account*, p. 34.

23. Greatrakes, *A Brief Account*, pp. 30–1.

24. David Lloyd, *Wonders No Miracles; or Mr. Greatrakes Gift of Healing Examined, upon Occasion of a Sad Effect of his Stroaking Mar. the 7, 1665 at one Mr. Cressets House in Charter-House Yard* (London, 1665/6), p. 9.

25. Lloyd, *Wonders No Miracles*, p. 14.

26. Greatrakes, *A Brief Account*, p. 11.

27. *Philosophical Transactions*, 21:256 (September 1699), p. 333.

28. Lloyd, *Wonders No Miracles*, p. 14.

29. Lloyd, *Wonders No Miracles*, p. 12.
30. Lloyd, *Wonders No Miracles*, p.12.
31. Tim Harris argues that this fear was a constant feature of the 1660s; see his *Restoration: Charles II and his Kingdoms, 1660–1685* (London: Allen Lane, 2005).
32. Stubbe, *The Miraculous Conformist*, preface.
33. Stubbe, *The Miraculous Conformist*, pp. 10–11.
34. Thomas Willis, *Of Fermentation of the Inorganical Motion of Natural Bodies* (London, 1659).
35. Stubbe, *The Miraculous Conformist*, p. 14.
36. Stubbe, *The Miraculous Conformist*, pp. 27, 15.
37. Daniel Coxe to Robert Boyle, 5 March 1666, *The Correspondence of Robert Boyle*, ed. Hunter et al., vol. 3, p. 84.
38. Stubbe, *The Miraculous Conformist*, p. 2.
39. Stubbe, *The Miraculous Conformist*, p. 26.
40. Stubbe, *The Miraculous Conformist*, p. 8.
41. She is referring, of course, to the interpretations made by historians of science; they are the historians who had paid the most attention to this case. Barbara Beigun Kaplan, 'Greatrakes the Stroker: The Interpretation of his Contemporaries', *Isis*, 73 (1982) pp. 178–85.
42. Eamon Duffy, in his article on Greatrakes, writes of 'the embarrassment' of the virtuosi, which, he claims, was the 'principal element in their response to the Stroker'. See Duffy, 'Valentine Greatrakes, the Irish Stroker: Miracle, Science, and Orthodoxy in Restoration England' in *Religion and Humanism*, Studies in Church History, vol. 17 (Oxford: Basil Blackwell, 1981), p. 269. However, the readiness of the virtuosi to observe Greatrakes at work, as well as those who claimed they were healed by him, suggests that they were curious and possibly did not know what to make of those claims, but *not* that they were embarrassed. On the contrary, such claims were the raw material of their enquiries.
43. Anthony Wood, *Athenae Oxonienses* (3 vols, London, 1913), vol. 3, p. 1071.
44. More to Conway, 28 April 1666, *The Conway Letters*, p. 273.
45. Coxe to Boyle, 5 March 1666, *The Correspondence of Robert Boyle*, vol. 3, p. 89.
46. Coxe to Boyle, 5 March 1666, *The Correspondence of Robert Boyle*, vol. 3, p. 89.
47. Larry Stewart, *The Rise of Public Science: Rhetoric, Technology, and Natural Philosophy in Newtonian Britain, 1660–1750* (Cambridge: Cambridge University Press, 1992), p. xxiii.
48. Boyle to Stubbe, 9 March 1666, *The Correspondence of Robert Boyle*, vol. 3, pp. 95, 97, 94–5, 95.
49. More to Anne Conway, 28 April 1666, *The Conway Letters*, p. 273.
50. Robert Boyle, *Work Diary XXVI (Accounts of Cures performed by Valentine Greatrakes, 1666)*, BL, Add MS 4293, fol. 52r.
51. Boyle, *Work Diary*, fols. 50r, 51r, 52r, 53r, 50v, 51v.
52. Greatrakes, *A Brief Account*, p. 40.
53. Greatrakes, *A Brief Account*, p. 60.
54. See Steven Shapin, 'Pump and Circumstance: Robert Boyle's Literary Technology', *Social Studies of Science*, 14, (1984), pp. 481–520; Steven Shapin and Simon Schaffer, *Leviathan and the Air Pump: Hobbes, Boyle and the Experimental Life* (Princeton: Princeton University Press, 1985) and Steven Shapin, 'The House of Experiment in Seventeenth-Century England' *Isis* (1988), pp. 373–404.
55. Greatrakes, *A Brief Account*, p. 31.
56. Greatrakes to Conway, 24 April 1666, *The Conway Letters*, p. 272.
57. Shapin, 'Pump and Circumstance', p. 489.
58. Rust to Glanvill, no date, *The Conway Letters*, p. 274.
59. More to Anne Conway, 28 April 1666, *The Conway Letters*, p. 273.

60. Quoted in Simon Schaffer, 'Self Evidence', *Critical Enquiry*, 18 (Winter 1992), p. 328.
61. Shapin, *A Social History of Truth: Civility and Science in Seventeenth-Century England* (Chicago: Chicago University Press), p. 328.
62. Shapin, *A Social History of Truth*, p. 78. See chapter 3 for a wider discussion of these issues of credibility and witnessing.
63. Stubbe, *The Miraculous Conformist*, p. 4. This passage indicates that Stubbe was keenly aware of all the 'technologies' that were necessary in writing his own, reliable account of what he had observed, in order to establish what he calls 'matter of fact' (*The Miraculous Conformist*, p. 3). James R. Jacob has made much of Stubbe's hostility towards the Royal Society generally and towards Boyle in particular, arguing that this hostility can be seen in the case of Valentine Greatrakes, and that Stubbe's and Boyle's disagreement represents a profound ideological difference that shaped the social and political context in which the early Royal Society emerged. This is part of a larger case that he and Margaret Jacob have made suggesting that the tensions between moderate Anglicans and more radical Protestants (such as Stubbe) ultimately produced modern science. (For a summary of this position, see James R. Jacob and Margaret C. Jacob, 'The Anglican Origins of Modern Science: The Metaphysical Foundations of the Whig Constitution', *Isis*, 71 (1980), pp. 211–33.) Nicholas Steneck, in challenging James Jacob's argument, points out that Stubbe's hostility towards the Royal Society really emerged at a point later than the Greatrakes case. For this debate, see James R. Jacob, *Henry Stubbe, Radical Protestantism and the Early Enlightenment* (Cambridge: Cambridge University Press, 1983) and Nicholas H. Steneck, 'Greatrakes the Stroker: The Interpretation of Historians', *Isis*, 73 (1982), pp. 161–77. Jacob was able to reply to Steneck's article in an epilogue to his book (pp. 161–74), written when his book on Stubbe was at proof stage.
64. Barbara Shapiro, 'The Concept 'Fact': Legal Origins and Cultural Diffusion', *Albion*, 26: 2 (Summer 1994), p. 247.
65. Robert Boyle, *The Works of the Honourable Robert Boyle: In Six Volumes* (London, 1722) Volume 4, p. 182.
66. See, for example, on witnessing in early modern culture, David Cressy, 'Monstrous Births and Credible Reports: Portents, Texts and Testimonies' in Cressy, *Travesties and Transgressions in Tudor and Stuart England* (Oxford and New York: Oxford University Press: 2000).
67. Doe, *The Narrative of the Miraculous Cure of Anne Munnings*, unpaginated.
68. Hillel Schwartz, *The French Prophets: The History of a Millenarian Group in Eighteenth-Century England* (Berkeley and Los Angeles: University of California Press, 1980), p. 69.
69. Glanvill, *Sadducismus Triumphatus*, p. 100.
70. Greatrakes, *A Brief Account*, p. 59.
71. Stubbe, *The Miraculous Conformist*, p. 2.
72. Beckett, *A Free and Impartial Enquiry*, pp. 27, 28, 30, 31.
73. Similarly, when Boyle investigated cases of Second Sight (the ability to foresee future events) in Scotland, in 1678, he was interested in investigating the cases, but tentative in his conclusions about their meaning. See Michael Hunter, *The Occult Laboratory: Magic, Science and Second Sight in Late Seventeenth-Century Scotland* (Woodbridge: Boydell Press, 2001).
74. More, *Enthusiasmus Triumphatus*, p. 40.
75. Conway to Rawdon, 9 February 1666, *The Conway Letters*, p. 268.
76. Oldenburg to Boyle, 13 March 1666, *The Correspondence of Henry Oldenburg*, vol. 3, 1666–7, p. 59.
77. 'Some Observations of the Effects of Touch and Friction', *Philosophical Transactions*, 12, 7 May 1666, p. 207. Barbara Beigun Kaplan suggests this article may have been written by Oldenburg. See her 'Greatrakes the Stroker', pp. 181–2.

78. Greatrakes, *A Brief Account*, p. 60.
79. Rust to Glanvill, no date, *The Conway Letters*, p. 274.
80. Greatrakes, *A Brief Account*, p. 59.

Chapter 5   Fasting women

1. For an important and influential analysis of such fasting practices in the middle ages, see Caroline Walker Bynum, *Holy Feast and Holy Fast: The Religious Significance of Food to Medieval Women* (Berkeley and Los Angeles: University of California Press, 1987).
2. See Keith Thomas, *Religion and the Decline of Magic* (Harmondsworth: Penguin, 1971), pp. 134–5.
3. Elaine Hobby, *Virtue of Necessity: English Women's Writing 1649–88* (Ann Arbor: University of Michigan Press, 1988), p. 26; see also her full bibliography of women's writing in this period, pp. 228–252.
4. Phyllis Mack, *Visionary Women: Ecstatic Prophecy in Seventeenth-Century England* (Berkeley: University of California Press, 1992).
5. See, for example, Richard Baxter, *The Saints Everlasting Rest* (1650) (reprinted in vols 22 and 23 of *The practical works of the Rev. Richard Baxter: with a life of the author, and a critical examination of his writings, ed.* W. Orme (23 vols, London: James Duncan, 1830)). For a discussion of the Puritan art of suffering, see Ann Thompson, *The Art of Suffering and the Impact of Seventeenth-Century Anti-Providential Thought* (Aldershot: Ashgate, 2003), chapters 1–3.
6. Diane Purkiss, 'Producing the Voice, Consuming the Body. Women Prophets of the Seventeenth Century' in *Women, Writing, History 1640–1740*, eds Isobel Grundy and Susan Wiseman (Athens, GA: University of Georgia Press, 1992), p. 144.
7. See Anna Trapnel, *The cry of a stone. Or A relation of something spoken in Whitehall, by Anna Trapnel, being in the visions of God* (London, 1654) for details of these prophecies. For an interesting discussion of the place of Trapnel and her prophecies in the civil war context, see Nigel Smith, *Perfection Proclaimed: Language and Literature in English Radical Religion 1640–1660* (Oxford: Clarendon Press, 1989).
8. Trapnel, *The cry of a stone*, p. 3.
9. Trapnel, *The cry of a stone*, p. 2.
10. Trapnel, *The cry of a stone*, pp. 5 and 7.
11. Jessey, *The Exceeding Riches of Grace Advanced*, pp. 27–30.
12. Anna, Trapnel, *Report and Plea: Or, a Narrative of a Journey from London into Cornwal, the occasion of it, the Lord's Encouragement to it, and Signal Presence with Her in It* (London, 1654), pp. 6–7.
13. See Bynum, *Holy Feast and Holy Fast*.
14. Mack, *Visionary Women*, pp. 80, 81.
15. Trapnel, *The cry of a stone*, p. 3.
16. Trapnel, *Report and Plea*, pp. 19, 21, 22.
17. Mack, *Visionary Women*, p. 80.
18. Trapnel, *The cry of a stone*, p. 3.
19. Jessey, *Exceeding Riches*, Postscript to the Reader.
20. See Dailey, 'The Visitation of Sarah Wight', p. 446.
21. Mack, *Visionary Women*, p. 116.
22. For a general overview of the case, see Janet Wadsworth, 'Martha Taylor – the Fasting Maid of Over Haddon 1651–?1687', *Derbyshire Miscellany* 8:3 (Spring 1978), pp. 77–83. Wadsworth documents the evidence carefully but interprets it in modern terms, concluding that it was a case of anorexia nervosa. For the perspective of an historian of science on the case, who presents the case in its particular political, medical and religious context, see Simon Schaffer, 'Piety, Physic and Prodigious

Abstinence' in *Religion Medici: Medicine and Religion in Seventeenth-Century England*, eds Ole Peter Grell and Andrew Cunningham (Aldershot: Scolar, 1996), pp. 17–203.

23. H.A., *Mirabile Pecci: or the Non-Such Wonder of the Peak in Derbyshire. Discovered in a full, though succinct and sober, Narrative of the more than ordinary Parts, Piety and Preservation of Martha Taylor, one who hath been supported in time above a year in away beyond the ordinary course of Nature, without the use of Meat or Drink* (London 1669), p. 5.

24. H. A., *Mirabile Pecci*, pp. 7–11.

25. H. A. *Mirabile Pecci*, p. 77.

26. H. A., *Mirabile Pecci*, p. 25.

27. H. A. *Mirabile Pecci*, p. 29.

28. H. A., *Mirabile Pecci*, p. 76.

29. On Robins, see Green, *Print and Protestantism in Early Modern England*, p. 475.

30. Thomas Robins, *The Wonder of the World* (London, 1669), p. 11.

31. Thomas Robins, *News from Darby-shire – or the Wonder of all Wonders* (London, 1668), pp. 3–6.

32. Schaffer, 'Piety, Physic and Prodigious Abstinence', p. 185.

33. Schaffer interprets the Quaker Richard Farnsworth's description (in his *England's Warning Piece Gone Forth* of 1653) of Thomas Robins as 'England's blind guide' as signifying Robins' Calvinism; this makes sense in the context of Interregnum politics. See Schaffer, 'Piety, Physic and Prodigious Abstinence', p. 201, n. 40.

34. *A Journal of the Life of that Ancient Servant of Christ, John Gratton* (London, 1720), pp. 31–2. This is not, however, evidence enough to support Schaffer's claim that 'he reported meeting many different sectaries' when he visited Taylor.

35. Schaffer, 'Piety, Physic and Prodigious Abstinence', p. 186. See *A Journal of John Gratton*, pp. 35–40 for an account of his conversion.

36. See William H. G. A. Bagshawe, *A Memoir of William Bagshawe (of Ford Hall) styled 'The Apostle of the Peak' with extracts from his unpublished writings* (London, 1887).

37. Dorothy Riden, ed. 'The Autobiography of Leonard Wheatcroft, of Ashover, 1627–1706', *Derbyshire Record Society*, 20 (1993), p. 85.

38. John Reynolds, *A discourse upon prodigious abstinence occasioned by the twelve moneths fasting of Martha Taylor, the famed Derbyshire damosell: proving that without any miracle, the texture of humane bodies may be so altered that life may be long continued without the supplies of meat & drink* (London, 1669), p. 4. This was republished at least twice, in 1745 and 1809.

39. For details of John Reynolds' life, see A. G. Matthews, *Calamy revised: Being a revision of Edmund Calamy's Account of the Ministers and others ejected and silenced 1660–2* (Oxford: Oxford University Press, 1988), p. 409.

40. Reynolds, *Discourse upon Prodigious Abstinence*, p. 9.

41. Taylor responded in a pamphlet, *Ignorance and Error Reproved* (1662).

42. Hobbes to Brooke, 20 [/30] October 1668/9, *The Correspondence of Thomas Hobbes*, ed. Noel Malcolm (2 vols, Oxford: Clarendon Press, 1994) vol. 2, pp. 701–3; *Calendar of State Papers, domestic Series, of the reign of Charles II . . . 1668–69* eds Mary Anne Everett Green, F. H. B. Daniell and F. L. Bickley (28 vols, London: Longman, Green, Longman & Roberts, 1860–1938), Car, II, No. 17, 1669, p. 145.

43. The publication of these reports continued well into the eighteenth century. See, for example, *Philosophical Transactions* 31: 364 (Jan–Apr 1720), pp. 28–30; 42: 466 (Nov–Dec 1742), pp. 240–2.

44. Hobbes to John Brooke, 20 [/30] October 1668/9, *Correspondence of Thomas Hobbes*, p. 702.

45. H. A., *Mirabile Pecci*, p. 16; Robins, *The Wonder of the World*, p. 11.

46. Robins, *Newes from Darby-shire*, p. 3.

47. Robins, *The Wonder of the World*, pp. 9–10.

48. Schaffer, 'Piety, Physic and Prodigious Abstinence', p. 180. Schaffer draws on the work of historians such as Adrian Wilson who depicts the lying-in ritual, as Laura Gowing puts it in her critique of Wilson, as 'a uniquely supportive and validating atmosphere for women . . . an all-female atmosphere [which] protects the labouring woman and the new mother from the outside world'. Gowing sees the lying-in scene as rather less rosy: 'A closer examination of the dynamics between women at lyings-in suggests . . . conflicts and tensions. This was not a world in which all-female environments were necessarily associated with support and validation . . . The divisions between women that helped reinforce gender order outside the birthroom were likely to be reinforced inside it.' Laura Gowing, *Common Bodies: Women, Touch and Power in Seventeenth-Century England* (New Haven and London: Yale University Press, 2003), p. 150. For Adrian Wilson's interpretation, see *The Making of Man-Midwifery: Childbirth in England, 1660–1770* (Cambridge, MA: Harvard University Press, 1998).
49. Gowing, *Common Bodies*, p. 154.
50. Hobbes to Brooke, 20 October 1668, *Correspondence of Thomas Hobbes*, p. 702
51. H. A., *Mirabile Pecci*, 'Preface to the Reader'.
52. See Lisa Forman Cody, *Birthing the Nation: Sex, Science and the Conception of Eighteenth-Century Britain* (Oxford and New York: Oxford University Press, 2005) especially chapter 6, and Wilson, *The Making of Man-Midwifery*.
53. See Mark Goldie, 'Johnston, Nathaniel (*bap.* 1629?, *d.* 1705)', *DNB*, http://www.oxforddnb.com/view/article/14946. Johnston was also an antiquary.
54. Johnston to Clarke, 29 June 1669, reprinted in Thomas Birch, *The History of the Royal Society of London* (4 vols, London, 1756), vol. 2, pp. 389–92. Timothy Clarke was an Oxford MD (Balliol, 1652), Fellow of the Royal College of Physicians, one of the original members of the Royal Society and physician in ordinary to Charles II. See Gordon Goodwin, 'Clarke, Timothy (*d.* 1672)', rev. Michael Bevan, *DNB*, http://www.oxforddnb.com/view/article/5535.
55. Letter from Johnston to Clarke, 29 June 1669, Birch, *History of the Royal Society*, p. 390 (my translation from the Latin).
56. Letter from Johnston to Clarke, 28 June 1669, Birch, *History of the Royal Society*, p. 391 (my translation).
57. Letter from Johnston to Clarke, 29 June 1669, Birch, *History of the Royal Society*, pp. 391–2 (my translation).
58. Birch, *History of the Royal Society*, p. 389.
59. Hobbes to Brooke, 20 October 1668, *Correspondence of Thomas Hobbes*, p. 702.
60. Wadsworth, 'Martha Taylor', p. 83.
61. Daniel Lysons and Samuel Lysons, *Magna Britannia, a concise topographical account of the several counties of Great Britain* (6 vols, London: Cadell and Davies, 1817), vol. 5, pp. 27–8.
62. For longer lists of fasting stories and some observations about how these seventeenth-century stories fit into a longer (Roman Catholic and Protestant) tradition, see Hyder E. Rollins, 'Notes on Some English Accounts of Miraculous Fasts', *Journal of American Folklore* 34 (1921), pp. 357–76; Petr Skrabanek, 'Notes Towards the History of Anorexia Nervosa', *Janus* 70 (1983), pp. 109–28; and Joan Jacobs Blumberg, *Fasting Girls: The History of Anorexia Nervosa* (New York: Plume Books, 1988), chapter 2; Joseph A. Silverman, 'Anorexia Nervosa in Seventeenth Century England as Viewed by Physician, Philosopher and Pedagogue', *International Journal of Eating Disorders* 5 (1986) pp. 847–53.
63. Hobbes to Brooke, 20 October 1668, *Correspondence of Thomas Hobbes*, p. 702.
64. H. A. *Mirabile Pecci*, p. 4.
65. H. A. *Mirabile Pecci*, pp. 23–4.
66. Hobbes to Brooke, 20 October 1668, *Correspondence of Thomas Hobbes*, p. 702.

67. H. A., *Mirabile Pecci*, p. 31.
68. Gowing, *Common Bodies*, p. 5.
69. Hobbes to Brooke, 20 October 1668, *Correspondence of Thomas Hobbes*, p. 702.

Chapter 6   Perfectly Protestant Miracles

1. *An Exact Relation of the Wonderful Cure of Mary Maillard* (London, 1730), p. 6.
2. *An Exact Relation*, p. 9.
3. Ian Green situates this ballad in the broader context of godly ballads; see his *Print and Protestantism in Early Modern England*, p. 453, especially n. 35.
4. See Jane Shaw, 'Maillard, Marie (1680–1731)' in *DNB*, http://www.oxforddnb.com/view/article/66115.
5. *A Narrative of the late Extraordinary Cure Wrought in an Instant Upon Mrs Elizabeth Savage (lame from Birth) without the use of any Natural Means* (London, 1694), pp. 14, 9–10.
6. *A Relation of the Miraculous Cure of Susannah Arch, of a Leprosy and Physick* (London, 1695), p. 9.
7. *A Relation of the Miraculous Cure of Susannah Arch*, p. 13.
8. *A Relation of the Miraculous Cure of Susannah Arch*, p. 15.
9. *A Relation of the Miraculous Cure of Susannah Arch*, p. 17.
10. *A Relation of the Miraculous Cure of Mrs Lydia Hills of a Lameness of Eighteen Years Continuance* (London, 1696, 2nd edn, with additions), p.7.
11. *A Relation of the Miraculous Cure of Mrs Lydia Hills*, p. 8.
12. *A Relation of the Miraculous Cure of Mrs Lydia Hills*, pp. 14–15.
13. *Light in darkness, or, a Modest Enquiry into, and humble improvement of Miracles, in General, Upon Occasion of this late Miraculous Cure of Marianne Maillard* (London, 1694), pp. 7, 22.
14. *A Narrative of . . . Mrs Elizabeth Savage*, p. 13.
15. *Light in darkness*, p. 22.
16. For cases of Bible-dipping in seventeenth-century England, see David Cressy, 'Books as Totems in Seventeenth-Century England and New England', *The Journal of Library History: Philosophy and Comparative Librarianship*, 21: 1 (Winter 1981), pp. 100–2.
17. On the significance of reading and domestic piety in this period, see Andrew Cambers and Michelle Wolfe, 'Reading, Family Religion, and Evangelical Identity in Late Stuart England', *Historical Journal*, 47: 4 (2004), pp. 875–96.
18. *A Plain and True Relation of a very Extraordinary Cure of Marianne Maillard* (London, 1693), p. 9.
19. *A Relation of the Miraculous Cure of Mrs Lydia Hills*, pp. 10–11.
20. *A Relation of the Miraculous Cure of Susannah Arch*, pp. 16–17.
21. *Light in Darkness*, pp. 13, 14, 15.
22. *A Relation of the Miraculous Cure of Mrs Lydia Hills*, pp. 5–6, 8.
23. *A Relation of the Miraculous Cure of Susannah Arch*, p. 13.
24. On providence and the interpretation of prodigies in the 1690s, see Craig Rose, *England in the 1690s: Revolution, Religion and War* (Oxford: Blackwell, 1999), chapter 6, and William E. Burns, *An Age of Wonders: Prodigies, Politics and Providence in England 1657–1727* (Manchester: Manchester University Press, 2002), chapter 4.
25. Warren Johnston places these apocalyptic expectations of the 1690s in a broader context in his 'The Anglican Apocalypse in Restoration England', *Journal of Ecclesiastical History* Vol. 55, No. 3, July 2004, pp. 467–501.
26. *A True Copy of a Letter of the Miraculous Cure of David Wright, a Shephard, at Hitchin in Hertfordshire* (London, 1694), p. 1.

27. Letter from Keach to John Watts, 20 December 1693, in Morgan Edwards, *Materials Towards a History of the Baptists*, eds Eve B. Weeks and Mary B. Warren (2 vols, Danielsville, GA: Heritage Papers, 1984), vol. 1, p. 54.

28. Marsin, see William E. Burns, "By Him the Women will be delivered from that Bondage, which some has found Intolerable": M. Marsin, English Millenarian Feminist', *Eighteenth-Century Women: Studies in Their Lives, Work and Culture*, ed. Linda V. Troost (3 vols, New York: AMS Press, 2001), vol. 1, pp. 19–38.

29. M. M[arsin], *The Near Approach of Christ's Kingdom, Clearly Proved by Scripture* (London, 1696), p. 19.

30. M. M[arsin], *The Figurative Speeches: by which God has veiled his secrets contained in his Word, until the end of the Time* (London, 1697), p. 255.

31. Thomas Beverly, *A Discourse Upon the Powers of the World to Come: or, The Miraculous Powers of the Gospel and Kingdom of our Lord Jesus Christ* (London, 1694), pp. 85–6.

32. *A Relation of the Miracle Cure of Susanna Arch*, p.15.

33. For Thomas Beverly, see W. M. Lamont, *Richard Baxter and the Millennium: Protestant Imperialism and the English Revolution* (London: Croom Helm, 1979) and Johnston, Warren, 'Beverly, Thomas'. *DNB*, http://www.oxforddnb.com/view/article/66364.

34. *Light in Darkness*, pp. 17, 24, 19.

35. Pead, Deuel, *Jesus is God: or, The deity of Jesus Christ vindicated, an abstract of some sermons* (London, 1694), pp. 4–5.

36. *A Relation of the Miraculous Cure of Susannah Arch*, p. iv.

37. *Light in Darkness*, p. 27.

38. *Light in Darkness*, p. 20.

39. D. W. R. Bahlman, *The Moral Revolution of 1688* (New Haven: Yale University Press, 1957).

40. John Spurr, '"Virtue, Religion and Government": The Anglican Uses of Providence', in *The Politics of Religion in Restoration England*, eds T. Harris, P. Seaward and M. Goldie (Oxford: Oxford University Press, 1990), p. 30.

41. On the societies for the reformation of manners, see Bahlman, *Moral Revolution of 1688*; T. Isaacs, 'The Anglican Hierarchy and the Reformation of Manners, 1688–1738', *Journal of Ecclesiastical History*, 33 (1982), pp. 391–411; A. G. Craig, 'The Movement for the Reformation of Manners 1688–1715', PhD thesis, University of Edinburgh, 1980; John Spurr, 'The Church, the Societies and the Moral Revolution of 1688' in *The Church of England c. 1688–c. 1833: From Toleration to Tractarianism*, eds John Walsh, Colin Haydon and Stephen Taylor (Cambridge: Cambridge University Press, 1993), pp. 127–42.

42. For example, see James Illingworth, *A Just Narrative or Account of the Man whose Hands and legs Rotted off* (London, 1678) for the story of a man who in January 1677 was accused of stealing a Bible, denied that he had done so and then cursed himself wishing that his hands might rot off if it were true; by April, his arms, dangling by single ligaments, had to be cut off; in May, his legs, rotten to the knees, fell off, and in June he died. Sermons were preached about this 'providence' by the local rector: see Simon Ford, *A Discourse Concerning God's Judgements, preached at Old Swinford* (London, 1678).

43. M[arsin], *Near Approach of Christ's Kingdom*, p. 19.

44. 'The Happy Damsel' reproduced in *The Pack of Autolycus*, ed. Hyder E. Rollins (Cambridge, MA: Harvard University Press, 1927), p. 234.

45. *An Astrological Diary of the Seventeenth Century: Samuel Jeake of Rye 1652–1699*, eds Michael Hunter and Annabel Gregory (Oxford: Clarendon Press, 1988), p. 236.

46. Pledger Diary, Dr Williams's Library, MSS 28.4, f.60v.

47. *An Exact Relation . . . Mary Maillard*, p. 10.

48. *An Exact Relation . . . Mary Maillard*, pp. 11–12.
49. 'Letter of Dr Welwood', in *An Exact Relation . . . Mary Maillard*, pp. 44–5.
50. 'Letter of Dr Welwood', *An Exact Relation . . . Mary Maillard*, p. 47.
51. 'Letter of Dr Welwood', *An Exact Relation . . . Mary Maillard*, p. 38.
52. *A Relation of the Miraculous Cure of Susannah Arch* pp. 22, 23. There was some hostility between the Royal College of Physicians and apothecaries.
53. *A Narrative of . . . Mrs Elizabeth Savage*, p. 24.
54. *A Narrative of . . . Mrs Elizabeth Savage*, p. 5.
55. *A Relation of . . . Susannah Arch*, p. viii.
56. *Light in Darkness*, p. 12.
57. *A Plain and True Relation of . . . Marianne Maillard*, p. 2.
58. *A Narrative of . . . Mrs Elizabeth Savage*, pp. 27, 33, 40–1.
59. Tony Claydon, *William III and the Godly Revolution* (Cambridge: Cambridge University Press, 1996). On the 1690s, see especially Rose, *England in the 1690s*.
60. Quoted in Spurr, 'The Church, the Societies and the Moral Revolution of 1688', p. 128.
61. Edward Stillingfleet, *Origines Sacrae, or a Rational Account of the Grounds of Christian Faith* (London 1662), Book II, chapters IX and X.
62. Edward Stillingfleet, *A Rational Account of the Grounds of Protestant Religion* (1664) (2 vols, Oxford, 1844) vol. 1, p. 219.
63. On Welwood, see Elizabeth Lane Furdell, *The Royal Doctors 1485–1714: Medical Personnel at the Tudor and Stuart Courts* (Rochester, NY: University of Rochester Press, 2001), pp. 207–8 and Elizabeth Lane Furdell, *James Welwood: Physician to the Glorious Revolution* (Conshohoken, PA: Combined Publishing, 1998).
64. On Richard Morton, see Stephen Wright, 'Morton, Richard (*bap.* 1637, *d.* 1698)', *DNB*, http://www.oxforddnb.com/view/article/19369.
65. On Dunton, see his autobiography, John Dunton, *The life and errors of John Dunton . . . written by himself* (London, 1705); S. Parks, *John Dunton and the English Book Trade* (New York: Garland, 1976) and Helen Berry, 'Dunton, John (1659–1732)', *DNB*, http://www.oxforddnb.com/view/article/8299.
66. 'Letter of Dr Welwood', in *An Exact Relation . . . Mary Maillard*; pp. 47, 36–8.
67. *A Narrative of . . . Mrs Elizabeth Savage*, pp. 33, 39.
68. On the *Athenian Mercury*, see Helen Berry, 'An Early Coffee House Periodical and its Readers: The *Athenian Mercury*, 1691–1697', *The London Journal*, 25: 1 (2000), pp. 14–33. For a discussion of the treatment of prodigies and providence in the *Athenian Mercury*, see Burns, *An Age of Wonders*, pp. 133–5.
69. *The Athenian Mercury* (Saturday, 4 April 1691), Vol.1, No.4. No pagination.
70. Michael Hunter, 'The Problem of "Atheism" in Early Modern England', *Transactions of the Royal Historical Society*, 5th series, 35 (1985), p. 156.
71. For a further discussion of these features of the 'atheist' or sceptic, see John Spurr, '"Rational Religion" in Restoration England', *Journal of the History of Ideas*, 49:4 (1988), pp. 563–85.
72. Hunter discusses the complex relationship between the fiction of the atheist, the use of that fiction and the actual phenomenon of atheism in his 'The Problem of "Atheism" in Early Modern England', pp. 135–58.
73. J. Samuel Preus, 'The Reified Heart in Seventeenth-Cenury Religion' in *Religion in History: The Word, the Idea, the Reality*, eds Michel Despland and Gerard Vallee (Waterloo, ON: Wildred Laurier University Press, 1992), p. 46. See John Locke, 'A Discourse on Miracles' in *John Locke: Writings on Religion* ed. Victor Nuovo (Oxford: Clarendon Press, 2002) pp. 44–50, and John Locke, *The reasonableness of Christianity* (London, 1695).

Chapter 7   Miracles and the Philosophers

1. Steven Connor makes a similar point in his book, *Dumbstruck: A Cultural History of Ventriloquism* (Oxford and New York: Oxford University Press, 2000), p. 185.
2. A huge number of pamphlets was published on miracles in the first half of the eighteenth century, and the flow of writings on the subject even continued into the 1760s and 1770s, albeit at a lesser rate. This caused Charles Wallace Jr, reviewing James Herrick's 1997 book on the philosophical debate on miracles, to comment: 'More power to anyone with the patience to survey the seemingly interminable outpouring of pamphlets and books attacking and defending miracles, the Bible, and revelation in general in the early eighteenth century.' See *Church History*, 67, (1998), pp. 590–2. R. M. Burns writes that, 'At its height – around the 1720s – the debate had received enormous attention; so much so that almost every English theologian, philosopher, or even simply man of letters of the period made some contribution to it.' *The Great Debate on Miracles*, p. 10.
3. See especially Burns, *The Great Debate on Miracles* and James Herrick, *The Radical Rhetoric of the English Deists: The Discourse of Skepticism, 1680–1750* (Columbia: University of South Carolina Press, 1997). There are many analyses of this debate by philosophers, most of whom are especially concerned with Hume's work on miracles. Recent examples include: David Johnson, *Hume, Holism and Miracles* (Ithaca and London: Cornell University Press, 1999); John Earman, *Hume's Abject Failure: The Argument Against Miracles* (Oxford: Oxford University Press, 2000); Robert J. Fogelin, *A Defense of Hume on Miracles* (Princeton, NJ and Oxford: Princeton University Press, 2003).
4. There has been much debate in recent years amongst historians about the scope and extent of the deist critique of orthodox Christianity. Most recently, S. J. Barnett has argued that there was no large group of deists, as is often assumed, and that the Enlightenment was not just about radical critiques of Christianity but also concerned debates within Christianity, as the work of B. W. Young and others has shown. Indeed, Barnett claims that, 'there is good evidence that . . . when he [Toland] wrote his most notorious work, *Christianity Not Mysterious* (1696), he was a Presbyterian of the Unitarian (Socinian) type and commonly known as such'. Barnett, *The Enlightenment and Religion*, p. 29. Undoubtedly, the term 'deist' was often used as a political and religious slur against certain sceptical writers.
5. John Toland, *Christianity Not Mysterious, or a treatise shewing that there is nothing in the Gospel contrary to reason, nor above it and that no Christian doctrine can be properly call'd a mystery*, 2nd edn (London, 1696), p. 145.
6. Toland, *Christianity Not Mysterious*, p. 146.
7. For a discussion of Spinoza on miracles, see Jonathan I. Israel, *Radical Enlightenment: Philosophy and the Making of Modernity 1650–1750* (Oxford: Oxford University Press, 2001), chapter 12.
8. On the impact of the expiry of the Licensing Act on religious life, and especially on the status of the Church of England, see Mark Goldie, 'The Theory of Religious Intolerance' in *From Persecution to Toleration: The Glorious Revolution and Religion in England*, eds O. P. Grell, Jonathan I. Israel and Nicholas Tyacke (Oxford: Clarendon Press, 1991), pp. 331–68. The Blasphemy Act of 1698 made it illegal to deny Christ's divinity and to reject the doctrine of the Trinity (except for Jews, who were exempt). For the reception of Toland's *Christianity Not Mysterious*, see Justin Champion, *Republican Learning: John Toland and the Crisis of Christian Culture* (Manchester: Manchester University Press, 2003), chapter 3.
9. Toland, *Christianity Not Mysterious*, p. 147.
10. Fowler wrote *A vindication of a late undertaking of certain gentlemen, in order to the suppressing of debauchery, and profaneness* (London, 1692) to publicise the work of the

societies and their prestigious supporters such as Queen Mary and Bishop Stillingfleet.

11. Moses Pitt, *An Account of one Ann Jeffries. Now living in the county of Cornwall, who was fed for six months by a small sort of Airy People call'd Fairies. And of the strange and wonderful cures she performed with salves and medicines she received from them, for which she never took one Penny of her Patients. In a Letter from Moses Pitt to the Rt Revd Father in God, Dr Edward Fowler, Lord Bishop of Gloucester* (London, 1696), pp. 5–6.

12. Pitt, *An Account of one Ann Jeffries*, pp. 10, 16, 17.

13. Pitt, *An Account of one Ann Jeffries*, pp. 12, 22.

14. See James Herrick, 'Miracles and Method', *Quarterly Journal of Speech*, 9 (1989), pp. 321–34, and, for a longer exposition of his argument, *The Radical Rhetoric of the English Deists*.

15. Anthony Ashley Cooper, Third Earl of Shaftesbury, 'A Letter Concerning Enthusiasm' (1707) in *Characteristics of Men, Manners, Opinions, Times*, ed. Lawrence E. Klein (Cambridge: Cambridge University Press, 1999), pp. 5–6.

16. For a full discussion of the French Prophets in England, see Schwartz, *The French Prophets*.

17. According to Hillel Schwartz, this meeting took place on 5 July 1707; see his *The French Prophets*, p. 93n.

18. Shaftesbury, 'Letter Concerning Enthusiasm', pp. 15–16.

19. Henry Morley, *Memoirs of Bartholomew Fair* (London: George Routledge, 1892).

20. Shaftesbury, 'Letter Concerning Enthusiasm', p. 22.

21. Shaftesbury, 'Letter Concerning Enthusiasm', p. 23; footnote Q on page 23 suggests 'that the "signal miracle" referred to Pierre Claris, who safely walked through fire in 1703'. Later writers frequently referred to this miracle, as discussed below. The name Claris was often anglicised to Clary.

22. Shaftesbury, 'Letter Concerning Enthusiasm', p. 23.

23. See Heyd, *'Be Sober and Reasonable'*.

24. Schwartz, *The French Prophets*, p. 241.

25. John Lacy, *Warnings of the Eternal Spirit by the Mouth of his servant, John, sirnam'd lacy. The Second Part* (London, 1707), pp. 110–11, 194–5.

26. John Lacy, *A relation of the dealings of God to his unworthy servant John Lacy, since the time of his believing and professing himself inspir'd* (London, 1708), p. 25.

27. Sir Richard Bulkeley, *An Answer to Several Treatises lately published on the Subject of the Prophets* (London, 1708), p. 113.

28. Bulkeley, *An Answer to Several Treatises*, pp. 114–15.

29. See Schwartz, *The French Prophets*: 'It was not simply the powers of the prophets or the relief of illness that brought these healed men into the group; it was also the spiritual drama of the cure. The experience of physical disruption and restoration could contribute positively to an awareness of the spiritual side of life. Prophecy and miracle promised to meet the desire for an understanding of that providence through which one had been so strangely blessed', p. 219. Some Quakers also used miracles as a missionary tool, as discussed in chapter 3.

30. Hillel Schwartz, *Knaves, Fools, Madmen and that Subtile Effluvium: A Study of the Opposition to the French Prophets in England, 1706–1710* (Gainesville, FL: The University Presses of Florida, 1978), p. 40.

31. Edward Fowler, *Reflections Upon a letter Concerning Enthusiasm* (London: H. Clements, 1709), p. 56.

32. I am indebted to Schwartz's helpful discussion of these various explanations for the Prophets' behaviour: see Schwartz, *Knaves, Fools, Madmen*, chapter 2.

33. See the forthcoming Oxford doctoral thesis of my graduate student, Ahmed Weir, on gentleman prophets in England, 1660–1730.

34. The Philadelphians were followers of Jane Lead, much influenced by Jacob Boehme's mystical theology. The Philadelphian group, which Roach had helped Jane Lead to found, collapsed in 1704, but Roach still had hopes of reviving it, and when he got involved with the French Prophets, he hoped he might convert them to his Behmenist beliefs.

35. Richard Roach, Miscellaneous Papers, Bodleian Rawlinson MSS D.832, 77v.

36. Richard Roach, Miscellaneous Papers, Bodleian Rawlinson MSS D.833, 33–34v.

37. Greatrakes, *A Brief Account*, p. 31.

38. Richard Kingston, *Enthusiastick Impostors no divinely inspir'd prophets* (London, 1707), p. 115.

39. Lacy, *A relation of the dealings of God*, p. 24.

40. Peter Annet, *The Resurrection Reconsidered* (London, 1744), p. 363.

41. Kingston, *Enthusiastick Impostors*, p. 81

42. This is a common trope in predictions of resurrection: for example, the prophet Joanna Southcott's body was kept warm in bed for several days after her death in December 1814, as her followers awaited her resurrection.

43. *Predictions concerning the Raising the Dead Body of Mr Thomas Emes* (London, 1708), p. 2.

44. *A Collection of Prophetical Warnings of the Eternal Spirit pronounc'd by the following persons, viz. Mary Aspinal, Mary Beer, aged 13. Thom. Dutton. Emes, John Glover* (London, 1708), p. 2.

45. *The Flying Post: Or, The Post-Master*, 2040, Tuesday 25–Thursday 27 May 1708.

46. Schwartz, *Knaves, Fools, Madmen*, p. 24. Schwartz provides a helpful summary of the Emes episode on pp. 22–4. There is also a selection of texts about the Emes prediction by the French Prophets and their critics, and a discussion about how the events related to the broader popular culture, in *Eighteenth-Century Popular Culture: A Selection*, eds. John Mullan and Christopher Reid (Oxford and New York: Oxford University Press, 2000), pp. 86–114.

47. George Hickes, *The Spirit of Enthusiasm Exorcised: in a sermon preach'd before the University of Oxford &c.*, 4th edn (1709), epistle dedicatory, A6.

48. Shaftesbury, 'The Moralists, A Philosophical Rhapsody, Being a Recital of Certain Conversations on Natural and Moral Subjects' in *Characteristics*, ed. Klein, p. 292.

49. Shaftesbury, 'The Moralists', p. 293.

50. Thomas Chubb, *A Discourse on Miracles, considered as evidences to prove the divine original of a revelation* (London, 1741), p. 87.

51. This was an Anglicisation of the French: Jean Chevalier.

52. Chubb, *A Discourse on Miracles*, pp. 85, 86, 87.

53. Chubb, *A Discourse on Miracles*, p. 83.

54. Chubb, *A Discourse on Miracles*, pp. 89, 90, 91.

55. Chubb, *A Discourse on Miracles*, pp. 93–4.

56. Chubb, *A Discourse of Miracles*, p. 96.

57. Peter Annet, *Supernaturals examined: in Four Dissertations* (1749) in Annet, *A collection of the tracts of a certain free enquirer*, with a new introduction by John Valdimir Price (London: Routledge/Thoemmes Press, 1995) p. 138.

58. Annet, *Supernaturals examined*, pp. 139–41.

59. Hume is often taken to be the high point of the philosophical debate on miracles – and certainly his text has garnered a lot of attention – but R. M. Burns suggests that the essay 'was very much a tail-end contribution to a flagging debate', and some current scholarship on Hume's text on miracles suggests that 'it is in fact a largely derivative work'. Undoubtedly, such scholars are trying to provide a corrective to philosophical treatments of Hume's text, which have tended to analyse it in isolation from the rest of the philosophical debate on miracles. See Burns, *Great Debate on Miracles*, p. 10 and Earman, *Hume's Abject Failure*, p. 14. Herrick nevertheless points to the

considerable number of texts published in the decades after Hume's essay. See his *The Radical Rhetoric of the English Deists*.

60. David Hume, *Of Miracles* (1748) (Las Salle, IL: Open Court Publishing, 1985), introduced by Anthony Flew, p. 32. 'Of Miracles' was originally published as section 10 of Hume's *An Enquiry Concerning Human Understanding*.

61. Hume, *Of Miracles*, p. 50.

62. Hume, *Of Miracles*, p. 51.

63. John Toland, *Tetradymus* (London, 1720), p. ii.

64. Thomas Woolston, *A Discourse on the Miracles of our Saviour, in view of the present controversy between the infidels and apostates* (London, 1727), p. 19.

65. Woolston, *A Discourse on Miracles*, pp. 32–3.

66. Woolston, *A Discourse on Miracles*, pp. 35–6.

67. Thomas Ray, *Our Saviour's Miracles Vindicated. On occasion of a late discourse on the miracles of our Saviour by Thomas Woolston* (London, 1727), p. vi.

68. Voltaire, *Letter addressed to His Highness the Prince of *****, containing, comments on the writings of the most eminent authors, who have been accused of attacking the Christian Religion* (Glasgow, 1769), pp. 46, 47, 48.

69. Stephen, *History of English Thought*, pp. 231–2.

70. Herrick, *The Radical Rhetoric of the English Deists*, p. 77.

71. Voltaire, *Letter addressed to His Highness the Prince of *****, p. 46.

72. William H, Trapnell, 'Woolston, Thomas (*bap.* 1668, *d.* 1733),' *DNB*, http://www.oxforddnb.com/view/article/29963.

73. Abraham Le Moine, *A Treatise on Miracles, wherein their nature, conditions, characteristics and true immediate cause are clearly stated* (London, 1747) p. 24. The *Treatise* was serialised in the *Gentleman's Magazine*, 1st series 19 (1749), pp. 161–3. Le Moine was Chaplain to the French Hospital in London from 1723 to 1743 and then Rector of Eversley in Wiltshire.

74. Fowler, *Reflections Upon a letter Concerning Enthusiasm*, p. 67.

75. Le Moine, *A Treatise on Miracles*, pp. 419, 420, 425, 426, 427, 428, 437.

76. Thomas Sherlock, *The Trial of the Witnesses of the Resurrection of Jesus* (London, 1729), p. 4.

77. George Wade, *Two Discourses: The First an Appeal to the Miracles of Jesus as Proofs of His Messiahship. The Second, a Demonstration of the Truth and Certainty of His Resurrection from the Dead* (London, 1729), p. 29.

78. Wade, *Two Discourses*, pp. 35, 38, 40.

79. Herrick, *The Radical Rhetoric of the English Deists*, p. 95.

80. *An Answer to the Jewish Rabbi's Two Letters Against Christ's Resurrection, and his raising Lazarus from the Dead; in a letter to Mr Woolston* (London, 1729), pp. 18. 15, 16.

81. John Williams, *Twelve Sermons Preach'd at the Lecture Founded by Robert Boyle Esq. Concerning the Possibility, Necessity, and Certainty of Divine Revelation*, 2nd edn (London: R. Chiswell, 1708), sermons 8 and 9, pp. 288–9.

82. Offspring Blackall, *A defence of natural and revealed religion: being a collection of the sermons preached at the lecture founded by Robert Boyle Esq.* (3 vols, London, 1739), vol. 1, sermon 7, pp. 609–10, 617–20.

83. William Law, *The Case of Reason, or natural religion, fairly and fully stated* (London, 1731). For the criticisms of Law, see Philip Doddridge, *The Perspicuity and Solidity of the Evidences for Christianity* (London, 1742); George Benson, *The Reasonableness of Christian Religion as Delivered in the Scriptures* (London, 1743); John Leland, *Remarks on a late Pamphlet, Entitled, 'Christianity not Founded on Argument'* (London, 1744) and the chapter on Dodwell in Leland's *View of the principal deistical writers that have appeared in England in the last and present century* (1757); Thomas Randolph, *The Christian's Faith a Rational Assent* (London, 1744); in addition, Dodwell's own brother, William, preached two sermons at Oxford, attacking Henry's work.

84. Joseph Butler, *The Analogy of Religion, natural and revealed, to the constitution and course of nature*, 2nd edn (London, 1736), pp. i, 363, 356.
85. Arthur Ashley Sykes, *A Brief Discourse Concerning the Credibility of Miracles and Revelation* (London, 1742), pp. 24–5.
86. Sykes, *A Brief Discourse*, pp. 35, 29–30, 42.
87. Jonathan Sheehan has noted that before the middle of the eighteenth century biblical scholarship in England was necessarily stagnant or 'engaged in a rearguard defense of the Bible per se'. Thus, he argues, 'It was only late in the century – deism effectively dead, and religion once more on the march with the revivals of Hutchinsonianism, and more importantly, Methodism – that the English project of Bible translation began to pick up steam, as the objectives of Biblical scholarship drifted slowly away from protection and toward renewal.' Sheehan, *The Enlightenment Bible*, p. 53. Leslie Stephen attributed the doubt about miracles in this period in part to 'certain rudimentary symptoms of the tendency which developed with time into genuine historical criticism'. See his *History of English Thought in the Eighteenth Century*, p. 246. On the 'demystification' of the Bible in early to mid eighteenth-century English scholarship, see also David S. Katz, *God's Last Words: Reading the English Bible From the Reformation to Fundamentalism* (New Haven and London: Yale University Press, 2004), chapter 4.
88. See *A Letter to Mr Fleetwood Concerning Miracles* (London, 1702).
89. Matthew Tindal, *Christiainity as old as the creation, or the gospel, a republication of nature* (London, 1730), vol. 1, p. 31.
90. Annet, *Supernaturals examined*, pp. 128, 127.
91. Annet, *Supernaturals examined*, pp. 125–6.
92. Hume, *Of Miracles*, p. 32.
93. Peter Harrison, 'Newtonian Science, Miracles and the Laws of Nature', *Journal of the History of Ideas* 56 (1995), p. 537.
94. For an interesting discussion of the arguments about this, see Frederick C. Beiser, *The Sovereignty of Reason: The Defense of Rationality in the Early English Enlightenment* (Princeton, NJ: Princeton University Press, 1996), chapter 6.

Chapter 8　　Conclusion

1. Annet, *Supernaturals Examined*, p. 168.
2. *Gentleman's Magazine*, 1st Series, 18, September 1748, p. 413.
3. William Harding was the curate of Coppenhall from October 1729 until his death on 9 July 1775; the rectors at this time were absentees.
4. *Gentleman's Magazine* 1st series, 18 (September 1748), p. 414.
5. John Bennett, Journal MS, JRL, Methodist Archives and Research Centre, 20 September 1748 and 29 March 1749.
6. *Gentleman's Magazine*, 1st series, 18 (1748), pp. 448, 450, 513.
7. *Gentleman's Magazine*, 1st series, 19 (1749), p. 343.
8. *Monthly Magazine* 25 (June 1808) and 26 (August 1808).
9. John Toland, *Pantheisticon: or The form of celebrating the Socratic-society* (1720) (New York: Garland, 1971 (reprint of the 1751 edition), p. 5.
10. Frank E. Manuel, *The Eighteenth Century Confronts the Gods* (New York: Athenum, 1967), p. 66
11. Connor, *Dumbstruck*, p. 186.
12. See E. J. Clery's discussion of the case in her *The Rise of Supernatural Fiction, 1762–1800* (Cambridge: Cambridge University Press, 1995) pp. 13–32.
13. *The Universal Magazine*, February 1762, p. 103.
14. On Mary Toft, see Lisa Cody, '"The Doctor's in Labour"; or a New Whim Wham

from Guildford', *Gender and History*, 4: 2 (Summer 1992), pp. 175–96, and Dennis Todd, *Imagining Monsters: Miscreations of the Self in Eighteenth-Century England* (Chicago and London: University of Chicago Press, 1995). Todd comments on the lack of religious interpretations of the case, and is therefore surprised that Hogarth included it in an engraving about enthusiasm.

15. See Robert G. Ingram, '"The Trembling Earth is God's Herald": Earthquakes, Religion and Public Life in Britain during the 1750s' in *The Lisbon Earthquake of 1755: Representations and Reactions*, eds Theodore E. D. Braun and John B. Radner (Oxford: Voltaire Foundation, 2005), pp. 97–115.

16. Thomas Sherlock, *A Letter from the Lord Bishop of London, to the Clergy and People of London and Westminster; on Occasion of the Late Earthquakes* (London, 1750).

17. W. S. Lewis, *Letters of Horace Walpole* (London: The Folio Society, 1951), p. 64.

18. T. D. Kendrick, *The Lisbon Earthquake* (London: Methuen, 1956).

19. Clark, 'Providence, Predestination and Progress', p. 572.

20. Henry D. Rack, *Reasonable Enthusiast: John Wesley and the Rise of Methodism* (Philadelphia: Trinity Press International, 1989), p. 432. See also Henry D. Rack, 'Doctors, Demons and Early Methodist Healing', *The Church and Healing*. Studies in Church History 19, ed. W. J. Sheils (Oxford: Basil Blackwell, 1982).

21. Rack, *Reasonable Enthusiast*, p. 388.

22. John Wesley, *Letters*, ed. J. Trelford (8 vols, London, 1931), vol. 8 p. 76. On Methodism and the miraculous, see the forthcoming Oxford doctoral thesis of Robert Webster.

23. Susan Juster, *Doomsayers: Anglo-American Prophecy in the Age of Revolution* (Philadelphia, PA: University of Pennsylvania Press, 2003).

24. On the nineteenth-century debates about miracles, see Robert Bruce Mullin, *Miracles and the Modern Religious Imagination* (New Haven and London: Yale University Press, 1996).

25. Martin, *On Secularization*, p. 3.

Bibliography

Manuscript Sources

British Library, London

Boyle, Robert, *Work Diary XXVI (Accounts of Cures performed by Valentine Greatrakes, 1666)* I, BL, Add MS 4293.

Bodleian Library, Oxford

Richard Roach, Miscellaneous Papers, Bodleian Rawlinson MSS D. 832, 77v. Richard Roach, Miscellaneous Papers, Bodleian Rawlinson MSS D. 833, 33–34v.

Dr Williams's Library, London

Pledger Diary, Dr Williams's Library, MSS 28.4, f.60v.

John Rylands Library, Manchester

Bennett, John, *Journal* MS, JRL, Methodist Archives and Research Centre, 20 September 1748 and 29 March 1749.

Primary Sources

Allen, Thomas, *Cheirexoke: The Excellency or Handy-work of The Royal Hand* (London, 1665).
Annet, Peter, *The Resurrection Reconsidered* (London, 1744).
—— *Supernaturals examined: in Four Dissertations* (1749) in Annet, *A collection of the tracts of a certain free enquirer*, with a new introduction by John Valdimir Price (London: Routledge/Thoemmes Press, 1995).

—— *A Collection of the Tracts of a Certain Free Inquirer* (London: Routledge/Thoemmes Press, 1995).

An Answer to the Jewish Rabbi's Two Letters Against Christ's Resurrection, and his raising Lazarus from the Dead; in a letter to Mr Woolston (London, 1729).

Ashley Cooper, Anthony, Third Earl of Shaftesbury, 'A Letter Concerning Enthusiasm' (1707) in *Characteristics of Men, Manners, Opinions, Times*, ed. Lawrence E. Klein (Cambridge: Cambridge University Press, 1999), pp. 4–29.

—— 'The Moralists, A Philosophical Rhapsody, being a recital of certain conversations on natural and moral subjects' in *Characteristics of Men, Manners, Opinions, Times*, ed. Lawrence E. Klein (Cambridge: Cambridge University Press, 1999), pp. 231–339.

A Miraculous Proof of the Resurrection: Or, The Life to Come Illustrated. Being a Strange Relation of What Hapned to Mris Anna Atherton (London, 1680).

Ayre, John, ed. *The Works of John Jewel, Bishop of Salisbury, The Third Portion* (Cambridge: Cambridge University Press, 1848).

Aubrey, John, *Miscellanies* (London, 1696).

Bagshawe, William H. G. A., *A Memoir of William Bagshawe (of Ford Hall) styled 'The Apostle of the Peak' with extracts from his unpublished writings* (London, 1887).

Baxter, Richard, *Reliquiae Baxterianae* (London, 1696).

—— *The practical works of the Rev. Richard Baxter: with a life of the author, and a critical examination of his writings*, ed. W. Orme (23 vols, London: James Duncan, 1830).

Beckett, William, *A Free and Impartial Enquiry into the Antiquity and Efficacy of Touching for the Cure of the King's Evil* (London, 1722).

Benson, George, *The Reasonableness of Christian Religion as Delivered in the Scriptures* (London, 1743).

Beverly, Thomas, *A Discourse upon the Powers of the World to Come: or, The Miraculous Powers of the Gospel and Kingdom of our Lord Jesus Christ* (London, 1694).

Blackall, Offspring, *A defence of natural and revealed religion: being a collection of the sermons preached at the lecture founded by the Honourable Robert Boyle, Esq.* (3 vols, London, 1739).

Blackwood, Christopher, *Expositions and Sermons upon the Ten First Chapters of the Gospel of Jesus Christ, According to Matthew* (London, 1659).

Boyle, Robert, *The Correspondence of Robert Boyle*, Michael Hunter, Antonia Clericuzio and Lawrence M. Principe, eds (6 vols, London: Pickering and Chatto, 2001).

—— *The Works of the Honourable Robert Boyle: In Six Volumes* (London, 1722).

Blome, Richard, *The Fanatick History, or An Exact Relation and account of the old Anabaptists and new Quakers* (London: J. Sims, 1660).

Browne, John, *Adenachoiradelogia: or, An anatomick-chirurgical treatise of glandules & strumaes. Together with the royal gift of healing* (London, 1684).

Bulkeley, Sir Richard, *An Answer to Several Treatises lately published on the Subject of the Prophets* (London: B. Bragg, 1708).

Butler, Joseph, *The Analogy of Religion, natural and revealed, to the constitution and course of nature*, 2nd edn (London, 1736).

By the King, A Proclamation for the Better Ordering of Those Who Repair to the Court for the Cure of the Disease Called the Kings-Evil (London, 1662).

Cadbury, Henry, ed. *George Fox's 'Book of Miracles'* (Cambridge: Cambridge University Press, 1948).

Calvin, John, *Commentary on the Gospel According to St John 11–21 and the First Epistle of John*, trans. T.H.L. Parker, eds David W. Torrance and Thomas F. Torrance (London and Edinburgh: Oliver and Boyd, 1961).

—— *Institutes of the Christian Religion*, I and II, trans. Ford Lewis Battles, ed. John T. McNeill (London, SCM Press, 1961).

—— *Commentary on the Acts of the Apostles*, Volume I (1552), trans. John W. Fraser and W. J. G. McDonald, David W. Torrance and Thomas F. Torrance, eds (Carlisle: Paternoster Press and Grand Rapids, MI: Erdmans, 1965).

Camm, J., *An Answer to a Book which Samuel Eaton put up to Parliament* (London: Giles Calvert, 1654).

Chaloner W. H., ed., *Bridget Bostock: The 'White Witch' of Coppenhall near Nantwich in Cheshire 1748–1749* (Crewe: Mayor of Crewe's Charity Committee, 1948).

Chubb, Thomas, *A Discourse on Miracles, considered as evidences to prove the divine original of a revelation* (London, 1741).

Clapham, Jonathan, *A Full Discovery and Confutation of the wicked and damnable doctrines of the Quakers* (London, 1656).

Clark, Henry, *His Grace the Duke of Monmouth Honoured in his Progress in the West of England in an Account of a most Extraordinary Cure of the Kings Evil: Given in a Letter from Crookhorn in the County of Somerset from the Minister of the Parish and many others* (London, 1680).

A Collection of Prophetical Warnings of the Eternal Spirit pronounc'd by the following persons, viz. Mary Aspinal, Mary Beer, aged 13. Thom. Dutton, Thom. Emes, John Glover (London, 1708).

Constitutions and Canons Eccleasiasticall . . . (London, 1604).

Conway, Anne, ed. Nicholson, Marjorie Hope, *The Conway Letters* (rev. Sarah Hutton) (Oxford: Clarendon Press, 1992).

Crashaw, William, *The Jesuites Gospel* (London, 1610).

Crouch, Nathaniel, *Surprizing Miracles of Nature and Art* (London, 1729).

Davis, R., *Truth and Innocency Vindicated* (London, 1692).

Deacon, John, *The Grand Impostor Examined* (London, 1656).

A Declaration from Oxford, of Anne Greene . . . that was lately . . . hanged . . . but since recovered (London: T. Clowes, 1651).

Doddridge, Philip, *The Perspicuity and Solidity of the Evidences for Christianity* (London, 1742).

Doe, Charles, *Narrative of the Miraculous Cure of Anne Munnings of Colchester, by Faith, Prayer, and anointing with Oil, on New Year's Day, 1705* (Totham: Charles Clark, 1848).

Dorcastor, N., *The Doctrine of the Masse Booke concerning the making of holye water, salt, breade, candels* (London, 1554).

Dunton, John, *The life and errors of John Dunton . . . written by himself* (London, 1705).

—— *The Athenian Mercury* (London, 1691–7).

Eaton, Samuel, *The Quakers Confuted, being an answer to nineteen queries* (London, 1654).

Edwards, Morgan, *Materials Towards a History of the Baptists*, Vol. 1, Eve B. Weeks and Mary B. Warren, eds (2 vols, Danielsville, GA: Heritage Papers, 1984).

Edwards, Thomas, *Gangraena: Or a Catalogue and Discovery of many of the Errours, Heresies, Blasphemies and pernicious Practices of the Sectaries of this time, vented and acted in England in these four last years* (London, 1646).

—— *The Third Part of Gangraena or, A new and higher Discovery of the Errors, Blasphemies, and insolent Proceedings of the Sectaries of these times; with some Animadversions by way of confutation upon many of the Errors and Heresies named* (London, 1646).

Ellwood, Thomas, *Journal* (London, 1694).

Evelyn John, *The Diary of John Evelyn*, ed. E. S. De Beer (London: Oxford University Press, 1959).

An Exact Relation of the Wonderful Cure of Mary Maillard (London, 1730).

Fanshaw, [Mrs], *A True and Wonderful Account of a Cure of the King's Evil, by Mrs Fanshaw, Sister to His Grace the Duke of Monmouth* (London, 1681).

Fanshaw, [Mrs], *An Answer to a Scoffing and Lying Libell, put forth and privately dispersed under the title of A Wonderful Account of the Cureing of the King's-Evil, by Madam Fanshaw the Duke of Monmouth's Sister* (London, 1681).

Farnsworth, R., *England's Warning Piece Gone Forth* (London, 1653).

Fleetwood, William, *An Essay upon Miracles in Two Discourses* (London, 1701).

The Flying Post: Or, The Post-Master (1708–10).

Ford, Simon, A *Discourse Concerning God's Judgements, preached at Old Swinford* (London, 1678).

Fowler, Edward, *A vindication of a late undertaking of certain gentlemen, in order to the suppressing of debauchery, and profaneness* (London, 1692).

—— *Reflections Upon a letter Concerning Enthusiasm* (London: H. Clements, 1709).

Fox, George, *The Great Misery of the Great Whore* (London, 1659).

—— *Journal of George Fox* (2 vols, Cambridge: Cambridge University Press, 1911).

—— 'The Cambridge "Journal of George Fox", xii', *Journal of Friends Historical Society*, 14: 2 (1917), pp.81–5.

Fox, George and R. Hubberthorn, *Truth's defence against the refined subtilty of the serpent held forth in divers answers to severall queries made by men (called ministers) in the North* (York: Thomas Wayt, 1653).

Gee, John, *The foot out of the snare* (London, 1624).

The Gentleman's Magazine: or, Monthly intelligencer . . . , collected chiefly from the public papers by Sivanus Urban 1731–1833 (103 vols, London, 1731–1868).

Gilbert, John, *An answer to the Bishop of Condon (now of Meaux) his Exposition of the Catholick faith etc. wherein the doctrine of the Church of Rome is detected and that of the Church of England expressed, from the publick acts of both churches* (London, 1686).

Glanvill, Joseph, *A Blow at Modern Sadducism* (London, 1668).

—— *Sadducismus Triumphatus* (London, 1689).

God's Great and Wonderful Work in Somersetshire. Or, The Charitable Farmer Miraculously Rewarded (London, 1674).

Grantham, Thomas, *Christianismus Primitivus* (London, 1678).

Gratton, John, *A Journal of the Life of that Ancient Servant of Christ, John Gratton* (London, 1720).

Greatrakes, Valentine, *A Brief Account of Mr Valentine Greatraks, and Divers of the Cures by him lately performed. Written by himself in a letter addressed to the Honourable Robert Boyle Esq.* (London, 1666).

—— *The Great Cures and Strange Miracles performed by Mr Valentine Gretrux* (London, 1666).

Green, Mary Anne Everett, F. H. B. Daniell and F. L. Bickley, eds, *Calendar of State Papers, Domestic Series, of the Reign of Charles II . . . , 1668–69* (28 vols, London: Longman, Green, Longman, & Roberts, 1860–1938).

H. A., *Mirabile Pecci: or the Non-Such Wonder of the Peak in Derbyshire. Discovered in a full, though succinct and sober, Narrative of the more than ordinary Parts, Piety and Preservation of Martha Taylor, one who hath been supported in time above a year in away beyond the ordinary course of Nature, without the use of Meat or Drink* (London, 1669).

Harsnet, Samuel, *A declaration of egregious popish impostures* (London: I. Roberts, 1605).

Hickes, George, *The Spirit of Enthusiasm Exorcised: in a sermon preach'd before the University of Oxford &c.*, 4th edn. (1709).

Hobbes, Thomas, *The Correspondence of Thomas Hobbes*, Noel Malcolm, ed., (2 vols, Oxford: Clarendon Press, 1994).

Hume, David, 'Of Superstition and Enthusiasm' (1741) in *Essays Moral, Political and Literary* ed. Eugene F. Miller (Indianapolis, IN: Liberty Classics, 1987), pp. 73–9.

—— *Of Miracles* (La Salle, IL: Open Court Publishing, 1985).

Illingworth, James, *A Just Narrative or Account of the Man whose Hands and legs Rotted off* (London, 1678).

Jeake, Samuel, *An Astrological Diary of the Seventeenth Century: Samuel Jeake of Rye 1652–1699*, Michael Hunter and Annabel Gregory, eds (Oxford: Clarendon Press, 1988).

Jessey, Henry, *The Exceeding Riches of Grace Advanced, By the Spirit of Grace, in an Empty Creature, viz. Mris. Sarah Wight* (London, 1647).

Kingston, Richard, *Enthusiastick Impostors no divinely inspir'd prophets* (London, 1707).

Knollys, Hanserd and William Kiffin, *The Life and Death of that old Disciple of Jesus Christ . . . Mr Hanserd Knollys . . . Written with his own Hand to the Year 1672, and continued in General, in an Epistle by Mr William Kiffin* (London, 1692).

Lacy, John, *Warnings of the Eternal Spirit by the Mouth of his servant, John, sirnam'd lacy. The Second Part* (London, 1707).

—— *A relation of the dealings of God to his unworthy servant John Lacy, since the time of his believing and professing himself inspir'd* (London, 1708).

Law, William, *The Case of Reason, or natural religion, fairly and fully stated* (London, 1731).

Leland, John, *Remarks on a late Pamphlet, Entitled, 'Christianity not Founded on Argument'* (London, 1744).

—— *View of the principal deistical writers that have appeared in England in the last and present century* (London, 1757).

Le Moine, Abraham, *A Treatise on Miracles, wherein their nature, conditions, characteristics, and true immediate cause are clearly stated* (London, 1747).

A Letter to Mr Fleetwood Concerning Miracles (London, 1702).

The Life and Death of Mr Henry Jessey (London, 1671).

The Life and Death of Mr. Vavasour Powell, That Faithful Minister and Confessor of Christ (London, 1671).

Light in darkness, or, a Modest Enquiry into, and humble improvement of Miracles, in General, Upon Occasion of this late Miraculous Cure of Marianne Maillard (London, 1694).

Lloyd, David, *Wonders No Miracles; or Mr. Greatrakes Gift of Healing Examined, upon Occasion of a Sad Effect of his Stroaking Mar. the 7, 1665 at one Mr. Cressets House in Charter-House Yard* (London, 1665/6).

Locke, John, *The reasonableness of Christianity* (London, 1695).

—— 'A Discourse on Miracles' in *John Locke: Writings on Religion*, Victor Nuovo, ed. (Oxford: Clarendon Press, 2002) pp. 44–50.

Lower, Sir William, *A Relation in the form of journal of the voyage and residence which the most mighty Prince Charles the II king of Great Britain, & c. hath made in Holland* (The Hague, 1660).

Luther, Martin, *Luther's Works*, trans. G.V. Schick, ed. Jaroslav Pelikan (56 vols, St Louis: Concordia Publishing House, 1955–86).

Lysons, Daniel and Samuel Lysons, *Magna Britannia, a concise topographical account of the several counties of Great Britain* (6 vols, London: Cadell and Davies, 1817).

M[arsin], M., *The Near Approach of Christ's Kingdom, Clearly Proved by Scripture* (London, 1696).

—— *The Figurative Speeches: by which God has veiled his secrets contained in his Word, until the end of the Time* (London, 1697).

Mather, Increase, *An Essay for the Recording of Illustrious Providences* (Boston in New-England, 1684).

Matthews, A. G., *Calumy revised: Being a revision of Edmund Calamy's Account of the Ministers and others ejected and silenced 1660–2* (Oxford: Oxford University Press, 1988).

Middleton, Conyers, *A free enquiry into the miraculous powers, which are supposed to have subsisted in the Christian Church, from the earliest ages through several successive centuries* (London, 1749).

The Miraculous Child or, Wonderfull news from Manchester. A most true account, how Charles Bennet doth speak Latine, Greek and Hebrew. (London, 1679).

Monthly Magazine 25 (June and August 1808).

More, Henry, *Enthusiasmus Triumphatus, or a Brief Discourse of The Nature, Causes, Kinds and Cure of Enthusiasm*, ed. M. V. Porte (2nd edn, 1662, facsimile) (Los Angeles: University of California Press, 1966).

A Narrative of the late Extraordinary Cure Wrought in an Instant Upon Mrs Elizabeth Savage (lame from Birth) without the use of any Natural Means (London, 1694).

Nayler, J. and Richard Hubberthorn, *A Short Answer to a Book called the Fanatick History: published by Richard Blome, against the Quakers* (London, 1660).

Nevinson, Charles, ed. *Later Writings of Bishop Hooper* (Cambridge: Cambridge University Press, 1852).

Newman, John Henry, *Two Essays on Biblical and on ecclesiastical miracles* (3rd edn) (London: Basil M. Pickering, 1873).

Oldenburg, Henry, *The Correspondence of Henry Oldenburg, 1663–1665*, ed. and trans. Rupert A. Hall and Marie Boas Hall (13 vols, Madison, Milwaukee and London: University of Wisconsin Press, 1966).

Pagett, Ephraim, *Heresiographie*, 5th edn (London, 1654).

Pead, Deuel, *Jesus is God: or, The deity of Jesus Christ vindicated, an abstract of some sermons* (London, 1694).

Petty, William, *The Petty Papers: some unpublished writings of Sir William Petty*, ed. Landsdowne, H. W. E. P. F. (London: Constable, 1927).

Philosophical Transactions 1666–1886 (177 vols, London: J. Martyn and J. Allestyry, 1886).

Pitt, Moses, *An Account of one Ann Jeffries. Now living in the county of Cornwall, who was fed for six months by a small sort of Airy People call'd Fairies. And of the strange and wonderful cures she performed with salves and medicines she received from them, for which she never took one Penny of her Patients. In a Letter from Moses Pitt to the Rt Revd Father in God, Dr Edward Fowler, Lord Bishop of Gloucester* (London, 1696).

A Plain and True Relation of a very Extraordinary Cure of Marianne Maillard (London, 1693).

Predictions concerning the Raising the Dead Body of Mr Thomas Emes (London, 1708).

Randolph, Thomas, *The Christian's Faith a Rational Assent* (London, 1744).

Rawlins, William, *A true copy of a letter from a minister of a dissenting congregation at Colchester, to a friend in London: concerning the miraculous cure of the daughter of Mrs. Muliner* (London, 1706).

Ray, Thomas, *Our Saviour's Miracles Vindicated. On occasion of a late discourse on the miracles of our Saviour by Thomas Woolston* (London, 1727).

Rehakosht, P. (pseud.), *A Plain and Just Account of a Most Horrid and Dismal Plague . . .* (London, 1692).

A Relation of the Miraculous Cure of Mrs Lydia Hills of a Lameness of Eighteen Years Continuance, 2nd edn with additions (London, 1696).

A Relation of the Miraculous Cure of Susannah Arch, of a Leprosy and Physick (London, 1695).

Reynolds, John, *A discourse upon prodigious abstinence occasioned by the twelve moneths fasting of Martha Taylor, the famous Derbyshire Damsell: proving that without any miracle, the texture of humane bodies may be so altered that life can be long continued without the supplies of meat and drink* (London, 1669).

Riden, Dorothy, ed. 'The Autobiography of Leonard Wheatcroft, of Ashover, 1627–1706' *Derbyshire Record Society*, 20 (1993).

Robins, Thomas, *Newes from Darby-shire; or the Wonder of all Wonders* (London, 1668).

—— *The Wonder of the World* (London, 1669).

Rollins, Hyder E., 'Notes on Some English Accounts of Miraculous Fasts', *Journal of American Folklore* 34 (1921), pp. 357–76.

—— ed. *The Pack of Autolycus; or, Strange and terrible news of ghosts, apparitions, monstrous births, showers of wheat, judgments of God, and other prodigious and fearful happenings as told in broadside ballads of the years 1624–1693* (Cambridge, MA: Harvard University Press, 1927).

Sheldon, Richard, *A Survey of the Miracles of the Church of Rome, proving them to be antiChristian* (London, 1616).

Sherlock, Thomas, *The Trial of the Witnesses of the Resurrection of Jesus* (London, 1729).

—— *A Letter from the Lord Bishop of London, to the Clergy and People of London and Westminster; on Occasion of the Late Earthquakes* (London, 1750).

A Short and Plain Narrative of Matthew Coker, touching some mistakes and misrecitals in reference to his gift of Healing &c. (London, 1654).

Sparrow, Anthony, *A Rationale or Practical Exposition of the Book of Common Prayer* (London, 1657).

Spinoza, Benedict de, *A Theologico-Political Treatise and A Political Treatise*, trans. R.H.M. Elwes (New York: Dover Publications, 2004).

Sprat, Thomas, *The History of the Royal-Society of London for the improving of natural knowledge* (London, 1667).

Spurrier, E., *Memorials of the Baptist Church Worshipping in Eld Lane Chapel, Colchester* (Colchester, F. Wright, 1889).

Stapleton, Thomas, *A fortresse of the faith first planted among us Englishmen* (Antwerp, 1565).

Stillingfleet, Edward, *Origines Sacrae, or a Rational Account of the Grounds of Christian Faith* (London, 1662).

—— *A Rational Account of the Grounds of Protestant Religion* (1664) (2 vols, Oxford, 1844).

Stubbe, Henry, *The Miraculous Conformist; or An Account of Severall Marvailous Cures Performed by a Stroaking of the Hands of Mr. Valentine Greatraik with a Physicall Discourse thereupon, In a Letter to the Honourable Robert Boyle, Esq.* (Oxford, 1666).

Sykes, Arthur Ashley, *A Brief Discourse Concerning the Credibility of Miracles and Revelation* (London, 1742).

Taylor, T. *Ignorance and Error Reproved* (London, 1662).

Tindal, Matthew, *Christianity as old as creation, or the gospel, a republication of nature*, vol. 1 (London, 1730).

Toland, John, *Christianity Not Mysterious, or a treatise shewing that there is nothing in the Gospel contrary to reason, nor above it and that no Christian doctrine can be properly call'd a mystery*, 2nd edn (London, 1696).

—— *Pantheisticon: or The form of celebrating the Socratic-society* (originally published 1720, reprint of the 1751 edition) (New York: Garland, 1971).

—— *Tetradymus* (London, 1720).

Trapnel, Anna, *The cry of a stone. Or A relation of something spoken in Whitehall, by Anna Trapnel, being in the visions of God* (London, 1654).

—— *Report and Plea: Or, a Narrative of a Journey from London into Cornwal, the occasion of it, the Lord's Encouragement to it, and Signal Presence with Her in It* (London, 1654).

A True Copy of a Letter of the Miraculous Cure of David Wright, a Shephard, at Hitchin in Hertfordshire (London, 1694).

A True Relation of the Wonderful Cure of Mary Maillard (London, 1694).

Turner, William, *A compleat history of the most remarkable providences, both of judgement and mercy, which have hapned in this present age* (London, 1697).

Tynley, Robert, *Two learned sermons* (London, 1609).

Underhill, Thomas, *Hell Broke Loose: or An History of the Quakers both old and new* (London, 1660).

The Universal Magazine, February 1762.

Voltaire, *Letter addressed to His Highness the Prince of *****, containing, comments on the writings of the most eminent authors, who have been accused of attacking the Christian Religion* (Glasgow, 1769).

Wade, George, *Two Discourses: The First an Appeal to the Miracles of Jesus as Proofs of His Messiahship. The Second, a Demonstration of the Truth and Certainty of His Resurrection from the Dead* (London, 1729).

Watkins, R., *Newes from the Dead. Or a True and Exact Narration of the Miraculous Deliverance of Anne Greene, who being executed at Oxford afterwards revived* (Oxford, 1651).

Werenfels, Samuel, *A Dissertation Upon Superstition in Natural Things. To which are added, Occasional Thought on the Power of Curing the King's Evil Ascribed to the Kings of England* (London, 1748).

Wesley, John, *Letters*, ed. J. Trelford (8 vols, London, 1931) vol. 8.

Whitehead, George, *The Christian Progress of that ancient servant and minister of Jesus Christ, George Whitehead* (London, 1725).

Williams, John, *Twelve Sermons Preach'd at the Lecture founded by Robert Boyle Esq. Concerning the Possibility, Necessity and Certainty of Divine Revelation*, 2nd edn (London: R. Chiswell, 1708).

Willis, Thomas, *Of Fermentation of the Inorganical Motion of Natural Bodies* (London, 1659).

The Wonderful Recompense of Faith: Or, Strange News from Dursly in Gloucestershire (London, 1675).

Wood, Anthony, *Athenae Oxonienses*, (3 vols, London, 1913).

Woolston, Thomas, *A Discourse on the Miracles of our Saviour, in view of the present controversy between the infidels and apostates* (London, 1727).

Secondary Sources

Adams, Marilyn McCord, *Horrendous Evils and the Goodness of God* (Ithaca, NY: Cornell University Press, 1999).

Albers, Jan, '"Papist Traitors" and "Presbyterian Rogues": Religious Identities in Eighteenth-Century Lancashire' in *The Church of England c.1689–c.1833: From Toleration to Tractarianism*, John Walsh, Colin Haydon and Stephen Taylor, eds (Cambridge: Cambridge University Press, 1993).

Armytage, Rushworth, 'Father Arrowsmith's Hand' in *Bygone Lancashire*, ed. Ernest Axon (London, Manchester and Hull: Simpkin, Marshall & Co., 1892).

Bahlman, D. W. R., *The Moral Revolution of 1688* (New Haven: Yale University Press, 1957).

Barnett, S. J., *The Enlightenment and Religion: The Myths of Modernity* (Manchester: Manchester University Press, 2003).

Beiser, Frederick C., *The Sovereignty of Reason: The Defense of Rationality in the Early English Enlightenment* (Princeton, NJ: Princeton University Press, 1996).

Berry, Helen, 'An Early Coffee House Periodical and its Readers: The Athenian Mercury, 1691–1697', *The London Journal*, 25:1 (2000), pp. 14–33.

—— 'Dunton, John (1659–1732)' in *Oxford Dictionary of National Biography*, H. C. G. Matthew and Brian Harrison, eds (Oxford: Oxford University Press, 2004), http://www.oxforddnb.com/view/article/8299.

Bhowmik, U., 'Facts and Norms in the Marketplace of Print: John Dunton's *Athenian Mercury*', *Eighteenth-Century Studies*, 36: 3 (2003), pp. 345–65.

Birch, Thomas, *The History of the Royal Society of London* (4 vols, London, 1756).

Bloch, M., *The Royal Touch, Sacred Monarchy and Scrofula in England and France*, trans. J. E. Anderson (London: Routledge & Kegan Paul, 1973).

Blumberg, Joan Jacobs, *Fasting Girls: The History of Anorexia Nervosa* (New York: Plume, 1988).

Bouwsma, William J., *John Calvin: A Sixteenth-Century Portrait* (Oxford and New York: Oxford University Press, 1988).

Braithwaite, William C., *The Beginnings of Quakerism* (London: Macmillan, 1923).

Brown, Peter, *The Cult of the Saints: Its Rise and Function in Latin Christianity* (Chicago: University of Chicago Press, 1981).

Buckley, Michael J., *At the Origins of Modern Atheism* (New Haven: Yale University Press, 1990).

Burke, Peter, *Popular Culture in Early Modern Europe* (New York: New York University Press, 1978).

Burns, R. M., *The Great Debate on Miracles from Joseph Glanvill to David Hume* (Lewisburg: Bucknell University Press, 1981).

Burns, William E. '"By Him the Women will be delivered from that Bondage, which some has found Intolerable": M. Marsin, English Millenarian Feminist', *Eighteenth-Century Women: Studies in Their Lives, Work and Culture*, vol. 1, ed. Linda V. Troost (3 vols, New York: AMS Press, 2001), pp. 19–38.

—— *An Age of Wonders: Prodigies, Politics and Providence in England 1657–1727* (Manchester: Manchester University Press, 2002).

Bynum, Caroline Walker, *Holy Feast and Holy Fast: The Religious Significance of Food to Medieval Women* (Berkeley and Los Angeles: University of California Press, 1987).

Cambers, Andrew and Michelle Wolfe, 'Reading, Family Religion, and Evangelical Identity in Late Stuart England', *Historical Journal*, 47: 4 (2004), pp. 875–96.

Capp, Bernard, 'Separate Domains? Women and Authority in Early Modern England' in *The Experience of Authority in Early Modern England*, Paul Griffiths, Adam Fox and Steve Hindle, eds (London: Longman, 1996), pp. 117–45.

Chadwick, Owen, *The Secularization of the European Mind in the Nineteenth Century* (1975) (Cambridge: Cambridge University Press, 1990).

Champion, J. A. I., *The Pillars of Priestcraft Shaken: The Church of England and its Enemies 1660–1730* (Cambridge: Cambridge University Press, 1992).

—— *Republican Learning: John Toland and the Crisis of Christian Culture* (Manchester: Manchester University Press, 2003).

Clark, J. C. D., *English Society, 1688–1832: Ideology, Social Structure and Political Practice during the Ancient Regime* (Cambridge: Cambridge University Press, 1985).

—— 'Providence, Predestination and Progress: Or, Did the Enlightenment Fail?' *Albion* 35: 4 (Winter 2003), pp. 559–89.

Claydon, Tony, *William III and the Godly Revolution* (Cambridge: Cambridge University Press, 1996).

Claydon, Tony, 'The sermon, the "public sphere" and the political culture of late seventeenth-century England', *The English Sermon Revised: Religion, Literature and History 1600–1750*, Lori Ann Ferrell and Peter McCullough, eds (Manchester: Manchester University Press, 2000), pp. 208–34.

Clery, E. J., *The Rise of Supernatural · Fiction, 1768–1800* (Cambridge: Cambridge University Press, 1995).

Cody, Lisa Forman, 'The Doctor's in Labour; or a New Whim Wham from Guildford', *Gender and History*, 4: 2 (Summer 1992), pp. 175–6.

—— *Birthing the Nation: Sex, Science and the Conception of Eighteenth-Century Britain* (Oxford and New York: Oxford University Press, 2005).

Collinson, Patrick, 'Truth, Lies and Fiction in Sixteenth-Century Protestant Historiography' in *The Historical Imagination in Early Modern Britain*, Donald R. Kelley and David Harris Sacks, eds (Cambridge: Cambridge University Press, 1997), pp. 37–68.

Connor, Steven, *Dumbstruck: A Cultural History of Ventriloquism* (Oxford and New York: Oxford University Press, 2000).

Cowan, Brian, 'What was Masculine about the Public Sphere? Gender and the Coffeehouse Milieu in Post-Restoration England', *History Workshop Journal*, 51 (2001), pp. 127–57.

—— *The Social Life of Coffee: The Emergence of the British Coffeehouse* (New Haven and London: Yale University Press, 2005).

Craig, A. G. 'The Movement for the Reformation of Manners 1688–1715' (PhD thesis, University of Edinburgh, 1980).

Crawfurd, Raymond, *The King's Evil* (Oxford: Clarendon Press, 1911).

Cressy, David, *Literacy and the Social Order: Reading and Writing in Tudor and Stuart England* (Cambridge: Cambridge University Press, 1980).

—— 'Books as Totems in Seventeenth-Century England and New England', *The Journal of Library History: Philosophy and Comparative Librarianship*, 21: 1 (Winter 1981), pp. 92–106.

—— *Travesties and Transgressions in Tudor and Stuart England* (Oxford and New York: Oxford University Press, 2000).

Curth, Louise Hill, 'Gell, Robert (1595–1665)' in *Oxford Dictionary of National Biography*, eds H. C. G. Matthew and Brian Harrison (Oxford: Oxford University Press, 2004), http://www.oxforddnb.com/view/article/10510.

Dailey, Barbara Ritter, 'The Visitation of Sarah Wight: Holy Carnival and the Revolution of the Saints in Civil War London', *Church History*, 55: 4 (1986), pp. 438–55.

Davies, Stevan L., *Jesus the Healer: Possession, Trance and the Origin of Christianity* (London: SCM Press, 1995).

Dear, Peter, 'Miracles, Experiments, and the Ordinary Course of Nature', *Isis* 81 (1990), pp. 663–83.

Dockrill, D. W., 'Spiritual Knowledge and the Problem of Enthusiasm in Seventeenth-Century England' in *The Concept of Spirit, Prudentia* (Auckland: University of Auckland, 1985).

Duffy, Eamon, 'Valentine Greatrakes, the Irish Stroker: Miracle, Science, and Orthodoxy in Restoration England' in *Religion and Humanism: Studies in Church History*, vol. 17 (Oxford: Basil Blackwell, 1981), pp. 251–73.

—— *The Stripping of the Altars: Traditional Religion in England 1400–1580* (New Haven and London: Yale University Press, 1992).

Dyton, S. C., 'Pagett, Ephraim (1574–1646)' in *Oxford Dictionary of National Biography*, H. C. G. Matthew and Brian Harrison, eds (Oxford: Oxford University Press, 2004), http://www.oxforddnb.com/view/article/21125.

Earman, John, *Hume's Abject Failure: The Argument against Miracles* (Oxford: Oxford University Press, 2000).

Elmer, Peter, 'Greatrakes, Valentine (1629–1683)' in *Oxford Dictionary of National Biography*, H. C. G. Matthew and Brian Harrison, eds (Oxford: Oxford University Press, 2004), http://ww.oxforddnb.com/view/article/11367.

Finucane, Ronald C., *Miracles and Pilgrims: Popular Beliefs in Medieval England* (London: J. M. Dent, 1977).

Flint, Valerie I. J., *The Rise of Magic in Early Medieval Europe* (Oxford: Clarendon Press, 1991).

Fogelin, Robert J., *A Defense of Hume on Miracles* (Princeton, NJ and Oxford: Princeton University Press, 2003).

Fox, Adam, *Oral and Literate Culture in England 1500–1700* (Oxford: Clarendon Press, 2000).

Freeman, Thomas, '"Great searching out of bookes and authors": John Foxe as an Ecclesiastical Historian' (PhD thesis, Rutgers University, 1995).

—— 'Texts, Lies and Microfilm: Reading and Misreading Foxe's *Book of Martyrs*', *The Sixteenth Century Journal*, 30: 1 (Spring 1999), pp. 23–46.

—— 'Demons, Deviance and Defiance: John Darrell and the Politics of Exorcism in Late Elizabethan England' in *Conformity and Orthodoxy in the English Church, c.1560–c.1660*, Peter Lake and Michael Questier, eds (Woodbridge: Boydell Press, 2000), pp. 34–63.

Funkenstein, Amos, *Theology and the Scientific Imagination* (Princeton, NJ: Princeton University Press, 1989).

Furdell, Elizabeth Lane, *James Welwood: Physician to the Glorious Revolution* (Conshohocken, PA: Combined Publishing, 1998).

Furdell, Elizabeth Lane, *The Royal Doctors 1485–1714: Medical Personnel at the Tudor and Stuart Courts* (Rochester NY, Rochester University Press, 2001).

Gay, Peter, *The Enlightenment, an Interpretation: The Rise of Modern Paganism* (New York: Vintage Books, 1968).

Glass, Norman, *The Early History of the Independent Church at Rothwell, alias Rowell in Northamptonshire* (London, 1871).

Goldie, Mark, 'The Theory of Religious Intolerance' in *From Persecution to Toleration: The Glorious Revolution and Religion in England*, O. P. Grell, Jonathan I. Israel and Nicholas Tyacke, eds (Oxford: Clarendon Press, 1991).

—— 'Johnston, Nathaniel (*bap.* 1629?, *d.* 1705)' in *Oxford Dictionary of National Biography*, H. C. G. Matthew and Brian Harrison, eds (Oxford: Oxford University Press, 2004), http://www.oxforddnb.com/view/article/ 14946.

Goodwin, Gordon, 'Clarke, Timothy (*d.* 1672)', rev. Michael Bevan, in *Oxford Dictionary of National Biography*, H. C. G. Matthew and Brian Harrison, eds (Oxford: Oxford University Press, 2004), http://www.oxforddnb. com/view/article/5535.

Gowing, Laura, *Common Bodies: Women, Touch and Power in Seventeenth-Century England* (New Haven and London: Yale University Press, 2003).

—— 'Greene, Anne (*c.*1628–1659)' in *Oxford Dictionary of National Biography*, H. C. G. Matthew and Brian Harrison, eds (Oxford: Oxford University Press, 2004), http://www.oxforddnb.com/view/article/11413.

Green, Ian, *Print and Protestantism in Early Modern England* (Oxford: Oxford University Press, 2000).

Gregory, Brad S., *Salvation at Stake: Christian Martyrdom in Early Modern Europe* (Cambridge, MA: Harvard University Press, 1999).

Gregory, Jeremy and Jeffrey S. Chamberlain, eds, *The National Church in Local Perspective: The Church of England and the Regions, 1660–1800* (Woodbridge: Boydell Press, 2003).

Grell, Ole Peter and Andrew Cunningham, eds, *Religion Medici: Medicine and Religion in Seventeenth-Century England* (Aldershot: Scolar Press, 1996).

Habermas, Jürgen, *The Structural Transformation of the Public Sphere*, trans. Thomas Burger (Cambridge, MA: MIT Press, 1989).

Hall, David D., ed. *Lived Religion in America: Towards a History of Practice* (Princeton, NJ: Princeton University Press, 1997).

Hardon, John A., 'The Concept of Miracle from St Augustine to Modern Apologetics', *Theological Studies* 15 (1954), pp. 229–57.

Harley, David, 'Explaining Salem: Calvinist Psychology and the Diagnosis of Possession', *American Historical Review*, 101: 2 (April 1996), pp. 307–30.

Harris, Tim, *Restoration: Charles II and his Kingdoms, 1660–1685* (London: Allen Lane, 2005).

Harrison, Peter, *'Religion' and the Religions in the English Enlightenment* (Cambridge: Cambridge University Press, 1990).

—— 'Newtonian Science, Miracles and the Laws of Nature', *Journal of the History of Ideas* 56 (1995), pp. 531–53.

Hayden, Roger, ed. *The Records of a Church in Christ in Bristol, 1640–1687* (Bristol: Bristol Record Society, 1974).

Hazard, Paul, *The European Mind: The Critical Years, 1680–1715* (1935), trans. J. Lewis May (Cleveland and New York: Meridian Books, The World Publishing Company, 1964).

Herrick, James, 'Miracles and Method', *Quarterly Journal of Speech*, 9 (1989), pp. 321–34.

—— *The Radical Rhetoric of the English Deists: The Discourse of Skepticism, 1680–1750* (Columbia: University of South Carolina Press, 1997).

Hesse, Carla, *The Other Enlightenment: How French Women Became Modern* (Princeton, NJ and Oxford: Princeton University Press, 2001).

Heyd, Michael, *'Be Sober and Reasonable': The Critique of Enthusiasm in the Seventeenth and Early Eighteenth Centuries* (Leiden: E. J. Brill, 1995).

Hill, Christopher, *The World Turned Upside Down: Radical Ideas during the English Revolution* (London: Penguin, 1972).

Hinds, Hilary, *God's Englishwomen: Seventeenth-Century Radical Sectarian Writing and Feminist Criticism* (Manchester: Manchester University Press, 1996).

Hobby, Elaine, *Virtue of Necessity: English Women's Writing 1649–88* (Ann Arbor: University of Michigan Press, 1988).

Hoppen, K. Theodore, 'The Nature of the Early Royal Society', parts 1 and 2, *British Journal for the History of Science*, 9 (1976), pp. 1–24, 243–73.

Hunter, J. Paul, *Before Novels: The Cultural Contexts of Eighteenth-Century English Fiction* (New York: W. W. Norton, 1990).

Hunter, Michael, *Science and Society in Restoration England* (Cambridge: Cambridge University Press, 1981).

—— *The Royal Society and its Fellows 1660–1700* (Chalfont St Giles: The British Society for the History of Science, monograph 4, 1982), p. 12.

—— 'The Problem of "Atheism" in Early Modern England', *Transactions of the Royal Historical* Society, 5th series, 35 (1985), pp. 135–58.

—— *The Occult Laboratory: Magic, Science and Second Sight in Late Seventeenth-Century Scotland* (Woodbridge: Boydell Press, 2001).

Hutton, Ronald, *The Restoration: A Political and Religious History of England and Wales, 1658–1667* (Oxford: Oxford University Press, 1986).

Iliffe, Rob, 'Lying Wonders and Juggling Tricks: Religion, Nature and Imposture in Early Modern England' in *Everything Connects: In Conference with Richard H. Popkin, Essays in his Honour*, James E. Force and David S. Katz, eds (Leiden: Brill, 1999).

Ingram, M. J. 'From Reformation to Toleration: Popular Religious Cultures in England 1540–1690', in Tim Harris, ed., *Popular Culture in England c.1500–1850* (Basingstoke: Macmillan, 1995), pp. 95–123.

Ingram, Robert G., '"The Trembling Earth is God's Herald": Earthquakes, Religion and Public Life in Britain during the 1750s' in *The Lisbon Earthquake of 1755: Representations and Reactions*, eds Theodore E. D. Braun and John B. Radner (Oxford: Voltaire Foundation, 2005), pp. 97–115.

Isaacs, T., 'The Anglican Hierarchy and the Reformation of Manners, 1688–1738', *Journal of Ecclesiastical History*, 33 (1982), pp. 391–411.

Israel, Jonathan I., *Radical Enlightenment: Philosophy and the Making of Modernity 1650–1750* (Oxford: Oxford University Press, 2001).

Jacob, James R. and Margaret C. Jacob, 'The Anglican Origins of Modern Science: The Metaphysical Foundations of the Whig Constitution', *Isis*, 71 (1980), pp. 211–33.

Jacob, James R., *Henry Stubbe, Radical Protestantism and the Early Enlightenment* (Cambridge: Cambridge University Press, 1983).

Johns, Adrian, *The Nature of the Book: Print and Knowledge in the Making* (Chicago and London: University of Chicago Press, 1998).

Johnson, D., *Hume, Holism and Miracles* (Ithaca and London: Cornell University Press, 1999).

Johnston, Warren, 'Beverly, Thomas' in *Oxford Dictionary of National Biography*, H. C. G. Matthew and Brian Harrison, eds (Oxford: Oxford University Press, 2004), http://www.oxforddnb.com/view/article/66364.

—— 'Revelation and the Revolution of 1688–1689', *The Historical Journal* 48: 2 (2005), pp. 351–89.

—— 'The Anglican Apocalypse in Restoration England', *Journal of Ecclesiastical History* 55: 3 (July 2004), pp. 467–501.

Jones, Rufus M., *Studies in Mystical Religion* (London: Macmillan, 1909).

Juster, Susan, *Doomsayers: Anglo-American Prophecy in the Age of Revolution* (Philadelphia, PA: University of Pennsylvania Press, 2003).

Kaplan, Barbara Beigun, 'Greatrakes the Stroker: The Interpretation of his Contemporaries', *Isis* 73 (1982), pp. 178–85.

Katz, David S., *God's Last Words: Reading the English Bible From the Reformation to Fundamentalism* (New Haven: Yale University Press, 2004).

Kendrick, T. D., *The Lisbon Earthquake* (London: Methuen, 1956).

Kiple, Kenneth F., ed. *The Cambridge World History of Disease* (Cambridge: Cambridge University Press, 1993).

Knox, R. A., *Enthusiasm: a chapter in the history of religion, with special reference to the XVII and XVIII centuries* (Oxford: Clarendon Press, 1950).

Kors, Alan Charles, *Atheism in France, 1650–1729. Volume I: the orthodox sources of disbelief* (Princeton, NJ: Princeton University Press, 1990).

Korte, Anne-Marie, ed. *Women and Miracle Stories: A Multidisciplinary Exploration* (Leiden: Brill, 2001).

Lamont, W. M., *Richard Baxter and the Millennium: Protestant Imperialism and the English Revolution* (London and Totowa, NJ: Croom Helm and Rowman and Littlefield, 1979).

Lang, Andrew, *Custom and Myth* (London: Longmans, Green and Co., 1884).

Langford, Paul, *A Polite and Commercial People: England 1727–1783* (Oxford: Clarendon Press, 1989).

Lewis, W. S., *Letters of Horace Walpole* (London: The Folio Society, 1951).

McDannell, Colleen, ed. *Religions of the United States in Practice* (2 vols, Princeton, NJ: Princeton University Press, 2001).

MacCulloch, Diarmaid, *Thomas Cranmer* (New Haven: Yale University Press, 1996).

MacDonald, Michael, 'Religion, Social Change and Psychological Healing in England, 1600–1800' in *The Church and Healing* (Studies in Church History, Volume 19), ed. W. J. Sheils (Oxford: Basil Blackwell, 1982), pp. 101–29.

MacIntosh, J. J., 'Locke and Boyle on miracles and God's existence' in *Robert Boyle Reconsidered*, ed. Michael Hunter (Cambridge: Cambridge University Press, 1994), pp. 193–214.

MacMullen, Ramsay, *Christianizing the Roman Empire: A.D. 100–400* (New Haven: Yale University Press, 1984).

Mack, Phyllis, *Visionary Women: Ecstatic Prophecy in Seventeenth-Century England* (Berkeley: University of California Press, 1992).

Manuel, Frank E., *The Eighteenth Century Confronts the Gods* (New York: Athenum, 1967).

Marshall, Peter, 'Forgery and Miracles in the Reign of Henry VIII', *Past and Present*, 178 (2003), pp. 39–73.

Martin, David, *On Secularization: Towards a Revised General Theory* (Aldershot, England and Burlington, VT: Ashgate, 2005).

Monod, Paul Kleber, *Jacobitism and the English People 1688–1788* (Cambridge: Cambridge University Press, 1989).

Morley, Henry, *Memoirs of Bartholomew Fair* (London: George Routledge, 1892).

Mullan, John, and Christopher Reid, eds, *Eighteenth-Century Popular Culture: A Selection* (Oxford and New York: Oxford University Press, 2000).

Mullin, Robert Bruce, *Miracles and the Modern Religious Imagination* (New Haven and London: Yale University Press, 1996).

Munck, Thomas, *A Comparative Social History 1721–1794* (London: Arnold, 2000).

Nicholls, David, 'The Theatre of Martyrdom in the French Reformation', *Past and Present*, 121 (1988), pp. 49–73.

Orsi, Robert A., *The Madonna of 115th Street* (New Haven and London: Yale University Press, 1985).

——, ed. *Gods of the City: Religion and the American Urban Landscape* (Bloomington: Indiana University Press, 1999).

Pagel, William, *New Light on William Harvey* (Baseland, NY: S. Karger, 1976).

Parish, Helen L., *Monks, Miracles and Magic: Reformation Representations of the Medieval Church* (London and New York: Routledge, 2005).

Park, Katherine and Lorraine Daston, 'Unnatural Conceptions: The Study of Monsters in Sixteenth- and Seventeenth-Century France and England', *Past and Present* 92 (1981), pp. 20–54.

—— *Wonders and the Order of Nature 1150–1750* (New York: Zone Books, 1998).

Parks, S. *John Dunton and the English Book Trade* (New York: Garland, 1976).

Pocock, J. G. A., *Barbarism and Religion*, vols 1 and 2 (Cambridge: Cambridge University Press, 1999).

Porter, Roy and Mikulás Teich, eds, *The Enlightenment in National Context* (Cambridge: Cambridge University Press, 1981).

Porter, Roy, *Enlightenment: Britain and the Creation of the Modern World* (London: Allen Lane, 2000).

Preus, J. Samuel, 'The Reified Heart in Seventeenth-Cenury Religion' in *Religion in History: The Word, the Idea, the Reality*, Michel Despland and Gerard Vallee, eds (Waterloo, ON: Canadian Corporation for Studies in Religion, 1992).

Purkiss, Diane, 'Producing the Voice, Consuming the Body. Women Prophets of the Seventeenth Century' in *Women, Writing, History 1640–1740*, Isobel Grundy and Susan Wiseman, eds (Athens, GA: University of Georgia Press, 1992), pp. 139–58.

Rack, Henry D., 'Doctors, Demons and Early Methodist Healing' in *The Church and Healing*, Studies in Church History 19, ed. W. J. Sheils (Oxford: Basil Blackwell, 1982).

—— *Reasonable Enthusiast: John Wesley and the Rise of Methodism* (Philadelphia: Trinity Press International, 1989).

Redwood, John, *Reason, ridicule and religion: the Age of Enlightenment in England, 1660–1750* (London, Thames and Hudson, 1976).

Rollins, Hyder E., 'Notes on Some English Accounts of Miraculous Fasts', *Journal of American Folklore*, 34 (1921), pp. 357–76.

—— ed. *The Pack of Autolycus* (Cambridge, MA: Harvard University Press, 1927).

Rose, Craig, *England in the 1690s: Revolution, Religion and War* (Oxford: Blackwell, 1999).

Schaffer, Simon, 'Self Evidence', *Critical Enquiry*, 18 (Winter 1992), pp. 327–62.

—— 'Piety, Physic and Prodigious Abstinence' in *Religion Medici: Medicine and Religion in Seventeenth-Century England*, Ole Peter Grell and Andrew Cunningham, eds (Aldershot: Scolar Press, 1996), pp. 171–203.

Schwartz, Hillel, *Knaves, Fools, Madmen and that Subtile Effluvium: A Study of the Opposition to the French Prophets in England, 1706–1710* (Gainesville, FL: University Presses of Florida, 1978).

—— *The French Prophets: The History of a Millenarian Group in Eighteenth-Century England* (Berkeley and Los Angeles: University of California Press, 1980).

Shapin, Steven, 'Pump and Circumstance: Robert Boyle's Literary Technology', *Social Studies of Science*, 14 (1984), pp. 481–520.

—— and Simon Schaffer, *Leviathan and the Air Pump: Hobbes, Boyle and the Experimental Life* (Princeton: Princeton University Press, 1985).

—— 'The House of Experiment in Seventeenth-Century England', *Isis*, 77 (1988), pp. 373–404.

—— *A Social History of Truth: Civility and Science in Seventeenth-Century England* (Chicago: Chicago University Press, 1994).

—— *The Scientific Revolution* (Chicago and London: University of Chicago Press, 1996).

Shapiro, Barbara, 'The Concept 'Fact': Legal Origins and Cultural Diffusion', *Albion*, 26: 2 (Summer 1994), pp. 227–52.

Shaw, Jane, 'Fasting Women: The Significance of Gender and Bodies in Radical Religion and Politics, 1650–1813' in *Radicalism in British Literary Culture, 1650–1830*, Timothy Morton and Nigel Smith, eds (Cambridge: Cambridge University Press, 2002), pp. 101–15.

—— 'The Long Eighteenth Century' in *A Century of Theological and Religious Studies in Britain*, ed. Ernest Nicholson (Oxford: Oxford University Press, for the British Academy, 2003), pp. 215–36.

—— 'Bostock, Bridget (*c.* c. 1678, *d.* after 1749)' in *Oxford Dictionary of National Biography*, H. C. G. Matthew and Brian Harrison, eds (Oxford: Oxford University Press, 2004), http://www.oxforddnb.com/view/article/40526.

—— 'Maillard, Marie (1680–1731)' in *Oxford Dictionary of National Biography*, H. C. G. Matthew and Brian Harrison, eds (Oxford: Oxford University Press, 2004), http://www.oxforddnb.com/view/article/66115.

Sheehan, Jonathan, 'Enlightenment, Religion, and the Enigma of Secularisation: A Review Essay', *American Historical Review*, 108: 4 (October 2003), pp. 1061–80.

—— *The Enlightenment Bible: Translation, Scholarship, Culture* (Princeton, NJ: Princeton University Press, 2005).

Shoemaker, Robert, 'Gendered Spaces: Patterns of Mobility and Perceptions of London's Geography, 1660–1750' in *Imagining Early Modern London: Perceptions and Portrayals of the City from Stow to Strype, 1598–1720*, ed. J. F. Merritt (Cambridge: Cambridge University Press, 2001), pp. 144–65.

Silverman, Joseph A., 'Anorexia Nervosa in Seventeenth Century England as Viewed by Physician, Philosopher and Pedagogue', *International Journal of Eating Disorders*, 5 (1986), pp. 847–53.

Skrabanek, Petr, 'Notes Towards the History of Anorexia Nervosa', *Janus*, 70 (1983), pp. 109–28.

Smart, T. W. W., 'A Biographical Sketch of Samuel Jeake Senr. of Rye', *Sussex Archaeological Collections 13* (1861).

Smith, Nigel, *Perfection Proclaimed: Language and Literature in English Radical Religion 1640–1660* (Oxford: Clarendon Press, 1989).

Snape, M. F., '"The Surey Impostor": Demonic Possession and Religious Conflict in Seventeenth-Century Lancashire', *Transactions of the Lancashire and Cheshire Antiquarian Society*, 90 (1994), pp.93–114.

—— *The Church of England in Industrialising Society: The Lancashire Parish of Whalley in the Eighteenth Century* (Woodbridge: Boydell Press, 2003).

Spurr, John, '"Rational Religion" in Restoration England', *Journal of the History of Ideas*, 49: 4 (1988), pp. 563–85.

—— '"Latitudinarianism" and the Restoration Church', *The Historical Journal*, 31: 1 (March 1998), pp. 61–82.

—— '"Virtue, Religion and Government": The Anglican Uses of Providence' in *The Politics of Religion in Restoration England*, eds T. Harris, P. Seaward and M. Goldie (Oxford: Oxford University Press, 1990), pp. 29–46.

—— *The Restoration Church of England 1646–1689* (New Haven: Yale University Press, 1991).

—— 'The Church, the Societies and the Moral Revolution of 1688' in *The Church of England c.1688–c.1833: From Toleration to Tractarianism*, eds John Walsh, Colin Haydon and Stephen Taylor (Cambridge: Cambridge University Press, 1993), pp. 127–42.

Steneck, Nicholas H., 'Greatrakes the Stroker: The Interpretation of Historians', *Isis*, 73 (1982) pp. 161–77.

Stephen, Leslie, *History of English Thought in the Eighteenth Century* (London: Smith, Elder and Co., 1876).

Stewart, Larry, *The Rise of Public Science: Rhetoric, Technology, and Natural Philosophy in Newtonian Britain, 1660–1750* (Cambridge: Cambridge University Press, 1992).

Sullivan, Robert, 'Rethinking Christianity in Enlightened Europe', *Eighteenth-century Studies*, 34: 2 (Winter 2001), pp. 298–309.

Sykes, Norman, *From Sheldon to Secker: Aspects of English Church History 1660–1768* (Cambridge: Cambridge University Press, 1959).

Thomas, Keith, *Religion and the Decline of Magic: Studies in Popular Beliefs in Sixteenth- and Seventeenth-Century England* (Harmondsworth, Penguin, 1971).

Thompson, Ann, *The Art of Suffering and the Impact of Seventeenth-Century Anti-Providential Thought* (Aldershot: Ashgate, 2003).

Todd, Dennis, *Imagining Monsters: Miscreations of the Self in Eighteenth-Century England* (Chicago and London: University of Chicago Press, 1995).

Trapnell, William H., 'Woolston, Thomas (*bap.* 1668, *d.* 1773)' in *Oxford Dictionary of National Biography*, H. C. G. Matthew and Brian Harrison, eds (Oxford: Oxford University Press, 2004), http://www.oxforddnb.com/view/article/29963.

Underwood, T. L., *Primitivism, Radicalism and the Lamb's War: The Baptist–Quaker Conflict in Seventeenth-Century England* (New York and Oxford: Oxford University Press, 1997).

Wadsworth, Janet, 'Martha Taylor – the Fasting Maid of Over Haddon 1651–?1687', *Derbyshire Miscellany*, 8: 3 (Spring 1978), pp. 77–83.

Walker, D. P., *Unclean Spirits: Possession and Exorcism in France and England in the Late Sixteenth and Early Seventeenth Centuries* (London: Scolar Press, 1981).

—— 'The Cessation of Miracles' in *Hermeticism and the Renaissance: Intellectual History and the Occult in Early Modern Europe*, eds Ingrid Merkel and Allen G. Debus (Cranberry, NJ: Associated University Presses, 1988).

Wallace Jr, Charles, 'Book Review: Herrick, J. *The Radical Rhetoric of the English Deists: The Discourse of Skepticism, 1680–1750*', *Church History*, 67 (1998), pp. 590–2.

Walsh, J., C. Haydon, and S. Taylor, eds, *The Church of England c. 1689–c. 1833: From Toleration to Tractarianism* (Cambridge: Cambridge University Press, 1993).

Walsham, Alexandra, *Providence in Early Modern England* (Oxford: Oxford University Press, 1999).

—— 'Reforming the Waters: Holy Wells and Healing Springs in Protestant England' in *Life and Thought in the Northern Church c.1100–c.1700: Essays*

in Honour of Claire Cross (Studies in Church History Subsidia Volume 12),
ed. Diana Wood (Woodbridge: Boydell Press, 1999).

—— 'Miracles and the Counter-Reformation Mission to England', *Historical Journal*, 46: 4 (2003), pp. 779–815.

Ward, Benedicta, *Miracles and the Medieval Mind: Theory, Record and Event 1000–1215* (London: Scolar Press, 1982).

Watt, Tessa, *Cheap Print and Popular Piety, 1550–1640* (Cambridge: Cambridge University Press, 1991).

Weber, Harold M., *Paper Bullets: Print and Kingship under Charles II* (Lexington, KY: University Press of Kentucky, 1996).

Webster, Charles, *The Great Instauration: Science, Medicine and Reform 1626–1660* (London: Duckworth, 1975).

Webster, Charles, book review, *Journal of Ecclesiastical History*, 39 (1988), p. 597.

Westfall, Richard S., *Religion and Science in Seventeenth Century England* (New Haven: Yale University Press, 1958).

White, B. R., *The English Baptists of the Seventeenth Century* (London: Baptist Historical Society, 1983).

Wilson, Adrian, *The Making of Man-Midwifery: Childbirth in England, 1660–1770* (Cambridge, MA: Harvard University Press, 1998).

Wright, Stephen, 'Morton, Richard (*bap.* 1637, *d.* 1698)' in *Oxford Dictionary of National Biography*, ed. H. C. G. Matthew and Brian Harrison (Oxford: Oxford University Press, 2004), http://www.oxforddnb.com/view/article/19369.

Young, B. W., *Religion and Enlightenment in Eighteenth-Century England: Theological Debate from Locke to Burke* (Oxford: Oxford University Press, 1998).

Zaret, David, 'Religion, Science and Printing in the Public Spheres in Seventeenth-Century England' in *Habermas and the Public Sphere*, ed. Craig Calhoun (Cambridge, MA: MIT Press, 1992), pp. 212–35.

Index